CANADA IN SUDAN

PETER PIGOTT

CANADA IN SUDAN

War Without Borders

DUNDURN PRESS
TORONTO

Editor: Michael Carroll
Design: Erin Mallory
Printer: Friesens

Library and Archives Canada Cataloguing in Publication

Pigott, Peter
      Canada in Sudan : war without borders / Peter Pigott.

Includes bibliographical references and index.
ISBN 978-1-55002-849-2

      1. Sudan--History. 2. Canada--Foreign relations--Sudan.
3. Sudan--Foreign relations--Canada. I. Title.

DT156.4.P54 2008   962.4   C2008-904874-1

1 2 3 4 5   13 12 11 10 09

We acknowledge the support of the **Canada Council for the Arts** and the **Ontario Arts Council** for our publishing program. We also acknowledge the financial support of the **Government of Canada** through the **Book Publishing Industry Development Program** and **The Association for the Export of Canadian Books**, and the **Government of Ontario** through the **Ontario Book Publishers Tax Credit** program, and the **Ontario Media Development Corporation**.

Care has been taken to trace the ownership of copyright material used in this book. The author and the publisher welcome any information enabling them to rectify any references or credits in subsequent editions.

J. Kirk Howard, President

Printed and bound in Canada.
www.dundurn.com

Dundurn Press
3 Church Street, Suite 500
Toronto, Ontario, Canada
M5E 1M2

Gazelle Book Services Limited
White Cross Mills
High Town, Lancaster, England
LA1 4XS

Dundurn Press
2250 Military Road
Tonawanda, NY
U.S.A. 14150

For Marion, who was caught by the Janjaweed

CONTENTS

ACKNOWLEDGEMENTS

"The problems in the Sudan are so complex and detailed that it would take several books to describe and even then would likely fail to do the job," warned Major Sandi Banerjee, deputy commander of the Canadian Task Force, Khartoum. "The tribal factions as well as the religious and cultural strife all create additional layers that act in a logarithmic manner — nothing is simple in Africa."

A lot of people were surprised by the subject. Sudan? I am known as an aviation author, and in the book business, when you are successful in a niche topic, the smart thing to do is to write the same sort of book once a year for the remainder of your life. I knew little of the country, its people, or its history. The sum total of my knowledge was from the 1966 movie *Khartoum* and of a boyhood reading of A.E.W. Mason's novel *The Four Feathers*. Sudan evoked Martini-Henry rifles, proud desert warriors, and the soul-stirring public school sentiments from Sir Henry Newbolt's poem "Vitai Lampada":

> The sand in the desert is sodden red,
> Red with the wreck of the square that broke;
> The Gatling's jammed and the Colonel dead,
> And the regiment blind with dust and smoke.

Later on there was Roy MacLaren's *Canadians on the Nile, 1882–1898: Being the Adventures of the Voyageurs on the Khartoum Relief Expedition and Other Exploits*, and when working in Foreign Affairs, I made sure I got on the distribution list for Nick Coghlan's emails from Khartoum. Like everyone else, I followed the fortunes of the Canadian and Sudanese attachés being expelled and of the British schoolteacher arrested for insulting Islam after she allowed her seven-year-old pupils to name the class teddy bear "Muhammad." And like everyone else, I am outraged at what is taking place in Darfur, the first genocide of the twenty-first century. How can one understand a government that is so contemptuous of the International Criminal Court that not only does it refuse to surrender an individual for crimes against humanity but makes Ahmed Haroun the minister for humanitarian affairs? There is something Orwellian about that.

John Bul Dau's *God Grew Tired of Us: A Memoir* affected me deeply, but then so did Jeff Davis's article in *Embassy* magazine (March 5, 2008). Headlined "Diplomat Doesn't Know the Meaning of Genocide," the piece was about Robert Aguek, the newly appointed first secretary of Sudan's embassy in Ottawa. Aguek had replaced Mwada Omar, the Sudanese diplomat expelled the previous summer. When interviewed, the first secretary said that he wasn't very familiar with the situation in Darfur. "I know there is a war in Darfur and that the government is fighting the rebels in Darfur," he commented. "But I cannot tell you that the Government of Sudan [GOS] is killing the people in Darfur, because I didn't see. I did not see that." And when asked if genocide was occurring there, Aguek said he didn't know the meaning of the word. Perhaps Sir Henry Wotton was right: a diplomat is an honest man sent aboard to lie for his country. *Canada in Sudan: War Without Borders* attempts to bridge the gap between the romance and the tragedy of that country.

Knowing so little of Sudan and nothing of the Canadians there, I relied on many who did: archaeologists, humanitarian workers, members of the Canadian Forces, a former prime minister of Canada, and ordinary Canadians such as Waterloo Police Sergeant Debbie Bodkin, all of whom were so moved by the plight of the Sudanese that they gave up time with their own families and lucrative professions to devote their lives to them.

While many people helped in their own way, pride of place goes to three. A former Foreign Service officer, Roy MacLaren was a Liberal

Member of Parliament and was a federal minister in the governments of John Turner (minister of national revenue) and Jean Chrétien (minister of international trade), capping off his career as High Commissioner for Canada to the United Kingdom of Great Britain and Northern Ireland. Between stints of public office, he was president of Ogilvy & Mather Canada and president and publisher of CB Media Ltd. MacLaren's literary output has been equally prodigious. Besides *Canadians on the Nile*, he has published a number of other books, including *Canadians in Russia, 1918–1919* and *Canadians Behind Enemy Lines, 1939–1945*.

Halifax lawyer Peter Dalglish went to Africa to rescue destitute children, but by his own admission they rescued him. An 11-year-old thief breaking into his Land Rover showed him what he was to do for the remainder of his life. Dalglish collected the abandoned children from the alleys and dumpsters of Khartoum to start a bicycle courier business run entirely by them. He championed their cause against police and government and international agencies, returning to Canada to begin Street Kids International, which in 2008 celebrated its twentieth anniversary working with two million kids in more than 60 countries. Recipient of the Vanier Award from 1994 to 1997, Dalglish was the first director of Youth Service Canada.

With *Far in the Waste Sudan: On Assignment in Africa*, Nicholas Coghlan inspired and encouraged me, as did his emails, when I told him about my book. For Canada's first representative in Sudan, it was truly a case of "cometh the hour, cometh the man."

Canada in Sudan had many godparents who willingly gave of their time and energy to educate and enlighten me about Sudan's complexities. Emmanuel Isch (vice-president of World Vision Canada), Senator Mobina Jaffer, and Lieutenant-Colonel Paul Pickell took time out of busy schedules to meet with me. The same can be said of Canada's former prime minister, the Right Honourable Paul Martin, who when I told him about my book recalled: "I was never so impressed when Tom Niles, then the U.S. ambassador to Canada, brought some businessmen into my office and looking at a boat model I had said, 'Oh, my God, that's a voyageur boat used to rescue General Gordon on the Nile!'"

The youthful enthusiasm of Miriam Booy, the Fellowship for African Relief (FAR) program support manager deep in the Nuba Mountains, shone through her narrative. Somehow Adam Giambrone, chair of the Toronto Transit Commission (TTC), found the time in a busy year to enlighten me on the early history of Nubia. My name must be anathema in the Media Liaison Office at National Defence Headquarters so many times did I harass Captains Joanna Labonté and Carole Brown. John Morris, public affairs officer, Canadian Expeditionary Force Command (CEFCOM), not only found answers for me promptly but put me onto more sources.

A special debt is due to the following Canadian Forces officers: Lieutenant Dave Coulter for his comprehensive narrative of a United Nations observer's duties; Major Greg Penner for recounting his actions during the Battle of Malakal; and Major George Boyuk, who was laid up in hospital but still managed to convey to me detailed explanations of Operations Augural, Safari, and Saturn. I would like to think that one day all three accounts will be required reading in the school curriculum.

Major Sandi Banerjee replied to my queries with warmth and humour: "Our medical kits — yes, I have four of them — allow for … several procedures that shouldn't be contemplated by anyone who doesn't have an MD after their name." His immunizations before going to Sudan were "26 injections and enough morphine, codeine, and types of antibiotics to bring down a decent-sized herd of elephants …"

Thanks, too, go out to Captain Douglas Oggelsby, CFB Kingston, for his deeply moving words: "I am not the same person that I was before I went there. I know that for sure. I saw terrible things in those camps and graves of people killed that day and burning villages. Attacks from the Arab militia were taking place nightly. The women and children feared for their lives daily." Far from the ocean Lieutenant-Commander Nicholas Smith, Task Force Addis Ababa, took a sabbatical from his job as president of the Canadian subsidiary of Lloyd's of London to serve on Operation Augural. While based in Addis Ababa, he volunteered "at an orphanage helping the children with their English and math … as it was often a relief to escape from the negativity of the situation I was monitoring in Darfur."

Acknowledgements

Concerning humanitarian aid, I sorely tested the patience of Kristy Vanderplas, Street Kids International; Reyn Lauer, Canadian Desk Officer, FAR Sudan; and Don McPhee, Plan International. For help in the research of materials I am particularly grateful to Thérèse Horvath, personal assistant, Office of the Right Honourable Paul Martin; Kevin McKague, York University; Laurent Charette, director, Program Sudan, Canadian International Development Agency (CIDA); Library and Archives Canada; and the Media Relations Office of Foreign Affairs Canada.

Supportive throughout the writing of this book have been Christina and Bruce Gillies and my sister, Christine Tebbutt.

The impassioned, soft-spoken Debbie Bodkin told me of meeting Miriam, a 17-year-old girl in Darfur who had been shot and crippled by roving Janjaweed. "She smiled, she couldn't walk, but she said her life was okay because she hadn't been raped and that she could still get married." This book is dedicated to all the Miriams in Sudan ... because they couldn't tell their story.

INTRODUCTION

"I ll-provided," the eighteenth-century traveller W.G. Browne wrote of Sudan in 1808, "with any such thing which is necessary for the sustenance of man or beast." One hundred and thirty years later, a Royal Air Force officer flying between the Sudanese airfields El Geneina and El Fasher wrote: "Seven hundred miles of sheer nothingness: maps absolutely useless, nothing shown on them for the most part, and where something is shown, it was obviously incorrect."

The landscapes of Sudan, just like those in Canada, are drawn on a vast scale. In fact, both countries have much in common. First, they are both the giants of their respective continents, with Sudan covering 8 percent of Africa. Both are overshadowed by the energy and avarice of a neighbour — Egypt to the north of Sudan and the United States to the south of Canada. Each of those neighbours has harboured expansionist ambitions, and Egyptians have ruled, overrun, and exploited Northern Sudan since 2900 BC. The early history of each country has been tied to rivers — the Nile in Sudan's case and the St. Lawrence in Canada's. Power, for both nations, was centred along those rivers, and cities grew up on their banks whose hinterlands served as sources for commodities that were traded with the outside world. In Canada's case it was beaver pelts and grain, while for Sudan it was, tragically, humans. The current boundaries of each country — everything south of the tenth parallel in Sudan's case — owe a lot to colonial expansion and animosity, having been drawn up by the British in both cases to exclude the French from Sudan and the Americans from Canada. Oil and water have played major roles in the politics of both nations. Finally, both Ottawa and Khartoum have had to contend with separatist movements — and have dealt with them in their own way.

"Getting off the plane in Khartoum," says a young Canadian aid worker, "I'm always hit with a wave of warm air that lets me know right away that I've entered a desert climate. The temperature rises to over 45 degrees in the hot season, and even in the cold season will reach highs of 30 degrees almost every day. It is somehow clean air that I breathe, though, and doesn't have the same pollution that many big cities would have. It is also a dry desert heat that isn't as oppressive as humidity can be. Another dramatic natural occurrence in Khartoum is the *haboob* or dust storm. Approaching the city like a giant wall of dust, it gradually sweeps through, and the air is turned a reddish-brown and particles of dust and sand are everywhere."

The two winds that govern Sudan's seasons are an apt analogy for its ethnic and cultural divides — the dry Arabian winds that blow from the northeast from January to March and the wet Congo winds from the southwest that bring heavy rain from April to September. But to say there are two Sudans — North and South, desert and tropical, Arab and black, Islamic and religiously diverse, farmer and nomad — is to simplify. For the images aren't so clear-cut. To say that the North has been brought together as a nation by Islam, what some call "Arabization," and that the South still lacks that cohesiveness, is to ignore the opposition in the rest of the country where, in 2008, independence movements in the east and west have stirred. Sudan is like its languages. Officially, there are two: Arab and Dinka, followed by 14 minor ones, which are themselves divided into more than 100 dialects.

The country's name derives from the Arabic *bilad al-sudan*, which means "land of the blacks," and of the estimated population of 42 million, 52 percent are black and 39 percent are Arab. The crossroads of Africa, Sudan is ethnically diverse, with 19 major groups and 800 subgroups. In 1934 Wilfred Thesiger, perhaps the greatest traveller of the twentieth century, was a British assistant district commissioner in Darfur. He was fascinated by Sudan. Its vastness and diversity of cultures almost qualified it for, he wrote, the status of a miniature continent. To Thesiger, as he stated in his book *Arabian Sands*, Sudan encompassed a complete cross-section of Africa's landscapes, from the ultimate sterile desert in the North, which he loved, down through the desert scrub and savannah, to the tropical forest on its southern borders. In his day it was home for hundreds of different tribes that spoke more than 100 different languages. While he was posted in Sudan in the 1930s, "the country teemed with every kind of game: elephant, lion, buffalo, leopard, and any number of gazelles, antelopes, small mammals, and birds."[1]

The animals have dwindled to a pathetic few, but the human diversity remains. Seventy percent of Sudan's population is Sunni Muslim, with animists and Christians in the southern part of the country making up the rest. The word *Arab* is an ethnic and cultural term in Sudan, referring to those who can trace their ancestry to the original inhabitants who came from the Arabian Peninsula and whose mother tongue is Arabic. That language and culture may be official in Sudan, and the government has certainly attempted to impose Islamic sharia law (the religious law as set down in the Koran) since 1983, but less than half of the population identifies itself as Arab. And nor is being "Arab" a single entity.

There are two main tribes: the agricultural Jaalayin, who live along the Nile from Dongola to Khartoum, and the Juhayna, the cattle and camel herders in the west, of which the best known are the Baggara ("cattle people" in Arabic) in Darfur. The Beja nomads, an Arabized Muslim people with ethnic links to Cushitic-speaking tribes farther south, make up about 5 percent of the Sudanese population and are distinctive for their curly hair, camel herds, and the fact that they wear swords even today. Immortalized by Rudyard Kipling as the "Fuzzy-Wuzzies" who broke a British "square" and originally from the pasture lands between the Red Sea coast and the Atbara River, the Beja have preserved their independence throughout the centuries, fighting everyone from ancient Egypt's pharaohs to the British Army. Another Muslim people, the Nubians, live along the Nile between the Third Cataract and the Egyptian border. Their origins predating the arrival of both Christianity and Islam, the Nubians were scattered when the Aswan Dam was constructed and their ancient homeland was flooded.

The largest non-Arab group in Sudan is the Dinka pastoralists who dwell along the White Nile and Bahr-al-Ghazal. Sometimes allied with their traditional rivals, the Nuer, the Dinka dominate the Sudan People's Liberation Movement/Army (SPLM/A). Less populous tribes are the Muslim Fur and Masalit in Darfur, the farming Azande (Christian and animist) in southwestern Sudan, and the Nuba, the last straddling the North and South, Muslim and Christian worlds.

There is an ancient Arab saying that states: "When Allah created the Sudan, he laughed." And well might he have, with bitterness. For Hilary Bradt, the founder of Bradt travel guides, the Sudanese are mysterious, beautiful, and hospitable. "Anyone asking directions in the Sudan evokes their traditional laws of hospitality, which means a cup of tea or a cooling drink, at the very least. They'll bend over backwards to see that you're looked after ... their helpfulness is entirely without expectation of reward."

Archaeologist Adam Giambrone's connection with Sudan is strong "because of its long history and amazing archaeological sites along with the incredible kindness and openness of the Sudanese people." Deep in the Nuba Mountains, the young aid worker Miriam Booy thought the Sudanese were some of the most hospitable and generous people she had ever known, "reflecting both their Arab and African heritage, and when I introduce myself as a Canadian I always get a positive response! Canadian ideals we uphold in our work include gender equality, e.g., through women's empowerment programs, and environmental sustainability. The Sudanese people I have met will remain my friends and my family for life."

When Don McPhee was growing up in Richmond, British Columbia, in the 1950s, he went to Gordon School but never knew who it was named after. He came to Sudan in June 1983 with his wife and two daughters to teach for the Irish organization Agency for Personnel Services Overseas (APSO) in Wad Medani, Gezira Region. "The appeal of Sudan is the people. Relationships — family, marriage, friendship, connection with God — take precedent over everything. In all the years we've lived in Sudan, we spend every weekend with Sudanese friends, celebrate marriages, baptisms, attending funerals, celebrating Eid Ramadan, Eid Kabir, and other Islamic holidays. I've developed friendships that have endured until today. Work could be frustrating because all of these social obligations and responsibilities took priority over work, and whatever one did one couldn't change that reality. To succeed you have to adapt to the rhythm of life here. I've learned patience and also that getting angry with people had the effect of only slowing down the work or creating tension as Sudanese rarely get angry. By coming to understand and adapt to the culture, I was able to succeed."

Yet there are few other parts of the world where human security is so lacking, and where the need for peace and security — precursors to sustainable development — is so pronounced. Armed conflict in Sudan has been Africa's longest running civil war and shows no sign of abating. The war has continued through three periods of democratic government (1956–58, 1964–69, and 1986–89) and through military regimes (1958–64, 1969–86, and 1989–2003). For this is the cockpit where the Muslim and sub-Saharan African worlds have collided for centuries, pitting religions, racial antagonisms, economic expansion, and colonial exploitation against one another. Experienced "Sudan hands" say that the fault line that divides the Muslim North from the non-Muslim South (in both Sudan and Chad) is the 12th parallel. As the French did in Chad, the British treated Sudan as two distinct countries. At independence it was the Southerners in Chad who gained control of the central government in Fort Lamy, precipitating a revolt by Northerners. But in Sudan the roles were reversed. Both conflicts stem from ancient hostilities that the Europeans played on to their own advantage. The central state around the Nile has used its military or proxy militaries, from slave traders to Janjaweed, to exploit the resource-rich hinterlands for slaves and now oil, coercing the inhabitants into performing its will.[2]

Sudan has never been a nation in the modern sense; its capital city has rarely exercised complete control of — or sympathy for — its nomadic tribes, which explains why the famines in Darfur elicit no interest in Khartoum. The country itself is an artificial creation, its borders drawn up by the Foreign Office in London during the "Great Grab for Africa" in the 1880s. It was what was left after all the better portions were taken. Almost landlocked, Sudan is bordered by Egypt, Eritrea, Ethiopia, Kenya, Uganda, the Democratic Republic of the Congo, the Central African Republic, Chad, and Libya. It sprawls over a total area of 967,499 square miles, is more than a quarter the size of the United States, and equals the combined surface area of Quebec and Ontario. It can be divided into three geographic regions: the extensive flat plain between the Blue and White Nile Rivers, which includes the approximately 30,000-square-mile swamp of the Sudd (the size varies widely up and down depending on the time of year and other factors) and the Qoz, a land of sand dunes; the sparsely populated Nubian and Libyan Deserts in the northern part of the country, which are separated by the Nile Valley; and the mountain zones — the Red Sea Hills in the northeast, the Jebel Marra to the west, the Nuba Mountains in the centre, and the Immatong and Dongotona ranges to the south.

The single dominant feature of Sudan has always been the Nile. The river to which all life is owed, the Nile is the most ancient highway from the heart of Africa to the Mediterranean Sea and is the current source of all hydroelectric power. The river's cataracts and waterfalls, once the first line of defence against invaders, were also its national boundaries, delineating where Egypt ended and where the Nubian kingdoms of Nobatia, Makuria, and Alwa began. In Sudan the great serpent splits into two Niles, the White and Blue, and the city of Khartoum was built at their confluence. The Blue, which provides most of the water, rises in the Ethiopian Highlands, reaching its highest level in July and August. But it is the Blue Nile's slower sister, the White, that excited explorers from Herodotus to Henry Morton Stanley and was the cause of Sudan's discovery by the West. The White Nile is born in neighbouring Uganda, Rwanda, and Burundi, entering Sudan at Nimule, the country's southernmost city. What defeated the early British explorers from discovering its source was the Sudd, a crocodile-infested, papyrus-choked swamp the size of Belgium that the river flows through. Here most of the river's water evaporates, leaving what one explorer called neither land nor water. The White Nile is then replenished by the Sobat River just below the town of Malakal before joining the Blue Nile at Khartoum.

The capital of Sudan is, like Casablanca, mostly known to foreigners because of a movie named after it. "Khartoum — where the Nile divides, the great Cinerama adventure begins!" was the film of the same name's tagline. Major-General Charles Gordon was played by a stiff, gold-braided Charlton Heston, and the Mahdi was performed by Laurence Olivier in gleaming white burnoose, making his case in beautifully chiselled English. The movie was panned as an attempt to catch up with the box office success of *Lawrence of Arabia*. Despite its historical inaccuracies (Gordon and the Mahdi never met), *Khartoum* was filmed at Al Minyal, Egypt, and did give Western audiences an idea of the brick-red desert and the flatness of the Nile, but not of the complex historical drama that Sudan's capital was known for. Like the A.E.W. Mason novel *The Four Feathers* (made seven times into films), it was the romantic image of Sudan, resplendent with desert warriors, intrigue, and glory, that Westerners wanted to see. The reality for Canadians posted there has been quite different.

"Like any other large city, Khartoum has a level of tension that isn't immediately noticeable to foreigners, or *khawaja*, as we were known by the local Arabic-speaking communities," recalls Major Sandi Banerjee, deputy commander, Canadian Contingent, Operation Safari, Task Force Sudan. "The ability to detect subtle changes in the rhythm or feeling of the city would become invaluable to us, especially in areas like Omdurman where factions still fighting in the Darfur region would have their political arms looking for uneasy alliances with government forces in the capital. North of the Nile confluence, the risk to life and limb rose and fell like the mighty river itself, only without the predictability needed to ensure our safety. Our UNMOs, or U.N. Military Observers, would most often comment on the palpable tensions when back in Khartoum from their remote patrol bases. For them the country life, though not without its risks and threats, provided a contrast to the stares and cold feelings of the big city. Given the massive influx of foreign NGOs and their accompanying aid workers, the locals had differing opinions on the net benefits, especially given the continual upward spiral of inflation. To be sure, we foreigners arrived with spending power that could be rivalled only by the very wealthy in Khartoum, a growing percentage of the population but still a small minority in the city, especially so when the true population was included. The massive ring of squalid slums and permanent refugee camps that surround the inner city like layers on an onion may not have been recognized by the government, but the reality was that generations of internally displaced persons [IDPs] had begun to call these homes permanent. Their children had been born there and knew no other."

But within sight of the IDP camps, the skyline of twenty-first-century Khartoum is changing rapidly. Members of Sudan's urban middle class say that only the *khawaja* worry about famines and desertification in the far west of their country. What they care about is not so different from their Western counterparts — a better standard of living, gleaming shopping malls, and the latest electronics, which thanks to oil are now all within their grasp. The most prominent symbol of the oil-fuelled economy is Khartoum's five-star hotel, which is shaped like a boat's billowing sail and was copied from Dubai's Burj Al Arab. Indeed, even as the atrocities in Darfur claim the headlines, Africa's Dubai rises between the two Niles — the $4 billion Al-Mogran project, which on completion in 2014 is to have 10 five-star hotels, 1,100 villas, and 6,700 apartments. Because of the U.S. embargo, the investors in Sudan's boom are Chinese, Indian, Arab, and Malaysian. Forty miles from Khartoum is the "Detroit" of Sudan. The GIAD industrial complex, which opened in 2000, assembles Hyundai cars, Ashok Leyland buses, tractors, and Renault heavy trucks — and armoured vehicles for Sudan's military.

Since being posted there in the 1990s, Emmanuel Isch, World Vision Canada's vice-president, has returned to Sudan on several occasions, most recently in early 2008. "Each visit I saw much happening in and around Khartoum, and clearly visible signs that oil and other revenues are springing up," he says. "There were investments in infrastructure, in new buildings, new hotels, and new gated communities. But, overall, they benefit those who already have so much while the rest of the country remains neglected and little change is noticed. Human development indicators outside of the capital continue to place much of Sudan as a country where improved living conditions remain a hope at best."

Donor nations may pour millions of dollars into feeding dying Darfuris, de-mining the country, and vaccinating IDP children, but to the Sudanese urban elite, neither famine nor street children will ever be their problem. Nor is Sudanese society alone in such a belief. All the relief efforts in history will never change Africa's value system. Those who live among them daily are immune to the destitute and starving. Funds set aside for agricultural reform aren't a domestic priority for Sudan's government. The West's governments and NGOs, Sudan knows, can be relied on to provide agricultural aid. For example, on cue at a conference held in Norway in May 2008 Sudan's government demanded $6 billion from donor nations to make the transition from humanitarian to developmental aid. In his book *Breakfast in Hell*, relief worker Myles F. Harris compared the middle class in all of Africa to the aristocracy in pre-revolutionary Russia: "They could walk down a street crowded with beggars and see only people on it similar to themselves."

Climate-wise, Sudan is tropical in the South and arid desert in the North, with rain coming to the latter from April to October. Winter temperatures in the desert can drop as low as 40 degrees Fahrenheit after sunset to more than 110 at midday, with frequent *haboobs*. Southern Sudan, by contrast, suffers from excessive humidity and an average annual rainfall of more than 40 inches. As might be expected, there is little vegetation in the desert zones, and it is in the river valleys of the Blue and While Niles that the characteristic acacia forests abound. Hashab, talh, and heglig trees flourish, along with ebony, mahogany, and baobab. "There is life only by the Nile," wrote a young Winston Churchill in *The River War*. "It is the great melody that recurs throughout the whole opera." Along the lush riverbanks are cotton, papyrus grasslands, and castor oil and rubber plants.

Until recently, animal life was also abundant in the plains and equatorial regions of Sudan. The river valleys once featured numerous elephants, crocodiles, and hippopotamuses, while the tropical plains regions had giraffes, leopards, lions, monkeys, and poisonous snakes. However, all are much diminished in number, and certain animals are extinct in Sudan altogether or severely endangered (such as the elephant). Unfortunately, the same can't be said for the mosquitoes, seroot flies, and tsetse flies that infest the equatorial belt.

For nineteenth-century Europe, Sudan existed to produce ostrich feathers, gum arabic, and ivory for piano keys and billiard balls. Today, while there are no longer elephants to kill for the ivory, and ostrich feathers have gone out of fashion, Sudan remains the world's major exporter of gum arabic. Derived from the acacia tree, gum arabic is an essential ingredient in candy, perfumes, processed food, and pharmaceuticals.[3] Other forest products are beeswax, tannin, senna, and timber, especially mahogany, but most of the forest harvest is used for fuel. Although much of Sudan is desert, it has large areas of arable land, and the agricultural production of cotton and peanuts employs 80 percent of the workforce and contributes 40 percent of the gross domestic product. It is the mineral wealth that has plagued the country's history. The country's fabled gold deposits, well known in ancient times, were made famous in the West by Henry Rider Haggard's novel *King Solomon's Mines*.

The wars in Sudan differ from those of Africa's other miseries in that, unlike civil wars in Somalia, Sierra Leone, and Rwanda, they have dragged on for a very long time and there has never been a single, defining moment. If the signing of the Comprehensive Peace Agreement (CPA) on January 9, 2005, ended one war, those in Darfur and the northeast were only beginning. The famine in Ethiopia and the genocide in Rwanda saturated Western media enough to force solutions, however temporarily. In 1989 when Operation Lifeline Sudan (OLS) was created in response to a devastating famine, aid workers had hoped a defining moment had finally arrived for the country, but the wars, droughts, and war-induced atrocities have rolled on mostly out of sight of television cameras since then. Each side — North and South, GOS and rebel, Islamic fundamentalist and Christian, Nuer and Dinka, et cetera — has perpetuated the violence against its own nationals. The discovery of oil has only complicated matters. For Western governments, understanding Sudan is by necessity two-dimensional (North/South, Arab/African, government/rebel, Muslim/animist, pastoral/farmer, et cetera) and multi-layered.

Even the enemy is fragmented. The former commander of Operation Augural, Lieutenant-Colonel Paul Pickell, explains: "There is the whole issue of who actually are the rebels? Are they the group that is being supported by the Government of Sudan, is it one that has its own agenda in Darfur, or is it Chadian rebels that are actually across the border? In Darfur the reality is there are Chadian rebels fighting against the government of Chad, and Chad has Sudanese rebels that are fighting the

Government of Sudan. So they both run back and forth across a meaningless border — a kind of Vietnam mentality." It is a war without heroes on any side, government or rebel, not in the South and certainly not in the North. So it has been difficult for foreigners — both governments and their concerned citizens — to take sides and to hope that the issues will ever be resolved.

"Did the Canadian oil company ask our permission to take our oil and sell it?" the Canadian Assessment Team was repeatedly asked in 2000. "Why is Canada, a rich country, taking our oil without our permission and without any benefit to us?" Although Canadians had long been in Sudan as missionaries, aid workers, and archaeologists, the country really entered Canada's consciousness in the last years of the twentieth century because of its mineral deposits. "The reason Canada opened a diplomatic office in Sudan in 2000," wrote Nick Coghlan in *Far in the Waste Sudan*, "was oil."[4] That was the year Sudan's current financial account entered surplus for the first time since independence in 1956.

Known since ancient times for its ivory, gum arabic, and slaves, it is its massive oil reserves that today account for nearly all of Sudan's current export revenues — 80 percent of it going to the People's Republic of China. Exploration for oil in Sudan began in the 1960s off its Red Sea coast, but it was when the U.S. company Chevron and the Sudanese government formed the White Nile Petroleum Corporation in 1981 to oversee oil production that it exacerbated the conflict. Because of the civil war, oil exploration has been limited to the central and south-central regions of the country, and the majority of proven reserves are located in the South in the Muglad and Melut basins. According to *Oil and Gas Journal*, as of January 2007, the country had proven oil reserves of five billion barrels. But it is thought that even larger potential reserves are held in northwest Sudan, the Blue Nile basin, and the Red Sea shore in eastern Sudan, all areas for potential conflict. Naturally, both the North and South have claimed the oil fields as their own, each realizing that the billions of dollars brought in would ensure them the means of achieving their own aims. Human-rights activists have long known that the oil revenues allow the Government of Sudan to finance its "cleansing" campaigns against its own people — initially in the South and now in the eastern and western parts of the country — and hold that the foreign oil companies extracting the crude are as culpable as the pilots of the Hind gunships that eradicate the unfortunates who inconveniently live above the liquid wealth.

For Peter MacKay, formerly Canada's minister of foreign affairs and now minister of national defence, Sudan is an almost perfect storm of conflict, dislocation, underdevelopment, and brutality. "For decades, wars have raged in the South, in the Darfur region, and in eastern Sudan…. Some might ask why would the Canadian government, which spends billions on international development assistance programs, need groups like the Canadian Economic Development Assistance for Southern Sudan?"[5]

Canada's historic connection with Sudan is obscure. How many Canadians know of the First Nations voyageurs recruited by the British in the 1880s to rescue General Gordon? In more recent times some people may have heard of Canadian aid organizations like FAR in Sudan or learned about the history of Nubia at Toronto's Royal Ontario Museum. Less known would be the developmental aid in the 1980s funded by CIDA, specifically a mechanized farming project in the Sudanese province of Gedaref. However, everything changed in 1992 when Chevron sold (abandoned would be more truthful) its investment in Sudan to the locally owned Concorp International, which resold it to the little-known Arakis Energy Corporation of Canada. The compassionate image of Canadians overseas was further sullied in 1998 when Arakis sold out to Talisman Energy Inc. That a Calgary-based oil exploration company was seen to be aiding and abetting a rogue regime drew protests by church groups, students, and concerned Canadians alike, embarrassing Ottawa enough to take official notice of Sudan.

Until then, based in Cairo or Addis Ababa, Canadian diplomats had made periodic trips to Khartoum, and Canada had helped bankroll the African-run Intergovernmental Authority on Development (IGAD). But although there was a Sudanese embassy in Ottawa, no Canadian flag flew in Sudan. A consequence of then Foreign Minister Lloyd Axworthy's meeting with his Sudanese counterpart in New York City at the United Nations General Assembly in 1999 was his department's "October 26 Policy Statement on Sudan," the first prominent Canadian initiative on the war-torn nation. It stressed that Canada was deeply concerned about reports of intense fighting in the regions of oil development, and that oil extraction by a Canadian company might be exacerbating that conflict. What followed was a Canadian investigative commission headed by Africa expert John Harker. The commission toured Sudan, meeting with government officials, Talisman oil workers, warlords, and refugees, then returned home to issue "Human Security in Sudan: The Report of a Canadian Assessment Team." The report only confirmed what the church groups and aid workers already knew — that the oil being extracted by a Canadian company was worsening the civil war in Sudan and that the massive civilian displacement was a consequence of that oil extraction. Moral indignation apart, there was little that Ottawa could do.

Placing Sudan on the Area Control List for economic sanctions was inconsequential.[6] Canadian exports amounted to little more than machine parts, boring tools, valves, and tube fittings — all equipment used in the oil industry and readily available elsewhere. The recognition that Canada needed a permanent presence in Sudan to monitor the situation and to provide consular assistance to Canadians working for Talisman, aid agencies, and helicopter pilots drove Ottawa to open an "office" in Sudan. In August 2000, in the first step toward diplomatic recognition, Foreign Affairs officer Nick Coghlan was posted to Khartoum as "Head of Office." His successors were given the title of chargé d'affaires. One of those successors was expelled after being charged with interfering in the internal matters of Sudan, while another granted a Sudanese Canadian "temporary haven" within the embassy.

In 2002, bowing to pressure to exit on all fronts, Talisman sold off its Sudanese investment to the Chinese- and Indian-dominated Greater Nile Petroleum Operating Company. After that Canada redeemed itself publicly and returned to its sympathetic role in Sudan, its presence today personified by those of its nationals involved in humanitarian organizations such as CARE Canada, Doctors Without Borders, and World Vision. "In my opinion," said a Canadian Forces officer who had been to Sudan several times, "given the inherent dangers, those Canadians presently working in Darfur to facilitate humanitarian aid (where UNAMID has yet to establish a secure environment) are the real heroes."

One hundred and twenty-five years after the first Canadians came to Sudan the voyageur boats manned by Ottawa shantymen have given way to the fixed-wing aircraft and helicopters of SkyLink Aviation, nicknamed Canada's air force in Sudan. The Toronto-based air cargo operator was commended by the United Nations for maintaining the vital air bridge between Khartoum and Darfur. The few Canadian militia officers recruited to accompany the voyageurs were the forerunners of Canadian Forces personnel who since 2004, in Operations Safari, Augural, and Saturn, have heeded the call of the African Union and the United Nations to help monitor the Comprehensive Peace Agreement and now the crisis in Darfur. Through the "permanent loan" of surplus armoured personnel carriers and leased helicopters and by contributing to de-mining and food assistance, Canada has committed $441 million in aid since 2004. When Paul Martin visited Sudan on November 25, 2004, he became the first Canadian prime minister to do so, and the plight of the country's IDPs remains very close to his heart. In May 2005, Martin set up a Special Advisory Team with Senators Roméo Dallaire and Mobina Jaffer to help with the humanitarian crisis in Darfur.

In 2008 it was estimated that Sudan's never-ending wars had killed 1.8 million people, more than those killed in Somalia, Bosnia, and Rwanda combined. Children are saved from starvation in one year only to be abducted and brutalized as child soldiers to murder in the next. As the pharaohs and khedives once raped Sudan for slaves and ivory, foreigners continue to destroy the country's already fragile social system today for oil. Ultimately, despite the best intentions of movie stars, of U.N. and NGO aid organizations, of politicians in their foreign capitals and humanitarian workers in the country itself, Sudan's problems defy all comprehension and solutions remain elusive.

Why are Canadians so involved with Sudan? It could be because as the former commander of Operation Augural, Lieutenant-Colonel Paul Pickell, points out, "Canada is perceived by the Africans as having no baggage. And that is a virtue of us being Canadians — that we are in

Sudan out of the goodness of our hearts." Or when Lloyd Axworthy, the former minister of foreign affairs, outlined his human security agenda in June 2000, he pointed out that in Kosovo, East Timor, and Rwanda sovereignty had protected the perpetrators of genocide but not the millions of their victims. In the First World War, civilians accounted for 5 percent of the casualties. In Sudan, he said, they accounted for 97 percent.

"In my father's time it was a bipolar world — good guys and the bad guys who were the Soviet Union — and Canada had the role of honest broker between," says Paul Martin. "Today it is no longer that and we have to find those areas in the world where Canada can play a leading role. In my own judgment Darfur is one of them. It's a better 'fit' for us than Afghanistan — Canada is needed there, too, but Afghanistan does not lack for public attention, and with NATO and the U.S. military is well supplied. Our principal role is wherever other countries are not stepping up to the job. And it is also the overwhelming human tragedy in Darfur. Never again after Rwanda struck me heavily."

Every Canadian who has been to Sudan has been profoundly affected by it. This wasn't the romance of British novelists and Hollywood that they had been brought up with but that of dying children, burnt villages, and systematic government brutality. "There are few other parts of the world where human security is so lacking," concluded the Harker Report, "and where the need for peace and security — precursors to sustainable development — is so pronounced. Canada's commitment to human security, particularly the protection of civilians in armed conflict, provides a clear basis for its involvement in Sudan."

Peter Dalglish says about the Darfur famine of 1985: "I felt guilty just being there — healthy, well-fed, white, from a rich country. Despite our trucks of food and our good intentions, our role as relief workers was more as chroniclers than saviours."

Posted to Sudan with the United Nations in 2006, Canadian Forces logistics officer Captain Douglas Oggelsby couldn't stop feeling the pain: "It hurts me when I see more and more photos of Darfur. It is amazing that we are living in 2008 and things like this are going on. Things don't seem to be changing. All I can think about are the Sudanese friends I met and what is going on with their lives."

During the Battle of Malakal in November 2006, in which 200 civilians were killed and an estimated 500 injured, United Nations Mission in Sudan (UNMIS) observer Major Gregory Penner volunteered to lead patrols and medical evacuation. He would go back anytime, he says, "to do whatever it takes to prevent something like what I saw break out across the entire Southern countryside. My heart is broken for the people of Sudan."

Nick Coghlan, Canada's first permanent diplomat in Sudan, summed it up thus in *Far in the Waste Sudan*:

> Over the years the tragedy in Sudan has attracted the interest, the dedication, and the philanthropy of a wide variety of individuals, organizations, and nations. We have busied ourselves, analysed, agonized, and examined ad nauseam, and we have expended fortunes many times over; but in the end it has to be said that if there are some places we *did* get it right (East Timor?), Sudan has to be an example of our thus far getting it badly wrong.[7]

1

THE LAND BELOW EGYPT

For the ancients, Sudan was the source of the Nile, that great river of antiquity. The river had never been known to fail; it poured out of the desert and mysteriously flooded its banks every September, the hottest and driest time of the year. Only by its banks was there life, or any hope of it. The young journalist Winston Churchill wrote of the Nile in *The River War*:

> ... the Nile is naturally supreme. It is the life of the lands through which it flows.... Emir and Dervish, officer and soldier, friend and foe, kneel alike to this god of ancient Egypt and draw each day their daily water in goatskin or canteen. Without the river, none would have started. Without the river none might have continued. Without it none could ever have returned.

How was it, the ancients wondered, that the Nile, considered even then the longest river in the world, maintained its bounty without tributaries or rainfall, rolling seemingly effortlessly from south to north into the Mediterranean Sea? What was known was that on its banks all civilization began. Here the pyramids rose, Moses was found in bulrushes, Alexander the Great waded into its waters, and Cleopatra seduced Julius Caesar and Mark Antony. But where below Egypt the Nile originated was a mystery. In 460 B.C. the Greek historian Herodotus set out to locate the source of the river, which he theorized erupted from the bowels of the earth, since the temperature at the equator would make snow — the usual source of rivers — impossible. He got as far as the spray of the First Cataract, the outer limits of ancient Egypt, where the endless desert started. The Nile, Herodotus speculated, arose from "fountains" somewhere in Africa. In A.D. 61 two Roman centurions were sent by Emperor Nero into Nubia, ostensibly to find the source of the Nile but actually to assess the strength of the Nubian military. When history's first geographer, Ptolemy, drew the first map of the world in circa A.D. 140, he disagreed with Herodotus's speculation and thought that the source of the Nile lay in the melting snows of *Lunae Montes*, "The Mountains of the Moon," on the equator.

Scholars in medieval Europe knew of Sudan, since it was described in the Book of Isaiah as "the country of whirring [insect] wings," filled with people who "were to be feared as mighty and masterful." The Book of Ezekiel told of the people of Kush fighting against Gog, the chief prince of Magog, who was from the land below Egypt. "With plague and bloodshed" and "every sort of terror," God was going to pass judgment on Gog.

Little is known about the Scottish explorer James Bruce who traced the course of the Blue Nile in the 1770s from its source in modern Ethiopia. But it was the source of the White Nile that enticed and eluded everyone, prompting mapmakers to fill in the blank spaces below the confluence of both rivers with fantastic creatures such as griffins and cannibal dwarfs. If the mapmakers were especially imaginative, they sometimes added mountains that in the heat of the equator had snow on their peaks and had to be the source of the Nile. Perhaps the great river, wrote the French philosopher Montesquieu, was never meant to be traced to its source by mortals. No ordinary person, it was believed, ought to know such mysteries, so through the centuries, since no European dared travel upriver, Ptolemy's map was accepted as factual.

If Canadians know the early history of Sudan at all, it is because of archaeologists such as the University of Calgary's Peter Shinnie, the Royal Ontario Museum's (ROM's) Krzysztof Grzymski, and Adam Giambrone, who has worked as an archaeologist in Sudan and is currently a City of Toronto councillor and the chair of the Toronto Transit Commission. Complementing his field projects in Egypt and in

Sudanese Nubia, Grzymski's curatorial activities included developing the Egyptian and Nubian galleries of the Royal Ontario Museum, opened in 1992, and curating special exhibitions such as the *Gold of Meroe* (1994), *Meroe, the Capital of Kush: Old Problems and New Discoveries* (2002), and *Landscape Archaeology of Nubia and Central Sudan* (2003). In 1999 a joint ROM–University of Khartoum expedition to Meroe was mounted to explore and protect the ruins of the ancient capital of Sudan. On June 24, 2006, because of his archaeological research at Meroe and publication of the standard text on the civilization, Peter Shinnie was awarded one of Sudan's highest distinctions — the Order of the Two Niles.

"Most of our knowledge about Sudanese prehistory comes from archaeological remains found in Nubia, a region covering Southern Egypt and Northern Sudan," says Adam Giambrone. Compared to Nubia, far less is known about historical and cultural development in Southern, Eastern, and Western Sudan, likely because relatively limited archaeological work has been done in those areas. This can be attributed to the many years of war in Southern Sudan as well as the logistical challenges associated with excavating in the East and West.

The earliest signs of human habitation in Sudan were found in Nubia and are estimated to be as much as 300,000 years old. While little is known of the Stone Age in Sudan, we do know these early people were nomadic. They lived in small groups, hunting and gathering for food as their primary means of survival. The Neolithic Revolution, the coming of agriculture, started in Nubia around the fifth to the sixth millennium B.C., as it did across North Africa. During this period, there was an increasing trend toward a sedentary lifestyle as people switched from hunting and gathering to farming. With agriculture larger populations were possible, and the first signs of civilization became evident. By 3500 B.C., a specific Neolithic culture had clearly taken hold across Northern Sudan. Around 2500 B.C. this culture had developed into a state with a high degree of organization.

The period and civilization of 2500–1500 B.C. is referred to as Kerma. The centre of power for Kerma culture appears to have been concentrated at the modern-day town of Kerma in the Third Cataract region of the Nile. Given its geographic proximity, the Egyptian state had a strong influence over the cultural and religious development of the Kerma civilization. The power of Kerma peaked in the eighteenth century B.C. when Egypt was preoccupied by an invasion of Asian nomads known as the Hyksos. Exposure to the Egyptian way of life was facilitated through trade.

Nubia is often referred to as "the corridor to Africa" because of its significance as an early trade conduit. Early trade patterns throughout Nubia reveal products such as ebony, ivory, and gum arabic being traded to Northern Sudan in exchange for products from the Mediterranean basin and grain from the fertile Nile Valley. As the Egyptian empire grew through the Old Kingdom (circa 2649–2150 B.C.) and the Middle Kingdom (circa 2030–1640 B.C.), Egypt increased its military presence in Nubia. The area became known as "Kush," or the Land of the Punt, to the Egyptians. Today archaeological findings reveal many similarities between the Sudanese and Egyptian cultures of that time.

Despite Egypt's military and cultural dominance in this early period, Nubians occasionally occupied Egypt, taking the throne in the Eighteenth and again in the Twenty-Fifth Dynasties (circa 1550–1292 B.C. and circa 690–664 B.C. respectively). As the Egyptian empire began to disintegrate in the eleventh century B.C., its authority over Kush diminished. Over the next 300 years little is known of the history of Nubia. By the eighth century B.C., the Kingdom of Napata had emerged in Nubia. The Napatan Empire was focused around the current city of Meroe, but in the third century B.C. the capital was moved to ancient Meroe near today's Shendi. The empire stretched from the Second Cataract to just south of what is now Khartoum. Despite having its own language, the culture of the Napatan Empire drew heavily on the Egyptian religion, with the pharaonic tradition continuing. Many pyramids and temples in Sudan date from this period. Indeed, remains from this time, including temples, palaces, and baths, attest to a centralized political structure that commanded the labour of a large and wealthy empire. In addition, an irrigation system allowed for a higher population density than later periods experienced. By the first century B.C., the use of hieroglyphs gave way to an indigenous Merotic script. As in the Napatan period, many fortified towns, temples, and pyramids were built at this time. The culture showed a mixture of Egyptian, African, and Roman influences.

For the ancient Egyptians, Nubia, the region past the First Cataract at Aswan, was known for its warriors. It was called Ta-Seti, or the Land of the Bow, the effect of which Egyptian invaders must have felt. After conquering Nubia and enslaving its people, the Egyptians appropriately called it Kush or "Wretched." Whatever the name, Nubia remained a hunting ground for slaves and a source of gold and stone. The pattern of a centralized power around the Nile exploiting the vast hinterlands for its own gain through slave raiding (or geological exploration today) was begun early.

The Egyptians built a number of forts up the Nile for their raiding parties, supplying them by the river. Near the Third Cataract the Nubian city state of Kerma grew rich as the exchange point for goods from Egypt and the south. By 2181 B.C., when the Egyptians withdrew their armies to fight the Hyksos, the citizens of Kerma seized their chance at independence and removed the Egyptian presence as far as the Second Cataract. But the superpower returned with a vengeance and exacted its revenge on Kerma at the beginning of the fifteenth century B.C., conquering Nubia and Kush as far as the Fifth Cataract. The Egyptians established themselves more permanently in the south, building the great temple to the god Amun at Napata (now Jebel Barkal) and enslaving the Nubians as the reliefs on the walls of Rameses II's temple at Abu Simbel demonstrate. Down through the centuries the Egyptian viceroys in Kush grew rich and restive enough to declare their independence from the mother country. By 780 B.C., they claimed the title of "pharaoh" for themselves and built pyramids locally for the burial of their own kings. This was the golden age of the Kingdom of Kush when its armies not only invaded Egypt itself but raided as far away as Libya and Palestine, the Kushites retreating only when the Assyrian armies conquered Egypt.

About the third century B.C., the Kushite kings moved from Napata to Meroe, a wetter, more fertile region that also had large deposits of iron ore. Sometimes called the capital of the first civilization of Black Africa, Meroe was a rambling city with temples that had steam baths leading down to the Nile and a royal cemetery with more pyramids (albeit smaller) than Egypt. At the same time Egyptian culture seems to have been replaced with an indigenous one — Egyptian hieroglyphics for example, with a cursive script that hasn't yet been deciphered.

In the first century B.C., the Romans ended the Ptolemaic Dynasty in Egypt and entered into a war with Kush. As neither side could defeat the other, for the next 300 years they tolerated each other in a form of armed truce. A Roman legion did venture south of the Egyptian border in 23 B.C. but determined that what lay ahead was "too poor to warrant its conquest." The eventual fall of Rome coinciding with the rise of the Ethiopian Kingdom of Axum in the east led to a decline in Meroe's importance as a trading city. It then mostly vanished into the desert sands, only to be used by nomadic tribes and early Christian missionaries.

The Nubian kingdom divided itself along the banks of the Nile: Nobatia was between the First and Third Cataracts, Makuria from the Third to the Sixth Cataracts, and Alwa on the Blue Nile. The three kingdoms entered a Christian phase, influenced in religion, culture, and politics by faraway Byzantium. Cathedrals and monasteries sprang up, decorated with frescoes that might have been copied from those in Constantinople. Religion superseded politics as kings slipped in importance to priests and the quasi-religious "eparchs" or prefects. Christian Nubia soon found itself isolated from Byzantium by a new religion that swept in from Arabia — Islam. But as the Romans had discovered, the Nubians clung to their independence tenaciously, and the Arabs, too, sued for peace. The *baqt* or peace treaty lasted 300 years, both sides profiting from it with security and trade.

The Arabs introduced both horses and currency to the region, but the indigenous population knew intimately the institution that substituted for both. As far back as the third millennium B.C., for the pharaohs the land above the Nile's cataracts had been the source of limitless manpower. The Kingdoms of Kush and Meroe on the Egyptian border had long since established themselves as the middlemen in the slave trade between equatorial Africa and Egypt. The taking of captives, whether by war, kidnapping, or alliances, had been the norm, each tribe raiding others for warriors, women, and children for armies, procreation, or labour.

Since time immemorial, without beasts of burden or a metallurgy industry, Sudan has had two currencies — cattle and slaves. However, the Arabs elevated the latter to a whole new level. In Islamic belief while it was immoral to enslave other Muslims it was divinely ordained that slavery was a suitable punishment for the defeated and infidels. The pagan black tribes south of Egypt were of the Dar al Harb, "the House of War," and in accordance with sharia, owning a nonbeliever was permissible. A fringe benefit (a justification also used by Catholic missionaries who accompanied the Spanish conquistadores to South America) was that the animist tribes were now exposed to the true religion and were thus civilized.

Isolated from Constantinople, the Nubian Christian kingdom gradually converted to Islam, with the cathedrals becoming mosques. The conversion to Islam brought more than literacy in Arabic. Adoption of Islamic legal principles and, more important, the genealogical link with Mecca were part of the transfer. Henceforth, the Sudanese elite families would be able trace their family origins to the Abbasid and Ummayid Dynasties. This further divided those who lived on the Nile, creating a greater chasm between urban Muslims with legal rights and advantages and distant hinterland peoples who had neither. In order to reap the benefits of Muslim protection, tribes such as the Beja readily converted to the new religion.

By 1275, the Mamelukes in Egypt had taken control of Nubia, with only distant Alwa retaining its Christian traditions for another two centuries at least. The power vacuum created led to the rise of the Funj, nomadic tribes from Ethiopia who pushed the Arabs back and built their own Muslim kingdom. The Funj not only provided the Arabs with slaves but even made contact with Europeans. The Mamelukes were absorbed by the Ottomans, remembered for opening the country's first port, Suakin, on the Red Sea. With the Funj, they encountered a new power in present-day Chad, the Fur Sultanate of Darfur. In the seventeenth century, the Sultanate raided for slaves in the Dar Fartit — modern Bahr al-Ghazal in Sudan. But whatever the tribe, the currency for trade remained ivory, gold, and slaves, with both the Arabs and Funj mounting expeditions deeper and deeper into the South, looking for fresh sources of all three. In doing so they came up against migrating tribes along the White Nile (near current Malakal) such as the Nilotic Shilluk, the

Dinka tribe with their herds of cattle moving into the Sobat region, and the Azande warriors emigrating from the Congo area.

With the emergence of the Muslim Funj Kingdom at the beginning of the sixteenth century, Islam spread across Sudan. Its teachers brought with them the new Sufi movement from the centres of Muslim learning — Cairo and Baghdad. Believing that God is reached by a mystical path separate from the orthodox Muslim prayer ritual, Sufism continues to play an important role in Sudan today, each of its brotherhoods (*tariqa*) led by a charismatic sheikh.[1] Although Sufis accept sharia, orthodox Muslims hold that the practices of Sufism border on heresy. But Sufis remain defiantly independent. One of the *tariqa*, the Khatmia, even fought with the British and Egyptians against the Mahdi. Politically astute, Sudanese Sufis today remain a political power through their control of Sudan's Democratic Unionist Party.

Napoleon's defeat by the British on the Nile led to the Ottomans reasserting control over their Egyptian colony from Istanbul. When Muhammad Ali was made Egyptian wali or viceroy in Cairo in 1805, he lost no time in hiring an army of Albanian mercenaries and arming them with European weapons. Quickly defeated, the decrepit Mamelukes fled to the town of Dongola on the border of the Funj kingdom, and Muhammad Ali went on to conquer Damascus, Mecca, and Medina. In 1820, consolidating his gains, he looked for slaves to replace the expensive mercenaries. This led him to Sudan, and the following year he sent his third son, Ismail Kamil Pasha, with an army of 4,000 soldiers up the Nile. Their mission was simple: build a network of forts along the river and use them as bases to raid farther south than the pharaoh's armies ever had to kidnap, transport, and sell the unfortunate locals in Middle Eastern markets.

"You are aware that the end of all our effort and this expense is to procure negroes," Muhammad Ali instructed Ismail's successor (the viceroy's son was killed in 1822). "Please show zeal in carrying out our wishes in this capital matter." This Turko-Egyptian invasion (and subsequent occupation) altered the economic and social balance of power in Sudan for all concerned. Not only did it devastate the fabric of Southern Sudanese society, but it forced the Northern Sudanese tribes that had succumbed to Islam earlier to turn on their future countrymen who had not. If there were tribes that rose up against this oppression, there were just as many who collaborated. The Shaiqiyya north of Khartoum, the Rufa'a on the Blue Nile, and the Baggara on the While Nile raided their brothers officially for the Egyptians and then for commercial companies. While not "Turks" themselves, the co-operating tribes soon had a personal stake in the exploitation of the South.

Muhammad Ali also sold licences to commercial companies to kidnap and transport the human cargo. In fact, the raiding and trading became a co-operative effort between the state and private enterprise. By the time the state monopoly was given up in the 1870s, the South had been carved into commercial fiefdoms that everyone, Egyptian and Sudanese, slave and free men, depended on. The invading slave raiders may have been Egyptians and Albanians, but to the Southerners they were all "Turks," and the new regime was remembered as the "Turkiyya."

Shendi was the largest trading city and traditional slave market in Sudan then. It was where the Nile was closest to the Red Sea and within easy reach of the caravans that brought with them Indian spices, German swords, and Ethiopian gold. But needing a collection and distribution centre for the slave caravans closer to the source, Muhammad Ali ordered Uthman Bey, governor general of Sudan, to build a town at the confluence of the Blue and While Niles in 1825. It was called Khartoum. There is a theory that the city was so named because the confluence of both Niles here takes on the shape of an elephant's trunk, which in Arabic was close enough to the word *Khartoum*.

With guns, and later steam-powered boats, the "Turks" penetrated far up the Nile into Sudan's South, enslaving tribes who had until then escaped the Arabs. By 1839, when the White Nile was opened to steamer navigation and the slavers of the Turkiyya had pushed as far south as Gondokoro (near modern Juba), it was the death knell for the freedom of the Shilluk, Dinka, Nuer, and Azande tribes. In the Nilotic language this period is referred to as "the time when the world was spoiled." Not for nothing is the Arabic word for "slave" synonymous with "black." Even the Southerners who converted to Islam and through the military won some social status remained stigmatized by their slave origins indefinitely. Douglas H. Johnson, in *The Root Causes of Sudan's Civil War*, says the incorporation of modern racial stratification in the country dates from this period, with Northerners believing that the inhabitants of the South are (and always will be) of lower status.[2]

It wasn't only the Southerners who suffered during Turko-Egyptian rule. The demand for more slaves and money became insatiable, causing Egypt to set taxes so high in Northern Sudan that domestic slaves could be confiscated from defaulters and sold for taxes. The heavy taxes on the riverine settlements in Nubia meant crop production had to be increased to pay them, which forced subsistence farmers to mortgage their crops in advance of harvests or drove them to abandon their farms altogether and hire out to the two new burgeoning industries in the South — the ivory and slave trades. Europeans, it was discovered, had a great hunger for the tusks of elephants whose herds were plentiful in the South. But getting the tusks to market required an inexhaustible supply of porters, making Khartoum's slave market the busiest since ancient Rome's and the whole Egyptian/Sudanese economy dependent on slaves. (Porters who took ill or faltered on the trail were immediately hanged, the fear being that if they recovered, they would be used by the next ivory trader.) Alan Moorehead, in *The White Nile*, aptly describes how all this worked:

> Any penniless adventurer could become a trader provided he was willing to borrow the money at anything up to 80 percent interest. On a normal expedition such a trader would sail south from Khartoum in December with two or three hundred armed men, and at some convenient spot would land and form an alliance with a native chieftain. Then together the tribesmen and the Khartoum slavers would fall upon some neighbouring village in the night, firing the huts just before dawn and shooting into the flames. It was the women that the slavers chiefly wanted, and these were secured by placing a heavy forked pole known as a sheba on their shoulders. The head was locked in by a cross-bar, the hands were tied to the pole in the front, and the children were bound

to their mothers by a chain passed round their necks. Everything the village contained would be looted — cattle, ivory, grain, even the crude jewellery that was cut off the dead victims — and then the whole cavalcade would be marched back to the river and await shipment to Khartoum. With the stolen cattle the trader would buy ivory. And sometimes too the trader would turn upon his native ally and despoil him in the same way as the others; but more often these alliances were kept up year after year, the native chief building up a fresh store of slaves and ivory while the trader was disposing of the last consignment in Khartoum. Every trader had his own territory and by mutual agreement the country was parcelled out all the way from Khartoum to Gondokoro and beyond. In a good season a slaver in a small way could reckon on obtaining 20,000 lb of ivory worth about £4,000 in Khartoum plus about 400 to 500 slaves worth about £5 or £6 each — an expedition total of perhaps £6,500. With this capital he paid off his debts, mounted a fresh expedition, and year after year expanded his business.[3]

Napoleon always maintained that Egypt was strategically the most important country in the world, and after his defeat there by the British in 1798, the Nile and its environs found a new prominence in the European consciousness. Steeped in the Bible and their own invincibility, it was incomprehensible to the British that the source of the most famous river in antiquity was still unknown. By the early nineteenth century, the Union Jack had already been planted in India, China, Canada, and other parts of Africa. That it was soon to fly from the Mountains of the Moon where Ptolemy's map imagined the Nile originated was a given. It might be inexplicable to us today with satellite mapping and global positioning systems, but as recently as the late nineteenth century the interior of the continent of Africa was very much *terra incognita*. Portuguese sailors had mapped its coastline thoroughly as they made their way to Goa in the fifteenth century, but a hundred miles inshore the continent was a mystery even 500 years later. With steamboats the great rivers — the Congo, Zambezi, and Nile — offered the most convenient highways inland.

From 1830 onward, for a certain type of Englishman, eccentric trekking up the Nile past the First Cataract was akin to the quest for the Holy Grail. None knew of the dangers ahead — death by bandits, snakes, malaria, dengue fever, or crocodiles — and the few who returned to the drawing rooms of London to tell the tale served only to whet the public's curiosity at a time when the popular press was looking for heroes. In 1855, in a bid to bypass the cataracts of the treacherous Nile, the British explorers Richard Francis Burton and John Hanning Speke set out to locate its source not as Herodotus had done by going up the Nile but by cutting across the jungle from the port of Mombasa. Speke made it to the Sudanese village of Gondokoro in 1863 and then travelled down the Nile as far as Cairo. When he returned to London, he published *Journal of the Discovery of the Source of the Nile*, the first study of the river since Herodotus.

It wasn't for exploration alone that such interest in the Nile grew. The "celebrity author" profession had begun, necessitating book tours and signings, lecturing at the Royal Geographic Society in London, and the opportunity to meet a royal fan of African exploration — Her Majesty Queen Victoria herself. At a baser level there was also the opportunity to make a quick fortune in the ivory trade. But more than both of these an expedition up the Nile was required to report on the ancient African institution of slavery. In 1807 Britain made the slave trade illegal in its empire, then abolished slavery altogether in its colonies in 1834. After that, with all the fanaticism of a reformed slaver, Britain sought to prevent the traffic in humans everywhere it could, especially in Africa. That it had the Royal Navy to enforce this on the high seas wasn't enough. Earlier, in 1823, the father of all human-rights movements, the Anti-Slavery Society, was founded in Britain. Backed by groups such as the Quakers, the society pressured the British government to use its military might and diplomatic clout to end slavery in Africa once and for all. If nothing could be done about the ownership of human beings in the

African colonies of the Portuguese, the French, or the Belgians, the dissolute Ottoman Empire in Egypt and Sudan was another matter.

Debates among the learned societies in London about the slave trade in Sudan were all very well. To eradicate it completely, though, required an Englishman "on the ground." The timing for such an individual was perfect when, in 1863, Muhammad Ali's grandson ascended to the throne as khedive in Cairo. Educated in Vienna, Ismail Pasha cast himself in the role of a reformer, an enlightened, liberal-thinking sovereign but a monarch nevertheless who would rule from the Nile Delta to the southern tip of Sudan. At 39 he was wealthy (the national treasury and his personal bank account were one and the same), and the blockading of the ports in the U.S. South during the American Civil War had inflated the price of Egyptian cotton. More important, nine years earlier, his uncle, Muhammad Said Pasha, had sold a concession to the French engineer Ferdinand de Lesseps, allowing him to build a canal from the Mediterranean to the Red Sea.

When the Suez Canal opened on November 17, 1869, Ismail played host to all the European rulers who accepted his invitation — only the British who had opposed the building of the canal were noticeably absent. The khedive understood only too well that to keep London's good wishes (and influence for further bank loans), slavery had to be banned in his domain. Besides, the exaction of tolls from the maritime nations of the world that used the canal was a source of income far less embarrassing than that of selling slaves.

Desiring that Egypt take its place among the modern nations of the world (and not be thought of as part of the savage African continent), Ismail set about spending on grandiose projects — opera houses, street lighting, and railways — and outlawing the slave trade in his kingdom on paper at least. (Once freed the slaves were to be "elevated" to the status of serfs, akin to the millions in Czarist Russia.) The government closed down the slave market in Khartoum, turning a blind eye when it reopened in the suburbs, and hired the British explorer and big game hunter Sir Samuel Baker to go up the Nile to enforce the khedive's wishes.

Ismail and Baker must have been aware that the annual trade now amounted to more than 50,000 slaves being brought out of Sudan, and that the livelihood of most Egyptians was dependent on the continuation of this practice. Baker himself had about as little sympathy for the slaves as the khedive and knew the trade well. He had already written: "However we may condemn the horrible system of slavery, the results of emancipation have proved that the negro does not appreciate the blessings of freedom, nor does he show the slightest feelings of gratitude to the hand that broke the rivets of his fetters."[4] But like the khedive, the Englishman recognized that the time had come to break with the custom. Besides, the salary of £40,000 over a four-year tenure that he had been offered was exceedingly generous.

It is to Baker that we owe a less-than-flattering description of early Khartoum: "A more miserable, filthy, and unhealthy place can hardly be imagined." Now almost 50 years old, the city of 30,000 was a collection of mud huts of burnt brick where dead animals lay in the streets, which were cleaned only when the Nile flooded. The Egyptians he saw didn't so much rule Sudan from the city as plunder it. And yet for Baker and his wife, Khartoum was fascinating. Civilization ended at this point and the unfathomable jungle began. Caravans and convoys met here, bringing with them the fruits of both — precious slaves, gold, and ivory jostling with biscuit tins from Fortnum & Mason, troops of light-skinned concubines on display beside exquisite Italian pianos and the latest Remington rifles, and French wines competing with elephant tusks. There were flowers, birds, and reptiles that hadn't been named by Europeans yet, and there were Stone Age people agog at the sight of mud huts.

Baker and his blond wife, Florence, departed from Khartoum on February 8, 1870, with boats that could be taken apart and carried in pieces across the desert by camels to be reassembled above the cataracts. The deeper south they went the more desolation caused by the slave trade was evident. The venal Egyptians were hated, the Arab slavers were feared, and the "Franks," as all Europeans were called by the Africans, were one step below both. But in 1871 Baker and his escort made it through the Sudd by damming the swamp so that boats could float through. When the Englishman raised the khedive's flag at Gondokoro where Austrian missionaries had been for two decades, he thought the River Styx must have been more attractive.

Here the Nile divided into a series of cataracts and swamps, effectively marking the navigable end of the river. So Baker paraded his Egyptian soldiers (all felons taken from prisons in Cairo), displayed paintings of Queen Victoria to the wondering locals, and dubbed the surrounding, unmapped countryside "Equatoria."[5] He eventually discovered a huge body of water, Luta Nzige, and with the intrepid Florence paddled it in a dugout canoe, proclaiming the lake the fabled source of the Nile. His subsequent books on Sudan and the Nile, *The Albert N'yanza* and *The Nile's Tributaries*, became the most read non-fiction in Victorian England. Known as "Baker of the Nile," he was knighted by Her Majesty (the royal recognition temporarily withheld when the queen discovered that the Bakers weren't formally married), and achieved a form of immortality when Henry Rider Haggard modelled the character Allan Quartermain after him in *King Solomon's Mines*, a novel about slaves and ivory.

Although later attacked by anti-slavery societies in England as a dupe of the khedive, Baker had made vigorous attempts to end slavery in Equatoria — at one point preventing the abduction of the blond Florence with his revolver. But when he returned to Cairo at the end of his contract in 1865, all he had done was push the slavers away from the Nile and into the deserts of Darfur and Kordofan. Here, out of sight from the European missionaries, Egyptian officials, and British anti-slavery observers, the slave-trading king Zobeir Pasha ruled all of Bahr-al-Ghazal, and the industry flourished so much that it was feared African tribes would soon be extinct. Now Zobeir was coming to Cairo to press the khedive into recognizing his power and making him the legal governor of Darfur.

2

GORDON, WOLSELEY, AND THE SIEGE OF KHARTOUM

The profligate nature of Khedive Ismail Pasha (matched only by that of King Farouk's 50 years later) had made the need for money more desperate than ever. With the end of the U.S. Civil War, the American cotton exports recovered sufficiently to undersell the Egyptian crop and the khedive was reduced to selling his shares in the Suez Canal to the British for £4 million. The country's international reputation was at stake, for besides ivory, ostrich feathers, and gum arabic, another source of revenue was about to open up — tourism — and Thomas Cook's agents were already offering "package tours" up the Nile. If Samuel Baker could pacify Equatoria, there must be an Englishman who could do the same for the remainder of Sudan.

At 41, Colonel Charles George Gordon of the Royal Engineers was one of the most famous men of his day. Hero of the Crimean War (with fellow officer Garnet Wolseley), he seemed ambivalent to danger as he had proven with his indifference to the Russian bullets whizzing around him at the siege of Sebastopol. Away from the "penny dreadful" hype, Gordon was a loner. He was an unhappy misfit in the British Army, eccentric in custom and mystical in religion, and something of a Victorian version of Lawrence of Arabia. When approached in Constantinople by the khedive's agent in 1872, he was already larger than life because of his role in leading the Ever Victorious Army of the Emperor of China to victory against the Taiping rebels. Legend had it that he had done so armed with only a walking stick, his moral superiority, and a Bible. If rebellious toward society's laws, he obeyed God's to the letter.

In an age of excess, Gordon was the Victorian ideal — a knight who was pure in heart and body (unmarried, he had no discernible sexual preference). His blue eyes, it was said, "allowed him to look into the very heart of his fellow man." And what he saw made him sick. He scorned the "hollow emptiness" of his own class. "I am like Moses who despised the riches of Egypt," he wrote to his sister, the only person of the opposite sex closest to him. If years later his character was attacked as that of a depressed alcoholic, what is generally agreed is that Gordon was a good soldier and was deeply concerned for his fellow man — whatever his colour, race, or religion. He also had such great faith in his own invincibility that, his critics alleged, he was a supreme egotist. Given a leave of absence from the British Army, he was hired by the khedive to accomplish three things: expand Egyptian rule in Southern Sudan, find the source of the Nile past Gondokoro, and abolish the slave trade.

It was an undertaking that any other man would have refused outright, but Gordon's belief in himself was such that it allowed him to reply that he accepted but refused the £40,000 salary given to Baker, saying that £2,000 was enough for his needs. Within two years he accomplished much: he built more forts in Equatoria, military discipline was strictly enforced within them, and by leading through his own honesty, his Egyptian soldiers didn't pillage, thereby earning the gratitude of the natives. In Khartoum he burned all debtors' records, stopped flogging in prisons, and forgave the peasants their tax debts. But even he soon realized that abolishing the slave trade was impossible, particularly since the Egyptian and Sudanese society and economy were built on it. Many Africans saw slavery as inevitable and felt there was nothing morally untoward about it. Without a wage-paying economy on the continent, slavery was the only acceptable currency and the sole form of employment.

Gordon himself had to buy his own servants — two Shilluk boys aged nine and twelve — and exchanged four pounds of grain for them. He knew he wasn't doing servants any favours by freeing them; they were fearful of walking back home and being re-enslaved or killed by neighbouring tribes along the way. Not surprisingly, Gordon and the Anti-Slavery Society in London soon fell out. In the latter's view,

Gordon wasn't doing enough to free slaves. Had the British abolitionists, Gordon wrote back, noticed who did all the labour in industrialized England — from factories to private homes? Eradicating the slave trade, he thought, required a more humane rule by the Egyptians, an impossibility given the involvement of the khedive and his friends. In 1876 Gordon resigned in disillusionment and returned to England.

The British Army, with a hero and celebrity on its hands, did what any large organization would in such circumstances: it posted Gordon to the obscurity of the Thames estuary, putting him in charge of coastal defences in case the French invaded. There he was so moved by the plight of homeless children on the streets of Gravesend that he spent his own salary (and sold the gifts given him by the Chinese emperor) to set up homes and schools for them (Gordon School in Gravesend flourishes today). And there he might have remained, dying in lonely exile, had not Ismail cabled him on January 17, 1877.

In a clever ploy that appealed to Gordon's vanity, the telegram said: "I refuse to believe that when Gordon has given his word as a gentleman, anything will ever induce him to go back on his word." The khedive was playing for time. He had kidnapped and imprisoned the slaver king Zobeir in Cairo and now needed someone to take charge of Sudan before the expected storm of unrest began. The incorruptible Englishman was to be made governor general of Sudan and would be given plenipotentiary powers to negotiate with local chiefs. More important, he would be allowed to punish and dismiss any Egyptian officials caught in corruption.

Gordon did return, and armed with his new powers he cleaned house in Khartoum, firing the corrupt "Turks" and riding a camel to distant parts of Sudan to negotiate peace with Zobeir's family in Darfur. Here he also won a pitched battle with the slave king's son after which 10,000 slaves were freed. Then he rode to the opposite end of the country to deal with the Abyssinian chiefs. Europeans and American bureaucrats were taken on to replace the corrupt Egyptians, and the Sudd was opened for regular navigation. Two truths caused Gordon to doubt his own mission: the gradual realization that freed slaves so far from home remained for their own protection in Khartoum (like the internally displaced persons a century later) inexorably starving to death, and second, that domestic slavery was the bedrock of Sudanese society and destroying it had inevitable consequences.

However, it was events in Cairo and Gordon's own ego that precipitated the British hero's downfall. Ismail's European creditors were pushing him to resign, so playing his only card, the khedive had Gordon brought to Cairo to intercede for him. That turned out to be akin to throwing gasoline onto a fire, since Gordon treated the "money men" with a patronizing attitude and was immovable to their entreaties to pressure Ismail to change his profligate ways. By attempting to end the slave trade, Gordon had also alienated many powerful Egyptians, to say nothing of Zobeir's henchmen.

In June 1879 the bankers lost patience with Ismail, and he was deposed and sent off in his yacht with more than £3 million of the treasury to a luxurious exile in a palace on the Bosporus. The knives were now out for the former khedive's protégé, and the following year Gordon was pushed to resign. Although he was respected in Khartoum, no one in Cairo was sad to see him leave. Worse, on his way back to England he stopped off in Paris and suggested to the French that they take over the wasteland that was Sudan, which only made him more unpopular in certain circles.

The British were already alarmed at French incursions into Arab Africa — Tunisia had just been colonized by France — but were hesitant at being sucked into the morass that was Egypt (and its colony Sudan) and installed successive puppet governments in Cairo to safeguard their investment in the Suez Canal. Egypt was, in effect, run by Sir Evelyn Baring (later Lord Cromer) of the banking family and now the British representative in Cairo, while Major-General (later Field Marshal and Viscount) Garnet Wolseley became the military commander of British troops in the country in 1882.

Like Gordon, who he called "Charlie," Wolseley had fought wars across the world, in his case in the Crimea, India, China, South Africa, and Canada. Wolseley was vain and pompous, his family origins were suspect (his father had been a bankrupt Irish major), and he had climbed the rungs of respectability and promotion through cultivating connections such as the author Henry James and the poet laureate Alfred Austin, who were friends. The major-general largely came to the attention of his superiors and the public thanks to his relentless search for methods to increase the efficiency of the British Army, so much so that he was lampooned as the "very model of a modern major-general" in Gilbert and Sullivan's *The Pirates of Penzance,* the operetta that premiered in London in 1880.[1]

As a 28-year-old lieutenant-colonel, Wolseley had arrived in Montreal in December 1861 to be the assistant quartermaster to the British Army in North America. He was posted to a militia officer training school at La Prairie outside Montreal. It was a crucial time for the snowbound colony. British Army engineers were just drawing up the North American boundary between an unexplored Canada and a bellicose United States, and Wolseley had been one of 11,000 British troops rushed to defend Canada against an expected invasion from below the border. A month before, a Union warship had seized the British passenger ship *Trent* to extract the Confederate passengers onboard. This act of piracy on the high seas only made a bad situation worse as, encouraged by Irish nationalists in the United States, it looked as though the victorious North would now annex Canada. Britain could spare few troops to defend a border that barely existed and encouraged its Canadian colonies to link up and join in a confederation.

While at La Prairie, Wolseley not only made trips across the U.S. border to observe the Civil War but also met Iroquois voyageurs at the settlement of Caughnawaga. The invasion never took place, but the very threat served to make the British North American colonies come together in 1867. The new country of Canada faced its first crisis three years later when Louis Riel sought to take the Red River settlement in southern Manitoba out of Confederation. Prime Minister Sir John A. Macdonald knew that a military force had to be sent to Fort Garry (now Winnipeg) to assert Ottawa's authority over Riel — and before the Americans did.

The quickest way would have been to send troops by rail to Minneapolis and then by boat on the Red River to Fort Garry, but Washington would never condone a foreign army crossing its border.

That left the arduous and largely unexplored route from Ottawa across the Great Lakes and then overland for 500 miles to Winnipeg and the Red River. The fur traders of another century knew the route well, not to mention the many rivers, bogs, waterfalls, and dense forest that had to be crossed.

Lieutenant-Colonel Wolseley was put in charge of leading 1,200 local militia and regular British soldiers to Fort Garry with wooden boats and military supplies. He recruited 400 voyageurs, mainly Iroquois from Caughnawaga but also some French Canadians from Trois-Rivières, to portage his force. Wolseley didn't know it at the time, but they were the last of their profession that had begun with the historic *coureurs de bois*.

By July 16, 1870, all had arrived by Canadian Pacific steamer at the far end of Lake Superior (now Thunder Bay) and set off through the morass to Fort Garry. The 25-foot boats had to be carried or rolled over no less than 50 portages, with Wolseley marching at the head of the force, which carried his own birchbark canoe.[2] The Englishman was deeply impressed both by the wiry voyageurs and the enthusiasm of the young Canadian officers, all of whom suffered through 13 weeks of drenching rain and torment by mosquitoes and blackflies. The first Canadian military expedition ever launched arrived at Fort Garry in late August to find that Riel had fled. But Macdonald and the War Office were pleased with the results — no lives had been lost and federal authority had been asserted in the West with the British government picking up the tab. Wolseley was knighted for his services and left Canada well pleased with himself, confident that he could reproduce the logistics of the expedition for the same results anywhere in the world — up the Nile if need be.

Britain's prime minister, William Ewart Gladstone, had no interest in Sudan. Domestic matters, which were boring to British newspaper editors, were his strength. The press was more interested in what was occurring up the Nile — a Messianic prophet rising out of the desert, slaves yearning to be free, the call for a plucky British officer with a Bible and a stiff upper lip who could be sent among (as Rudyard Kipling put it) "those lesser breeds without the law." The old prime minister foresaw that venturing upriver would inevitably cause the superpowers of the day, the English and the French (and possibly the Germans), to clash, precipitating a wider conflict. Hoping matters would settle themselves, he ignored the growing tension and calls for action for as long as possible. Then in September 1881, as in Colonel Gamal Abdel Nasser's time in the 1950s, a group of young Egyptian army officers attempted a coup to throw the foreigners out. In the ensuing unrest the Royal Navy evacuated all Europeans from Alexandria and, as an afterthought, bombarded the port's batteries, which had recently been built by former officers of the Confederate Army. Descending into chaos, Egypt was about to be hit by a force out of the Sudanese desert unlike any other.

Scholars accept that the Mahdi was born in Dongola Province in 1844 and that even as a young man he exuded an intense magnetism in his personality to the point of being possessed. Although no photographs of the Mahdi exist, those who met him never forgot his appearance. He had a heavy build with a mole on his left cheek, and his dark complexion was illuminated by white teeth in which there was a gap in the upper middle — a sign of good luck in Sudan. The man was soft-spoken, but there was no doubt that he possessed a fanaticism that could only come from the austerity of the desert. Although Muhammad Ahmad ibn as Sayyid Abdallah was the son of a poor teacher, he believed he was the reincarnation of the Prophet, as foretold, who would renew the faith. As such he called himself the Mahdi, or the Expected One.

To the Mahdi, the only thing worse than the corrupt Egyptians and proselytizing "Frank" missionaries were those Muslims who strayed from the true path and indulged in alcohol, smoking, dancing, swearing, and the company of women other than their relatives. His followers, called the Ansar, wore patched white smocks symbolizing their poverty and, like the Afghan Taliban a century later, they enforced a code of asceticism, meting out floggings and arm amputations for the most trivial of offences such as attendance at wedding feasts, the playing of music, and other amusements.

The Mahdi preached that there was a single way to live honourably — in his service in the war against the infidels. Beyond seizing power as a local warlord, he wanted to build a theocracy in Sudan, overthrow the Turks, and liberate the holy cities of Mecca and Medina. His popular appeal extended to desert tribes such as the Beja, traditionally anti-authoritarian, who threw their lot in with the Ansar and brought with them their camel herds and warrior fanaticism. The Egyptian government in Khartoum first sent an army to capture the Mahdi, looking forward to bringing this false prophet to Cairo in chains where he could be suitably tortured. Instead, in August 1882 without guns, the Ansar routed the Egyptians and captured the fort at El Obeid, massacring the garrison. Now armed with modern weapons, the Mahdi openly waged a jihad, or holy war, and took all of Kordofan.

The Egyptian government in Cairo, smarting from its humiliation first at the hands of the British and now a Sudanese wild man, next sent a well-equipped force of 7,000 infantry, 1,000 cavalry, and 2,000 camp followers against the Mahdi. It was led by William Hicks, a former British Indian Army officer who had no experience in the desert. A London *Times* correspondent summed the affair up suitably: "9,000 infants that 50 good men could rout in 10 minutes." Before long, Egypt's new army was out of water and then even its camels died. Lost and dispirited, Hicks's troops were an easy target for the Mahdi's dervishes, which now numbered 50,000. The ensuing massacre in November 1883 gave the Mahdi not only artillery and the latest Maxim machine guns but his prestige in Sudan grew in proportion. Slave dealers and tribesmen flying the green flag of the Mahdi adorned with texts from the Koran rose up against their Egyptian masters and joined the revolt. Fort after fort fell along the Nile, and panic ensued in Khartoum, Cairo, and London. Gladstone didn't want the British military involved. The Suez Canal was Britain's main interest in the region — and it was safe. The desert fanatic was an Egyptian problem. But in December 1883, after months of procrastination, the prime minister was forced into a decision about Sudan.

Since Egypt could no longer defend itself (the British had seen to that), it was to abandon Sudan and withdraw all garrisons upriver from Wadi Halfa. From now on Britain would assume responsibility for Egypt's defence. It was easy to sit in London and talk of abandoning Sudan to the Mahdi's followers, but as the British press pointed out: what about the evacuation of the 21,000 Egyptian soldiers in Khartoum and the forts along the Nile? Surely, Britain now had a moral responsibility to do so. Egged on by the retired Sir Samuel Baker who wrote incessantly to the *Times*, the British public soon learned the mantra: if Khartoum fell, it followed that Cairo would and then what would happen to the Suez Canal and the British Empire east of it? Only one man, the *Pall Mall Gazette* opined, could save the day — an Englishman, of course.

Very soon newspaper readers across the empire wanted to know: "Where is Gordon when his country needs him?" The question was much discussed in clubs, pubs, and the British Cabinet. The great man himself was about to be employed by King Leopold of the Belgians to deal with the Congo, but another appeal to his vanity, this time by supporters at the War Office, led to a change of mind. Seen off at Charing Cross Station, London, on January 18, 1884, by Wolseley and the commander-in-chief of the army, the old Duke of Cambridge, Gordon was given straightforward instructions: report on the situation from Khartoum and do nothing more. Later, Wolseley added that Gordon was also to evacuate all inhabitants from that city.

At the same time an expedition under the command of Major-General Gerald Graham, VC, was sent to the Sudanese Red Sea port of Suakin to relieve the Egyptian garrison besieged at Tokar by Osman Digma, one of the Mahdi's commanders. Graham was also tasked to crush the rebellious Beja tribe in the vicinity of Suakin. The British force landed by February 27, and two days later Graham led his column to relieve Tokar. En route the British force attacked the enemy at El Teb, and in the square formation that was adopted during the action, the Gordon Highlanders were put in the front face. The enemy couldn't break through and were soon routed. Soon after, Tokar was relieved.

Although Gordon received a rapturous welcome from the citizens of Khartoum exactly a month later, it was as much for his personal reputation as the assurance that Britain would now get involved and its military might save the day. "I come without soldiers, but with God on my side to redress the evils of Sudan," he told the crowd, few of whom understood English. "I will not fight with any weapons but justice." Given the choice, the audience would rather have had crates of Remington rifles than Gordon's delusions, but they cheered, anyway. In any case, the city of 34,000 inhabitants was well defended by both Niles, there were enough armoured steamers to get at least the Europeans out, and as long as the telegraph worked, the outside world knew that Gordon was alive. In the hope that they might rise up against the Mahdi, Tawfiq Pasha (Ismail Pasha's son and now the khedive) formally granted "the peoples of Sudan their freedom," and Gordon's first act on arrival was to allow all tribal chiefs to keep their slaves if they supported the Egyptians. But it was all too late. Centuries of brutality were a motive for outright massacre of any unfortunate Egyptians who fell into the wrong hands, and most tribal chiefs fearing what would happen to them when the Egyptians left had already gone over to the Mahdi.

Gordon could have escaped with his staff — he had eight armoured steamers at his disposal and the Mahdi had offered all Europeans safe passage through his lines — but he chose to stay, watching for the relief column from the roof of the palace. He warned Cairo that the Mahdi wouldn't be satisfied with the fall of Khartoum, that the Expected One would want all of Egypt. On February 26, 1884, in one of the last telegrams sent out before the line was cut, Gordon told Evelyn Baring: "If Egypt is to be quiet, Mahdi must be smashed up." But Gladstone stood firm. Gordon hadn't been asked to destroy the Mahdi, and by remaining in Khartoum, he was disobeying orders from his commander-in-chief.

Recognizing a fellow ascetic in the Mahdi, Gordon wrote that "he would sooner live like a Dervish with the Mahdi than go out to dinner every night in London." He had no faith in the Egyptian troops in his charge or the merchants who hoarded grain. The khedive's soldiers guarding the walls napped unless they knew he was watching through his telescope. "A more contemptible soldier than the Egyptian never existed," Gordon recorded in his journal. "Here we never count on them; they are held in supreme contempt, poor creatures."

Throughout the long summer London feared the worst. The Egyptian soldiers could be abandoned to the Mahdi. They weren't British citizens. But Gordon, "one noble-hearted Englishman, resolute, righteous, and fearless," to quote the *Times*, and now elevated to the cult of a saint, could not. He was selflessly giving up his own life for the citizens of Khartoum. There were mass demonstrations in London, the press took up the outcry, and Her Majesty Queen Victoria sent off strongly worded telegrams to her foreign secretary: "General Gordon is in danger; you are bound to try to save him … you have incurred fearful responsibility." The unfortunate Gladstone came to realize that not only his government's fate but his own reputation depended on Gordon's rescue. So on August 1, 1884, Wolseley (who had been preparing for the possibility all summer) was told to lead such an expedition. Major Herbert Kitchener, a Royal Engineer like Gordon and now seconded to the Egyptian Army, had been sent three months before to reconnoitre the siege and report back to London. Learning to ride a camel and disguised as an Arab (and carrying poison if he fell into the Mahdi's hands), Kitchener intercepted Gordon's increasingly desperate messages.

The staff at the War Office had already drawn up plans for the shortest route to relieve Gordon. As it had with Graham, the Royal Navy would land Wolseley's force at Port Suakin on the Red Sea from where he could make the quickest speed overland to Khartoum. With William Hicks's disaster still fresh, Wolseley countered with his own proposal. While he agreed that there should be an overland force to get to Khartoum before it fell, he wanted to take the vanguard by boat up the Nile. At some point that summer he recalled the events 14 years earlier when the tough Canadian voyageurs had taken his 1,400 men from Lake Superior to the Red River. The rapids (or cataracts) of the Nile, he held, were no different than those of the Canadian wilderness. The planners in the War Office disagreed. Thomas Cook had placed his tourist steamboats at the force's disposal to take the soldiers as far as they could. From that point the soldiers would go overland. Whatever means of transport was used, since the Mahdi controlled the desert, the rescue force had to be logistically self-reliant in food, ammunition, and water, which made the idea of using small boats unfeasible. Everyone was also aware that Gordon was running out of time. But the "very model of a modern major-general" was firm, and he had an ace up his sleeve.

3

VOYAGEURS ON THE NILE

On August 20, 1884, Garnet Wolseley had the Colonial Office cable Lord Lansdowne, the governor general of Canada:

> I would propose to send all the dismounted portion of the force up the Nile to Khartoum in boats, as we sent the little expeditionary force from Lake Superior to Fort Garry on the Red River in 1870. It is proposed to endeavour to engage 300 good voyageurs from Caughnawaga, Saint Regis and Manitoba as steersmen in boats for Nile expedition — engagement for 6 months with passage to & from Egypt. Will pay of 40 dollars a month with suit of clothes and rations free be sufficient? The voyageurs should arrive at Liverpool not later than the 1st of October, but if possible by the 15th of September. Three officers of Canadian militia might accompany party.[1]

Lansdowne had his private secretary, Major Lord Melgund (later the Earl of Minto), travel immediately to brief Prime Minister John A. Macdonald, who was vacationing at Rivière-du-Loup, Quebec. Macdonald agreed to sanction this project, but conscious of how it might play out in Quebec he stipulated it be made clear that the Canadians recruited were being paid by the British government and that this military expedition wasn't an officially sponsored one. Other British colonies later volunteered troops for Sudan — New South Wales, India, and Fiji, among them — but like Prime Minister Mackenzie King at the out-break of the Second World War, Macdonald was cautious about getting involved overseas. He didn't want Canada to be seen as automatically embroiled in what was a British imperial conflict. The Canadians might be under military discipline in the Sudan, but they were still civilians. When Melgund returned to Ottawa, he put advertisements in various newspapers across the country under the banner headline IMPORTANT TO BOATMEN and asked J.T. Lambert, an Ottawa timber broker, for help with the selection.

Unknown to Wolseley, though, by the 1880s there were few true voyageurs of the fur trade left. Railways and steamboats had made their canoeing and portaging feats obsolete. The lumber industry had replaced the fur trade, and instead of voyageurs there were now "shantymen," the French Canadians who rode herd on the great log rafts down rivers. Fiercely autonomous, hard-drinking, and boisterous in spirit, they were skilled in guiding small boats through rapids (except few could swim) and ideal for Wolseley's needs. For the British they still embodied the stereotype of the voyageur.

The first of the three Canadian militia officers Melgund obtained was Frederick Charles Denison, who had served on the Red River expedition. Educated at Upper Canada College and Osgoode Hall law school, Denison had been called to the bar in 1870. His older brother, Lieutenant-Colonel George Taylor Denison, was a famous military author whose books on cavalry had been translated into Russian, German, and Hungarian. Living in his brother's shadow, Frederick Denison was a major in the prestigious Toronto unit of the Governor General's Body Guard. Since most of the voyageurs were bound to be French-speaking and Denison wasn't, Captain Telmont Aumond from the Ottawa unit of the Governor General's Foot Guards was recruited. Not only was young Aumond fluently bilingual, but his father had a lumber business and he knew the river men well. The third officer chosen was Captain Alexander C. MacRae of the Seventh Battalion, Fusiliers, from London, Ontario. Like Denison, he had served with Wolseley on the Fort Garry force. The governor general's secretary noted of Aumond and MacRae: "We have succeeded in sending two of the toughest customers [to the Sudan], but I believe that they are both well suited to their work."

Canadian Minister for the Militia Adolphe Caron recommended that a Laval medical school graduate, Major John Louis Hubert Neilson, be taken to look after the force's medical needs. Neilson, also a veteran of the Red River expedition and a medical officer with the International Red Cross in Serbia during the Russo-Turkish War of 1877, was later hired by the *Toronto Star* as a correspondent. Conscious of the spiritual needs of the French-Canadian boatmen, Caron also recommended that a Catholic priest be invited. An enormous French Canadian with a bushy black beard, Father Arthur Bouchard was a fortunate asset for the expedition. Not only had he done missionary work in Sudan and spoke good Arabic, but his recent experience in Khartoum in 1879 would help prepare the Canadians for what lay ahead. However, Bouchard didn't think much of Wolseley's idea of rescue by boat. He felt the construction of a railway would be more practical. Still, he knew his shantymen well and was better prepared than the others for the voyage and for Sudan.[2]

Although Wolseley had asked for only three militia officers, he now had doubts about that number, so on August 28 he asked Melgund to telegraph a friend in Winnipeg for "50 good Manitoba men." Lieutenant-Colonel William Nassau Kennedy had founded the 90th Battalion of the Winnipeg Rifles, the only militia regiment west of Toronto. Originally from Ontario, Kennedy, a former house painter, had served in the Red River expedition and had remained in Manitoba afterward. There he promoted railway companies before being elected as the second mayor of Winnipeg. Kennedy ran advertisements in the *Manitoba Daily Free Press* and the *Winnipeg Sun* during the week of August 29 to September 6. They read: "Wanted Immediately 50 men to accompany GORDON RELIEF EXPEDITION in Egypt to take charge of small boats on the rapids of the Nile. Must be good boatmen. Men who were in Red River expedition preferred."

Many of the men accepted by Kennedy were bored young Winnipeg professionals and businessmen. Eight were lawyers who had no experience as boatmen but were looking for adventure in exotic Sudan. The recruits with real river experience were 12 Saulteaux headed by Chief

William Prince and also 25 of the last voyageurs from Rat Portage (now Kenora).

By August 29, the enthusiastic Kennedy cabled Wolseley that he had 50 voyageurs and that he and his second-in-command of the Winnipeg Rifles, Major Daniel McMillan, would accompany the party. Wolseley was pleased and then asked that a birchbark canoe be bought for his own use, with spare bark and gum. He also told Kennedy that each participant should bring his own paddle. Kennedy subsequently asked if he could also recruit 50 raftsmen in addition to his voyageurs, and that was also agreed to.

On September 6, Kennedy cabled Lord Melgund that he now had 80 men ready to go to the Nile. As the military historian Colonel C.P. Stacey later pointed out, the addition of the Manitoba contingent brought with it seeds of future problems. Not only did its young businessmen speak no French and had no river experience, but they were a social class above the rough-and-ready French Canadians from the East. Then there was the hierarchy of rank: Kennedy was a lieutenant-colonel and Denison was a major. So who would command the expedition? The influential Denison family lobbied on behalf of Frederick, and Melgund caved in. Kennedy might have brought 92 men to the force, but the British had specified that only three Canadian militia officers were to be accepted and there was no place for him. When a deputation of the Saulteaux asked that Kennedy accompany them as their "boss" or foreman in an unpaid role, the relieved Melgund agreed to this, as did Denison, who was now promoted to lieutenant-colonel to make sure there were no further misunderstandings. Once on the Nile, Kennedy was to be the acting quartermaster and paymaster of the expedition.

So, 17 years after Confederation, for the first time in its history, Canada provided aid and relief to another country, one that it continues to do so for to the present day. The average French Canadian, and probably all of the boatmen, had little idea of Sudan's state or who Major-General Gordon was. And if they had heard of the Nile, it was from the Bible. For English Canadians, though, the expedition was heeding the call of the British Empire, and Macdonald was taken to task by the Toronto newspapers for not doing more. The contract for the boatmen's six-month employment ran from September 9, 1884, to March 9, 1885, which was agreeable, since that would have them returning in time for the busy season of the logging industry.

On September, 13, 1884, after first being photographed in front of the Parliament Buildings in their slouch hats and new set of clothes, 200 of the boatmen were feted by the citizens of Ottawa and escorted by the band of the Governor General's Foot Guards down Wellington Street to the station to catch the train for Montreal.[3] It hadn't even been a month since Wolseley's initial telegram to Lansdowne. The efficient Melgund had organized the recruitment, outfitting, and embarkation with a minimum of fuss, a feat he would repeat as governor general when under his guidance Canada sent a contingent to the Boer War.[4] Of the more than 360 in the party, 159 came from around Ottawa, six from Sherbrooke, Quebec, 15 from Peterborough, Ontario, 39 from Trois-Rivières, Quebec, 56 from Caughnawaga, Quebec, and 92 from Manitoba.

But Wolseley's shopping list wasn't finished. While observing the U.S. Civil War, he had become quite taken by the use of Mississippi sternwheelers to supply the army. He cabled Lansdowne to purchase two such ships for the Nile and to find "eight good men accustomed to working and steering sternwheel steamers in rapids." Melgund was once more given the job of finding them, and 10 days later he telegraphed Wolseley that he also had men from Ottawa and the St. Lawrence River who, while not knowledgeable about sternwheelers, were used to taking steamers up and down the Lachine Rapids. The War Office agreed to hire the eight men — four each from Ottawa and Manitoba at $150 a month. The eight arrived in Alexandria, Egypt, on October 30, and the two sternwheelers *Water Lily* and *Lotus* followed soon after. Throughout the expedition the eight would pilot the sternwheelers between Aswan and Wadi Halfa, ferrying supplies to the jumping-off point of the expedition. The eight returned to Canada in March 1885, having had a romantic, if uneventful, paid vacation.

The War Office chartered the midsize steamer *Ocean King* to take them from Montreal to Alexandria. When it docked at Quebec City on September 15, the governor general visited the men, donating books and board games to help while away the voyage and exhorting them in both languages to acquit themselves credibly. Alcohol and the shanty-men's distaste for shipboard and military discipline plagued the voyage in Montreal, Quebec City, and Sydney, Nova Scotia (where the ship coaled, three of the boatmen deserted, and a stowaway was discovered) until, at Gibraltar, Denison had an armed guard surround the ship to prevent further drunken sorties ashore.[5]

The Canadians arrived at Alexandria on October 7, the port 1,600 miles downriver from Khartoum. Here they met another Canadian, Major James Frederick Wilson (nicknamed "Cupid" for a reason that history hasn't recorded) of the Regiment of the Canadian Artillery in Kingston, Ontario, who had permission to be seconded to Wolseley's rescue force that summer. The War Office allowed this on the understanding that all of Wilson's expenses would be borne by the Canadian government. Here, too, the voyageurs first saw the boats they were to handle. Standard Royal Navy whalers 30 feet long and six and a half feet wide, they had been somewhat enlarged and modified. They had to be capable of being rowed, poled, sailed, or towed, and able to carry a dozen fully armed soldiers and their supplies for 100 days. On August 12, 47 British shipyards had been given orders to build 800 such whalers. Amazingly, within 10 weeks all of them were stowed onboard 19 ships bound for Alexandria. When they got there, they were loaded onto trains and sent south to Aswan at the old border with Sudan. From here they were towed by the khedive's yacht *Ferooz* to Korti, a town between the Third and Fourth Cataracts.

The Canadians transferred for Cairo by train on October 8, with Kennedy remaining in Alexandria to draw some money with which to pay expenses and catching up later. Father Bouchard also left to report to his bishop in Cairo and would rejoin his flock farther upstream. They continued by rail to Assiut from where they boarded a steamer to Aswan. Here a portage railway bypassed the First Cataract, and then it was on by another small ship to Wadi Halfa and the Second Cataract, a series of waterfalls covering more than eight and a half miles of the river, the party arriving there on October 26. Going up the Nile was a source of wonder for everyone. They saw the ancient ruins mentioned in the Bible, camel caravans, and date palms, and gawked at the almost nude native women on the banks of the Nile who wore only lace breech clouts. Denison succeeded in purchasing one such piece of clothing from a maiden for 25 cents.

Called "Bloody Halfway" by the British troops because it was exactly 800 miles between Cairo and Khartoum, the logistical depot of Wadi Halfa was the end of the railway line and the launching point for the force. In 1884 the border town looked, as one correspondent wrote, as if "it were the goods station of a London terminus set in the middle of the desert." Here, on October 26, the instigator of their journey, Wolseley, welcomed the "rough-looking lot" of Canadians, as he wrote in his journal, but was especially pleased to see his comrades from the Red River days — Denison, Neilson, Kennedy, and MacRae.

Now the boatmen set to work, climbing the rapids and portaging around those they couldn't ascend. They were divided into independent groups, rowing, sailing, and working the modified whalers up the river, and living with the British regiments they had been assigned to. As soon as they got the troops over one cataract to another, they returned to the beginning for the next. By then, since the river channel might have changed course, they had to rediscover the whole system once more. Years later Denison described what the voyageurs had accomplished:

> As a usual thing, six men pulled. The voyageur took the rudder, sometimes the bow. When the boat came to a strong current, the men would pull their best, and with a good way on would get up; but if they failed and were carried back, I have seen them make the attempt a second and third time, straining every nerve and then succeed. If it were impossible to row up, all the crew but the boatman and the man at the rudder would disembark, get out their tracking line, put it over their shoulders, and walk along the bank, tracking the boat, until they reached smooth water again. When they came to a bad rapid, instead of having one crew on the rope, 3, 4 or 5 crews, according to the rush of water would be put on.... When it became necessary to place 30 or 40 men

on the line, it was generally necessary to unload the arms and perhaps part of the load.... Great care had to be exercised to see that there was not any slack rope so that on the Nile you would hear the words from morning until night, "Pull up the slack," "Haul away." ... If there was too much slack rope, the current would catch the boat, running her out into the stream broadside on, and sometimes filling the boat. She would turn over, throwing the voyageurs into the water.[6]

The long day began at first light, which quickly gave way to the burning sun and ended with the cool of sunset, allowing the boatmen to rest their muscles and repair clothes that had been made ragged by the hauling. The rations were standard British Army fare in North Africa — tinned bully beef supplemented by dates. The officers brought their own supplies of alcohol, and one man even enjoyed a plum pudding at Christmas. But, as in the forests back home, for the shantymen there was always time around the campfire for a pipe, songs, and conversation. Rowdiness wasn't a problem — the men were confined to the camps on the riverbanks, since one never knew the sympathies of the local population. However, on the last night of October, the very first Halloween was celebrated in Sudan, possibly in all of Africa, by the North Americans. Since there were no pumpkins to carve in the middle of the desert, they played tricks such as capsizing tents and stealing blankets from the no doubt befuddled British.

The Canadians were very aware that all of Canada, indeed the whole empire, was watching and that time was running out for Gordon. With few swimmers among them and the only "life jackets" available the large biscuit tins that bobbed to the surface when boats capsized, getting through each of the rapids must have been a harrowing ordeal for British and Canadian alike. A sergeant of the Black Watch later wrote: "Nothing less than the levelheadedness and surpassing skills of the voyageurs could have guided us. Many were the hairbreadth escapes from death; for once cast overboard would have meant doom sealed; not only a watery grave but even if we could float, a zigzag journey thereto with bangs and slams against rocks, a course over which one would have no more control than an insect."[7]

Much was of out of their control. The river channels changed almost daily and the too-heavy whalers had to be emptied, the supplies portaged over by camel to be reloaded. Then Thomas Cook's ships ran out of coal in October, and between October 25 and November 10 the supply line between Aswan and Wadi Halfa dried up. In November the Mahdi began shelling Khartoum with the ill-fated William Hicks's artillery. By then the city's inhabitants were weak with starvation and were subsisting on pet animals and visiting birds. Soon the only food left in Khartoum was a palm tree fibre that could be battered into paste but brought on stomach pains when eaten. Although Gordon exhorted them to stay, telling them that he had no fear of death, by the new year of 1885, Khartoum's citizens were nightly stealing away to the Mahdi's camp.[8] Each day brought new rumours that the relief column was near. Worst of all, the Nile was falling, making the ditch on the desert side of the town passable for the besiegers.

On November 16 a messenger got through the Mahdi's lines with a cryptic note from Gordon saying that he could hold out for 40 days more, after which, he wrote in typical British understatement, "it would be difficult." Since it had taken 12 of those 40 days to reach Wolseley, the most optimistic figured that Khartoum could fall by the end of December. To hasten his rescue (and reduce the starving mouths in Khartoum), Gordon dispatched four of his armoured steamers filled with the remaining Europeans to wait at Metemmeh, just below the Sixth Cataract. They fought off the Mahdi's parties until, out of firewood, they were forced to land and were slaughtered. Hearing of this, Gordon, perhaps seeing his own fate, wrote in his journal: "We are a wonderful people, it was never our government which made us a great nation; our government has ever been the drag on our wheels. It is of course on the cards that Kartoum [*sic*] is taken under the nose of the Expeditionary Force, which will be just *too late*."[9] If Wolseley could just cut across the curve of the Nile from Korti with a land force …

Wolseley ignored the opportunity but made a number of innovations to speed up the river rescue. He offered a prize of £100 for the regiment that made the best time between Wadi Halfa and the advance base at Korti, a reward that was won by the Royal Irish Rifles. The boats were also lightened by 500 pounds — only essential supplies were to be carried from now on. And, rather than staying with the British regiments, the Canadian boatmen were broken up into groups and permanently stationed at each of the worst rapids. That new measure was appreciated by the river men, since it enabled them to build better accommodations on the shore and get to know their respective channels better each day. What raised the morale of everyone was Father Bouchard's arrival on November 16 with letters from back home. As the first of many Canadian missionaries to Sudan, Bouchard must also have been the most loved. Louis Hylas Duguay, one of the shantymen from Trois-Rivières, wrote of him:

> Apart from his ministry, he has a marvellous knack of making come to him not only the meek but also the most rebellious. You can imagine that among a composite of voyageurs, men from the lumber yards, rafters, leapers of rapids ... there will be present those who don't follow the cross of St. Louis. I have met several of them, who after an interview with this missionary, exclaim with joyful heart, "That is a good father!" ... How many times has he not been of the greatest use to our officers in a thousand unforeseen circumstances? ... It is true that he has become indispensable and that he is considered among us like an envoy of Providence.[10]

In early January 1885, Kitchener intercepted a final message from Gordon: "Khartoum all right. 14.12.84." That note of optimism had been designed to fool the enemy if it was captured, for sewn into the strands of the messenger's camel saddle the real message told of the lack of provisions and the numerous Ansar ahead of the rescue force. On New Year's Day in 1885, Wolseley decided to divide his army in half. The Desert Column would be an overland force on camels racing from Korti and bisecting the curve of the Nile to Berber below the

Fifth Cataract where it would meet up with the River Column of 3,000 men. Then the two columns would rush up the Nile, each supporting the other. All would make for Metemmeh where Gordon's boats waited to speed them on to Khartoum. The land option had always been available to Wolseley — Kitchener and the War Office had lobbied for it long before — but Wolseley had clung stubbornly to his Red River–type rescue plan. As it turned out, few of the British "Tommies" were able to stay on their camels, and it would take two weeks to train them to do so.

Three Canadians accompanied the overland force: "Cupid" Wilson of the Regiment of Canadian Artillery, Commander Edmund van Koughnet of the Royal Navy, and war correspondent Alexander MacDonald, who was appalled at the cruelty the British subjected the camels to. He predicted that most would die of exhaustion soon and hinder the rescue.

With fewer men in the boats there was now less need for the voyageurs, which was just as well, for the Nile and Sudan had proved unforgiving to the Canadians. By New Year's Day of 1885, eight had died: five by drowning, two of smallpox, and one of typhoid. What Denison rightly feared was that as March approached and the six-month contract ended the boatmen would want to return home, especially with the heat of a Sudanese summer soon to come. And he was right. Financial, clothing, and travel inducements were made: an additional $20 a month, a new set of work clothes, and upon the return journey a sightseeing stop in London (instead of Alexandria). For a shantyman, though, London or even twice his salary held no attraction, and only 89 of the surviving Canadians signed up for another six months. Disappointed as he was to see so many go, there were some that Denison was glad to be rid of, especially the Winnipeg adventurers who were more tourists than river men. The British newspapers, looking for sensationalism, described them as "trippers" and said they were "photographers, cooks, bank cashiers … all out for a holiday."

Still, with Wolseley's initiative and the British troops themselves learning to navigate the boats that were now lighter, the voyageurs who wanted to return home could be spared. In late January, Father Bouchard and Captain Aumond accompanied them back to Cairo, the trip downriver being made with comparative ease. The Canadians even stopped briefly at Wadi Halfa to participate in a sports day. Two of the Ottawa boatmen were killed when they fell off the train and were carried under its wheels between Assiut and Cairo. Wolseley, despite his mounting problems, made arrangements for the Canadians to receive a hero's welcome in Cairo. A tour of the city in open carriages, including the Pyramids, was organized with 50 of "the most fashionable ladies" as escorts. The voyageurs might have preferred to sample some of the delights of the city's less-fashionable women, but that didn't happen until, loaded down with souvenirs and shepherded by Father Bouchard and Captain Aumond, they were hustled on to Alexandria.

The voyage home was less than memorable. Accommodation and meals aboard the troopship *Poonah*, hired to take them from Alexandria to Queenston, Ireland, via Malta, were so poor that the Canadians elected one of their own to cook their meals. On arrival in Ireland, seven chose to stay there, and on February 20 the remaining boatmen, now commanded by the only officer, Captain Aumond, transferred to the better-equipped *Hanoverian* and were reportedly drunk and seasick all the way from Queenston to Halifax. Three days before their contract ended they arrived at Union Station in Ottawa on the cold winter's day of March 6, tanned and wearing a variety of Turkish and Egyptian clothing. Weighed down with souvenirs of swords, shields, cockatoos, and even monkeys, they looked more like something from Barnum & Bailey's Circus than a victorious rescue expedition. Nevertheless, they marched up Wellington Street as the capital's citizens cheered them, and that night Lord Melgund threw a banquet for them at the Drill Hall. The *Ottawa Free Press*, in flamboyant praise, said it all: "Hurrah stout hearts, well and bravely have you done your duty. Welcome home, an honour to your cherished country which proudly salutes you and totally delights to honour you."

On January 14, Wolseley's flying force was finally able to leave Korti. It was to meet an advance party of the River Column at Berber. The Mahdi, now ensconced in Omdurman and enjoying the pleasures of a greatly expanded harem, was aware of what was happening and detached 14,000 Ansar to meet Wolseley's men. Three days later at the oasis of

Abu Klea they attacked the British regulars, which with customary discipline formed into an impenetrable square. The dervishes, some armed with only sticks, broke through the square for a few desperate minutes, an accomplishment greatly admired by the British. Not even Napoleon's crack Guards regiments or Zulu warriors had accomplished this feat. Although superior firepower and superb discipline won in the end, the near-defeat was romanticized by contemporary authors, among them Winston Churchill and Rudyard Kipling. The latter especially memorialized the Beja tribesmen who made the charge:

> Then 'ere's to you, Fuzzy-Wuzzy, an' the missis and
> the kid;
> Our orders was to break you, an' of course we went
> an' did.
> We sloshed you with Martinis, an' it wasn't 'ardly fair;
> But for all the odds agin' you, Fuzzy-Wuz, you broke
> the square.

Raw courage and fanaticism were no match for the devastating effects of machine guns and shrapnel, and after the first battle of the campaign an estimated 11,000 of the Mahdi's followers lay dead in heaps. With no time to lose, the victors pressed on to rendezvous with Gordon's ships. A second battle followed in which thousands more of the Ansar were mowed down before January 21 when the Desert Column arrived at Metemmeh. That same day Denison and 67 of the 89 remaining voyageurs were rushed to the head of the River Column to get it through the worst stretch of the Nile. With its fall the river had changed channels and its banks were no longer safe, since they were infested with crocodiles. As the voyageurs poled and hauled the boats through the treacherous waters, they did so aware that they were below cliffs where Arab riflemen could easily be hidden.

The River Column, not surprisingly, almost ground to a halt. The boats, now barely 215 left of the 800 built, were showing the wear and tear of rough usage. As more boats were lost, the rescued supplies had to be added to the remaining vessels, making them top-heavy and liable to tip. Supplies again confounded the column. Food was running out and the relief force was far from Wadi Halfa. Every tin of bully beef was precious, since the men knew that Khartoum would have no food to spare. Denison discovered that the British and Egyptian troops had been pilfering food along the way — a crime punishable by firing squad. When they reached Berber, they knew they were closing in on Khartoum and that any day the Mahdi might attack. There was now a chance, though, that they could arrive before the city fell.

Instead of dashing forward to at least show a "presence," as Gordon had hoped, the Desert Force vacillated 36 hours before Khartoum fell. Fearful of the Mahdi's strength, the relievers chose to send a reconnaissance party ahead in two of Gordon's waiting boats. Thirty soldiers were put onboard, but without river experience the expected occurred. On January 25, still 50 miles north of Khartoum, one of the ships ran aground navigating the Sixth Cataract's channel, and it took precious hours to get free.

The Mahdi's scouts saw how close the British were — the rescuers purposely wore red coats borrowed from the relevant Guards regiments because it was thought they frightened the Arabs. If he was to control both banks of the Nile and annihilate the rescue by river, the Mahdi knew that Khartoum had to be taken immediately. On January 26, after a speech reminding his Ansar that those who fell in battle would secure their place in paradise and that Khartoum had untold treasure to loot, the Mahdi attacked. The ditch was easily crossed under darkness at 3:00 a.m., and the city was bombarded as a diversion. Soon the city's walls were breached and the streets were quickly littered with corpses as the attackers made for the homes of the wealthy. There was no opportunity to surrender for civilians or soldiers alike; all were hacked to death.

Chain-smoking, Gordon stood on his rooftop and fired into the attackers. When his ammunition ran out, he went back into his house, put on his best white uniform, clutched a revolver and a sword in either hand, stood at the top of the stairs, and awaited his fate. Speared to death just before the sun rose, he was decapitated and his head was taken to the Mahdi. His body continued to be speared and was then thrown into the palace well. Gordon's death disappointed the Mahdi, who respected his opponent, saying that but for the fact that the British officer was Christian, he was perfect.

For two days Khartoum was looted, with all slaves and treasure becoming the property of the Mahdi and taken across the river to his camp. On January 28 the first of the two ships of the relief flotilla appeared to be driven off by Arab artillery from both sides of the river. Even if Wolseley had arrived in time to save Gordon, he couldn't likely have taken on the Mahdi and evacuated the city. Both of his columns were in pitiful condition — low on food and ammunition, boots and clothes in shreds, and most of the camels in the Desert Column dead through overuse, just as Canadian journalist Alexander MacDonald had predicted. The next day, after being driven off, one of the column's steamers hit a rock and sank. Finally, emboldened by the fall of Khartoum and hoping for their share of plunder, thousands more Mahdists made their way to the area.

For the Canadians guiding the River Column, the first and only battle they witnessed took place at Kirbekan on February 10. Not combatants, the voyageurs stood unarmed by their boats, listening to the skirl of the pipes as the Black Watch bagpipers led a bayonet attack on the massed army of the Mahdi. But not Denison. As a militia officer, he was determined not to miss the action and attached himself to the South Staffordshire Regiment.

Once more spears and clubs were pitted against Martini rifles and machine guns, and despite the ferocity and courage of the dervishes, the battle ended with the same sad, predictable results as at Abu Klea. Disgracefully, after the last shot was fired, the voyageurs rushed to the battlefield and "secured for themselves valuable mementos in the shape of guns, knives, and swords, etc." Three days later the River Column heard of Gordon's death and the city's fall. Without orders to the contrary they continued poling and dragging the boats until on February 24 outside the village of Abu Hamel a messenger from Wolseley appeared. All further advances were to stop and the River Column was to return to Berber to wait for the Desert Column. Berber had been chosen because it was as close to the port of Suakin on the Red Sea as possible and could be linked to the Royal Navy's supply lines. Thus, the village of Abu

Hamel became the most southern point for the Canadians, who were bitterly disappointed at not seeing Khartoum, their goal since the previous year. The desert was said to be "loud with their cursing."

With Denison in the lead the whalers turned around and started down the Nile on February 26. Going downstream, they covered an average of 30 to 50 miles daily. The danger now was going too fast and being swept up by the current and dashed against the rocks. The river had fallen, and new rocks had appeared that had been hidden on the way down. Exhausted, the boatmen steered the now-fragile whalers through the gorges. At one point Wolseley wrote of the Canadians:

> The channel turned to the left, and then sharply at right angles to the right. Just at this turn, two great rocks stood out in mid stream. It was necessary to pass between them. The least error in steering would have been fatal.... I watched this triumph of skill over a difficulty that to anyone unaccustomed to such work would have seemed insuperable. Boat after boat came down at lightning speed, the men giving way with might and main to steering power; the bowmen standing cool and collected ... the steersman bringing around the boat with marvellous judgment at the right moment.[11]

On the way back to Korti a single boat overturned, drowning two wounded soldiers, the accident taking place because, as Denison explained, there had been no voyageur with them. Here the River Column rested and waited for the ragged Desert Column to stagger in. On March 13 the Canadians began their journey home. Denison was sure they would renew fighting in the autumn, and Wolseley asked if Denison would return with "four or five hundred voyageurs" to smash up the Mahdi and avenge Gordon. However, as far as London was concerned, with Gordon murdered, the war was over and Wolseley was ordered to withdraw from Sudan. The Foreign Office was now more concerned about Russian expansion in Afghanistan and the threat to India than anything the Mahdi might do in Sudan.

Ottawa, too, now had other concerns. Riel had returned, and the North-West Rebellion was taking place even as the last of the voyageurs were embarking from Cairo. Two more of the voyageurs died before they left Egypt — not on the Mahdi's spears but of typhoid fever, bringing the number of Canadians buried in Egypt to 11. While Denison was suffering from typhoid in a Cairo hospital, Kennedy took charge of the remaining voyageurs and embarked from Alexandria for London. They were to be presented to Her Majesty, but smallpox had been discovered among them and the audience was cancelled. Kennedy died of the disease on May 3 and was buried with full military honours in Highgate Cemetery, not far from the grave of Karl Marx. House painter, mayor, railway promoter, and paymaster of the expedition, Kennedy is commemorated in Winnipeg by a street named after him.

Denison received the news of Kennedy's death while still in the Cairo hospital. After buying some Turkish delight as a souvenir, he left for England, arriving on May 27. He did all the tourist "sights" in London, even going to the Derby. Denison also met up with his three brothers, who were serving in the British military. On June 6, in gratitude for his service on the Nile, he was invited to dine with the commander-in-chief of the British Army, the Duke of Cambridge, who had seen Gordon off at Charing Cross Station 18 months earlier. That August Her Majesty awarded Denison the Cross of St. Michael and St. George (C.M.G.), and his joy showed in his diary. Not even his elder brother had been so honoured. He was "the first Denison in Canada," he noted, "to receive that order."

Unfortunately, his arrival home like that of the other voyageurs was somewhat overshadowed by the excitement of the North-West Rebellion. Nor did he return to Sudan as he had expected to. Although Denison went on to a career in federal politics and was twice elected as Conservative Member of Parliament for Toronto West, his subsequent militia dealings tarnished his legacy.[12] Neither did Father Bouchard return to Sudan. The priest served his time in various parishes in the Province of Quebec until 1891 when he was made a member of the Fathers of the Holy Sacrament in Brussels and died on a posting in Trinidad in 1896.

In Britain, Gordon's death was greeted by mass hysteria in the streets, and crowds thronged Downing Street to boo Gladstone.[13] TOO LATE! shrieked the headlines when the news hit London of Gordon's death. Sick with grief, Her Majesty was said to be inseparable from Gordon's Bible, which had been dispatched to Windsor Castle by his sister. As they did during the Suez Crisis in 1956, the British press and public looked for scapegoats, and poor Gladstone played the part Anthony Eden took on in the mid-twentieth century. He and his party were thrown out of office, it somehow being forgotten that Gordon's instruction were specifically to evacuate Khartoum. By refusing to do so and making himself a martyr, he had blackmailed the British government into taking action and assuming eventual responsibility for Sudan.

When Gordon's journals, which had made it out of the besieged city with the last messenger, were published, they were instant bestsellers, fuelling his canonization and stoking the desire to avenge his death in the British psyche. A statue was erected in Trafalgar Square (opposite the future Canada House), and boys' schools across the empire were named after him. Gordon was eulogized by Alfred Tennyson, and his epitaph on the wall of London's St. Paul's Cathedral reads: "Sacred to the memory of Charles George Gordon, who at all times and everywhere gave his strength to the weak, his substance to the poor, his sympathy to the suffering, his heart to God." With time Gordon's legacy would dim, never more so than in the 1920s when the essayist Lytton Strachey described him rather cruelly: "Ambition was in reality, the essential motive in his life — ambition, neither for wealth or titles, but for fame and influence, for the swaying of multitudes ..."[14]

But such was the effect of Gordon's death that across the empire, and even in the United States, young men volunteered to go to Sudan to avenge him. In Ottawa, Governor General Lansdowne was so deluged by such offers from every province begging him to set up another expedition that he referred the matter to Prime Minister Macdonald. It didn't help that the controversial and eccentric Colonel Sam Hughes, who would be the Canadian minister for the militia during the First World War, lobbied intensively for a full militia unit to be sent over immediately.

Once more, however, Macdonald was firm. Canadians could join the crusade, but not as part of their country's armed forces. If they wanted to fight the Mahdi, all they had to do was enlist in the regular British Army. Under the Canadian Militia Act of 1883, the Militia couldn't be mobilized unless there was a threat to Canada, and the Mahdi certainly didn't warrant that. When the Australians sent 500 infantry and a battery of artillery to Sudan, Sir Charles Tupper, Canada's High Commissioner in London, urged his friend Macdonald to do the same. The shrewd old prime minister wrote back:

> We do not stand in the same position as the Australians. The Suez Canal is nothing to us, and we do not ask England to quarrel with France or Germany for our sake.... Why should we waste men and money in this wretched business? England is not at war but merely helping the Khedive to put down an insurrection.... Our men and money would therefore be sacrificed to get Gladstone and Co. out of a hole they have plunged themselves into by their own imbecility.[15]

For the young country of Canada the overall effect of the expedition up the Nile was that of a romantic adventure. For some of the participants, such as Kennedy, it was the imperial sentiment to heed the Mother Country's call. For the French Canadians, the First Nations voyageurs, and the steamboat skippers, it was a well-paid job in an exotic locale that demanded their unique skills. The War of 1812, the Fenian Raids, and the Riel rebellions had given the Canadian military some prominence at home, but as Aumond, Neilson, MacRae, and Denison demonstrated in Sudan, Canadians could hold their own with British regulars anywhere. Historians have marked Canada's service in the Boer War and the First World War as the emergence of a Canadian character forged in a separate identity. But one could argue that such an identity began on the Nile, the first time that Canadians went overseas not to conquer or colonize but as they always have — to aid. "In the Sudan in 1884, Canadians for the first time served abroad in circumstances which allowed them to realize their own better natures," wrote diplomat and author Roy MacLaren. "It soon became clear to them — if they did not know it before — that they had unique skills, abilities and attitudes."[16]

None of the 16 Canadians who perished due to the Nile campaign are buried at home. But in the Memorial Chamber of the Peace Tower on Parliament Hill in Ottawa, with that of 267 of their countrymen who were soon to die in Africa during the Boer War, their names are recorded in the Book of Remembrance. Of the more than half a million visitors who view the book in its glass-topped case every year, some must go away wondering what Canadians were doing on the Nile River. A lesser-known reminder is the Egypt Medal authorized by Prime Minister John A. Macdonald's government on November 5, 1884. On the obverse the circular silver medal has a diademed, veiled effigy of Queen Victoria facing left and the legend VICTORIA REGINA ET IMPERATRIX, the same as the North West Canada Medal. But on the reverse is the Sphinx on a pedestal with the word EGYPT above. The ribbon consists of five equal stripes: blue, white, blue, white, and blue, with the recipient's name impressed on the rim in sloping capitals. Three hundred and ninety-two medals with THE NILE bar were awarded to the Canadian voyageurs, of which 46 also received the KIRBEKAN bar, given to those who took part in the Egyptian Campaigns between 1882 and 1889.[17]

4

A CANADIAN ENGINEER
IN SUDAN

Major-General Charles George Gordon's martyrdom was only the first act in the great drama of Sudan. The Mahdi survived Gordon by five months, dying on June 22, 1885, and was buried in Omdurman in a tomb with a silver dome.[1] It soon became a place of pilgrimage, holier it was said than that of Mecca. His successor, the Khalifa Abdullah from the Baggara tribe, chose to live on the Mahdi's prestige and attempted to govern within his principles. In case neither strategy worked, he brought his own tribe to Khartoum as a Praetorian Guard and army of occupation.

Slave markets were reopened, and the trade once more flourished, with life in Sudan no better or worse than it had been under the Egyptians. The ensuing Mahdiyya (1883–98) is seen as the first expression of an independent Sudan, since for the first time in its history the country was self-governing. Allegiance was now imposed through a theocracy with a personal oath to the Mahdi and later his khalifas or lieutenants. All regional administrators who replaced the Egyptians were from the Ansar, a measure that alienated those non-Muslims, particularly in the South, who had joined the Mahdi to throw off foreign oppression. Feudal ties were ignored as the power of imams superseded that of tribal autocracies, another move that estranged the powerful families in the Suakin and Kassala regions. The Mahdi's dream of a jihad was perpetuated as fanatical Ansar were dispatched to the far corners of Sudan to massacre all who had sought refuge in Gordon's remaining forts in Equatoria. In 1887 alone three of its armies were sent to invade Egypt, the Belgian Congo, and Ethiopia, all to be beaten back with horrific casualties.

The Sudanese economy suffered as the British and Egyptians cut all trade by preventing the export of gum arabic and ivory. The continual wars had devastated the population, all arable land had returned to wilderness, and smallpox and syphilis now raged through the country. Nature also conspired against the first Sudanese government; in 1886 a biblical plague of locusts blotted out the sky and ate any vegetation left.

Even if all of these disasters hadn't taken place, the khalifa's days were numbered. The new prime minister, Liberal Robert Arthur Gascoyne Cecil, the Marquess of Salisbury, was anything but liberal. He wrote to Evelyn Baring in November 1890: "Whenever you have money enough to go to Khartoum, the resources of civilisation will be adequate to the subjugation of the country." The British now considered Sudan their private Egyptian backyard. After all, the country had been won through the blood shed by Major-General Gordon, their soldier and saint. But in the last decade of the nineteenth century Sudan was also in a dangerous vacuum. The "Grab for Africa" was in motion all around the British, with the French taking the west, the Belgians the Congo in the southwest, the Italians attempting to conquer Ethiopia in the east, and the Germans firmly in Tanganyika in the southwest. Not only was it the largest country in Africa, but Sudan also controlled the headwaters of the Nile on which Egypt, the guardian of the Suez Canal, depended.

By the end of March 1895, it was obvious that Sudan had collapsed into anarchy and that the Mahdi's successors ruled no farther than the walls of Khartoum. No doubt there were many in the capitals of Europe who held that a well-equipped and European-led invading army would encounter no resistance. In Cairo, Baring, whose fiscal policies had by now made the Egyptian economy financially sound, feared that if Britain didn't stake its claim, others would. And he wasn't alone. When the old Duke of Cambridge retired as commander-in-chief of the British Army, he was succeeded by Garnet Wolseley, who was enthusiastic about a return to Sudan. His replacement in Egypt was Lieutenant-Colonel Kitchener, now famous in boys' adventure books for his clandestine operations in "mufti" to rescue Gordon. As "sirdar" or commander-in-chief of the Anglo-Egyptian Army, Kitchener was poised at Wadi Halfa to conquer Sudan.

When the Italians were defeated by the Ethiopians at Adowa, Ethiopia, on March 1, 1896, it was the excuse that Salisbury, Baring, and Kitchener needed to invade Sudan. The British claimed they had returned in force to avenge Gordon and help out their Italian allies next door, but in reality Salisbury wanted to checkmate the French who were preparing to annex Southern Sudan. The former Canadian governor general, Lord Lansdowne, now the British secretary of state for war, noted in a Cabinet memo: "With the object of effecting a diversion in [the Italians'] favour, we have announced to the European Powers that we intend to advance up the Valley of the Nile."

Kitchener had carefully assembled his force over two years, since unlike Wolseley, he wasn't playing for time. And if the latter had been parodied by Gilbert and Sullivan, Kitchener, with his ramrod stature and carefully trimmed moustache — soon to be famous in First World War recruiting posters — was dubbed "The Sudan Machine" by a foreign correspondent. Remembering the amateurism and logistical difficulties that had plagued Wolseley, Kitchener worked on methodically laid plans and machinery to take to Sudan. Instead of relying on untrained camels and undisciplined Canadian shantymen, the next British advance on Khartoum was run with Teutonic efficiency. But to do that Kitchener needed the expertise of a young Montrealer named Édouard Percy Cranwill Girouard.

A baby of Confederation, Girouard was born on January 26, 1867, to an Irish mother and a French-Canadian father. A Montreal lawyer and local Member of Parliament, his father, Désiré Girouard, would one day be appointed to the Canadian Supreme Court. He must have had great ambitions for his son, yet strangely Édouard Girouard wasn't sent to St. Jean de Brébeuf College in Montreal or to Laval University in Quebec City but instead attended that bastion of English-Canadian militarism, the Royal Military College (RMC) in Kingston, Ontario. Percy, as he was usually called, didn't distinguish himself in athletics, but did graduate at the top of his class at RMC with an engineering degree in 1886, becoming the first Catholic to do so. He accepted a position at Canadian Pacific Railway (CPR), obviously deeming it temporary, since in 1888 while building a branch rail line through Maine, he applied to join the

British Royal Engineers. His father, who wanted him to take up a career at home, refused to help, so Percy had to borrow money for his passage and uniform from an aunt.

Girouard knew that it had taken Wolseley three months of portaging to reach the Red River Rebellion in 1870, but 15 years later troops had reached Riel's second uprising in days because of the newly constructed CPR. To his generation of military engineers, the Riel rebellions, the U.S. Civil War, and the Franco-Prussian War had demonstrated that successful military campaigns no longer depended on laborious marches or dashing cavalry charges but the careful laying of track, the building of pontoon bridges, and the use of the telegraph. Appointed traffic manager at the giant Woolwich Arsenal outside London, Girouard learned how a railway line could provision an entire army no matter how far away it was. He must have gained some notoriety when he lectured to the Royal United Services Institute that the island of Britain could be better protected by moving armoured trains around its coast than relying on the forts it depended on. Although the young Canadian wore a monocle to correct a deficiency in his left eye, his fellow officers soon discovered that there was nothing "old school" and stuffy about the colonial they called "Gerry," and it came as a surprise to many that he wasn't French but French Canadian.

To Kitchener, Lieutenant Girouard, a fellow "sapper," was typical of the New Age Army, and by December 1895 it astounded no one that the 29-year-old found himself at Wadi Halfa. The British were intent on occupying the Sudan permanently this time, and they planned to do so in careful stages, going along the Nile as Wolseley had done but without the logistical headaches his expedition had suffered. Kitchener decided to extend the Nile Railway to carry his supplies. The first phase of the campaign was to take control of Dongola Province in Northern Sudan.

On March 20, 1896, Colonel (later General Sir) Archibald Hunter and a small force took possession of Akasheh at the head of the abandoned Sudan Railway. The 8th and 10th Railway Companies, with local labourers under the Royal Engineers, repaired the railway from Wadi Halfa to Akasheh, and a telegraph line was strung between the two towns. By August 4, 1896, Girouard had extended the railway as far as

Kosheh, 116 miles from Wadi Halfa. Each advance was halted until the railway caught up with supplies. The first base was Dongola, the largest town in Northern Sudan, chosen by Kitchener, it was thought, because its most famous son had been the Mahdi.

Girouard was given the task to extend the line (initially reusing the embankments of the khedive's old railway) from Wadi Halfa to Dongola. With a few brother Royal Engineers as young as he was from his Wadi Halfa headquarters, he recruited a workforce of 800 men for his Railway Battalion. Dervish prisoners, Sudanese pensioners, and local tribesmen were hired, except for the Beja, who refused to work for him. Most had never seen a locomotive before and couldn't be trusted to do more than dig in the sand. Since there was no one with any expertise in operating a railway, Girouard established two technical schools to train station masters, signallers, and yard shunters.

With dogged determination both he and Kitchener met one catastrophe after another. A cholera epidemic in August depleted the ranks more efficiently than the Mahdists' spears, killing labourers, engineers, and supervising officers alike. Rails, bolts, crowbars, and fishplates sent down from Egypt were stolen along the way or were faulty. Miles of laid track disappeared when the seasonal torrential downpours swept the sand from under them. Because of poor spiking of track and/or no maintenance, the tiny British-made locomotives were soon wrecked in such a hostile climate — it was said that the only parts of them still working were their whistles. But everyone knew about Girouard's railcar as it rushed up and down the line, its occupant personally supervising each mile of track laid.

The young Winston Churchill, a subaltern in the 4th Hussars in the Sudanese campaign, was particularly impressed by Girouard's meticulous attention to detail. Later, in 1899, he wrote about him in *The River War*:

> Sitting in his hut at Wadi Halfa, he drew up a comprehensive list. Nothing was forgotten. Every want was provided for; every difficulty was foreseen; every requisite was noted. The questions to be decided were

numerous and involved. The answers to all those questions were set forth by Lieutenant Girouard in a ponderous volume several inches thick; and such was the comprehensive accuracy of the estimate that the working parties were never delayed by the want of even a piece of brass wire.

When the decisive battle against the Mahdi took place at Hafir on September 19, 1896, it was the artillery fire from Royal Navy gunboats brought up the Nile that saved the day. Dongola was entered on September 24, and for his work Girouard was awarded the Distinguished Service Order. Encouraged by the speed of railway construction, Kitchener now planned a two-pronged attack on Khartoum. The next two bases, Abu Hamed and Berber, were to be conquered by the gunboats moving up the Nile from Dongola to Abu Hamed. Here they would meet with Girouard's rail construction crew from Wadi Halfa, which would short-circuit the curve of the Nile by going straight through the desert. It was a risk for the Canadian to do this, since exposed in the middle of the desert, he would be far from the boats that supplied and protected him. The members of the Railway Battalion were very aware how vulnerable they were to ambush by the desert warriors. Fortunately, petrified behind the city walls, the Mahdi's successors in Khartoum had lost the will to do so.

Promoted to director of railways for Sudan but still a lieutenant in rank, Girouard put his CPR experience to good use. Thought of as Kitchener's favourite, he was the only one who stood up to him. When the locomotives bought by Kitchener were too light for the desert, Girouard went to England himself in early 1897 to buy heavier ones, with some from the United States. He borrowed more from that other African railway builder, Cecil Rhodes, who envisioned a Cape-to-Cairo railway, and the gauge chosen by both men fitted into the scheme. Kitchener pushed for progress on the new line, the Railway Battalion working through the broiling summer heat (Girouard suffered from heatstroke) to accomplish his goals. On October 31, 1897, the first train entered Abu Hamed, just as news came that the Mahdists had abandoned Berber and were retreating to Atbara. The Railway Battalion was ordered to begin laying tracks immediately to that city. The rapidity of the advance caused a shortage of materials, which meant that Girouard had to rush up and down the line, cajoling and exhorting to move sleepers, signals, and switches to where they were needed.

Just above Berber was Atbara, where the Nile and Atbara Rivers met. Here Kitchener planned to orchestrate the final "push" on Khartoum. The khalifa assembled his forces there on April 8 to stage a mass attack, only to be once more devastated by the machinery and professional soldiers of the modern world — this time, thanks to Girouard's railway, possessing an unlimited supply of shells and food.[2]

The British moved on to Khartoum where outside the walls of Omdurman on September 2 the two armies met for a final battle. Like his nation, and perhaps the whole English-speaking world, Kitchener was intent on not only destroying the Mahdists but also avenging Gordon. The Royal Navy gunboats provided covering fire, and in what Churchill witnessed as the last mass charge in history, the khalifa's dervishes swept down upon the British lines. With the keen eye of a historian, Churchill caught the spirit of the battle. The Mahdi's followers, with their medieval chain mail, spears, and flags, were like combatants from the Crusades, while the disciplined forces of the British Army brought them down with volleys from their repeating rifles, artillery, and machine guns. It was, a war correspondent wrote, not a battle but an execution.

The dead and wounded Ansar fell in their thousands, with the survivors escaping into the desert. Proclaiming that he had given the enemy "a good dusting," Kitchener rode in triumph into Omdurman where the women were relieved to hear that for once in Sudanese history they wouldn't be killed, raped, or sold into slavery. Proving that he could be light-hearted, Kitchener telegraphed Lord Cromer that he now had 300,000 female cooks and concubines on his hands and that he had no use for the services of either. The Mahdi's tomb was blown up by a nephew of Gordon's, and his remains were dug up, decapitated, and flung into the Nile.[3] When his skull was offered to Kitchener for use as an inkstand, he had the decorum to refuse and it was reburied at Wadi Halfa.[4] A service was conducted where Gordon had been speared on the palace steps, and his favourite hymn, "Abide with Me," was sung. When this was related to Her Majesty, who felt as her subjects, though not as her prime minister, did, she wrote in her diary: "Surely he is avenged."

As for Girouard, when Kitchener entered Khartoum, he was far from the railhead, having been sent back to Egypt in March 1898 to rebuild the deteriorating Luxor-Aswan line. It had never been designed for such heavy traffic, and if it fell apart, it would have cut Kitchener's supply chain that stretched from the Alexandria docks to Khartoum. The hero of the hour by those who appreciated his part in the victory, the 33-year-old was offered by Cromer the position of president of Egyptian State Railways, which on Kitchener's approval he accepted. He was also knighted and made a Knight of the Grand Cross of St. Michael and St. George. Girouard then returned to Canada to buy new railway equipment and hire more engineers.

When the Boer War broke out, Girouard was appointed director of railways for the South African Field Force where his talents were once more put to use by Kitchener. Later, when Churchill was made undersecretary of state for the colonies in 1907, the northern Nigerian rebellions against British imperial rule were taking place. Unable to quell them, Frederick Lugard, the British High Commissioner in Lagos, resigned, and Churchill recommended Girouard as his successor.[5] Appointed governor (and the only one of two Canadians to attain that post in the British Colonial Service), the former desert railway engineer once more relished the challenge of moving troops quickly and built a railway across the 800 miles of jungle from the mouth of the Niger River to the northern capital of Kano, effectively ending the rebellion. He would go on to serve as governor of Kenya, as well, and write his own history of railways in wartime. Canada's most distinguished yet little known colonial governor is commemorated at home by Mount Girouard in Banff National Park and the Girouard Building at the Royal Military College. There is also a plaque in his honour at St. Paul's Cathedral in London.[6]

With the fall of Khartoum, Kitchener couldn't rest on his laurels. He had carried with him since leaving Cairo orders from the War Office that he was only to open once Khartoum had been retaken. He was to proceed farther upstream to block a French expedition heading for the Nile. Later the crew of a captured Arab steamer confirmed that a party of native soldiers commanded by white officers had taken the old Egyptian fort at Fashoda where now a strange flag flew. In a feat of endurance that ranks with Speke and Burton's adventures, French Army Captain Jean-Baptiste Marchand had set out from Brazzaville with 100 Senegalese, dragging their boats through the jungle. Marchand had arrived at Fashoda in July 1898, raised the French flag, and claimed the south Nile basin for France. The French government had been given to understand that after Gordon's death the British had left Sudan permanently and thought (with the scandal of the Dreyfus Affair growing daily) that an expedition like this might capture national admiration. Paris made it clear that it was willing to back up Marchand. No one really owned Southern Sudan, and it was better that the French moved in rather than the Belgians, or worse, the Germans. It looked as if Gladstone's fears had come true: the two superpowers of the Victorian era were preparing to go to war over Sudan!

Kitchener arrived in Fashoda, put on the uniform of an Egyptian general, and employed the level of diplomacy with the French that he would repeat in the Great War (he spoke fluent French). He told Marchand that while he had to take the tricolour down, the Frenchman could remain, pending orders from Paris. Rather than going to war over Sudan, cooler heads prevailed in London and Paris (or perhaps it was the fallout from the Dreyfus scandal), and in 1899 a treaty was signed that gave the British the Lower Nile and the French a free hand in what is today Chad, the Central African Republic, and Cameroon. Sudan was returned to Egypt and until 1924 was ruled by a governor general who was protected by Egyptian troops in the country.

Made governor general of Sudan, Kitchener set about rebuilding it. He did so with characteristic thoroughness, laying out the streets of Khartoum in interlocking Union Jacks so that one battery of artillery in the centre of each could command all streets. (He couldn't have foreseen the massive traffic problems that bedevil the city today as drivers negotiate the 120-degree turns.) In November he launched an appeal for £100,000 to establish a college in Khartoum in memory of Gordon. Through his prestige it was oversubscribed within a month. The Lower Nile was made navigable with a permanent channel dug through the

Sudd, tracks were laid for railways, and efforts were made to abolish slavery. Inevitably, even Sudan was too small a canvas for the ambitious Kitchener. Bored of it within six months, he left in late 1899 to meet Lord Roberts in Gibraltar where he was given charge of British forces in South Africa.

Thus, as the century turned, in the last years of her reign, Queen Victoria had succeeded where the pharaohs, Caesars, and khedives had failed. She ruled the banks of the ancient river along its entire length from the Mountains of the Moon to the Mediterranean Sea.

5

REBELS, OIL, AND DARFUR

After the First World War, Germany's African colonies were shared out among the victors, with Ethiopia, the single East African country managing to remain independent for a while longer. Then, having staked their claims and redrawn the map of Africa, the European powers, exhausted by the Great War, neglected their African colonies, there being (with the exception of the Belgian Congo and South Africa) few prospects of immediate wealth obtainable from them. Little money was expended on them, colonial influence barely extended beyond their capitals, and only missionaries and the few administrators ventured into their hinterlands. Between the wars it was estimated that barely 140 British colonial officials ruled over a population of nine million Sudanese. The prestigious Sudan Political Office attracted so many public school/Oxford graduates (all of whom had been trained in classical Arabic rather than the dialects) that someone quipped that Sudan was a land of blacks ruled by "blues." To keep law and order in distant parts, rather than mounting expensive military expeditions to punish marauding tribes, the British discovered that a bombing raid by Royal Air Force biplanes served equally well, be it the North-West Frontier in Afghanistan or the desert wastes of Sudan.

The Anglo-Egyptian return to Sudan in 1899 followed different patterns in the North and South. On July 19, 1899, a treaty establishing an Anglo-Egyptian Condominium of the Sudan was signed: "Its purpose was to protect, instruct and assist a backward country to a point at which it could govern itself and take over the administration of its assets ... for proving that government on the principles of trusteeship can be successful, Kitchener, by that first year in Sudan, undoubtedly deserves credit."[1] The Condominium, which lasted until 1947, was responsible for the two power structures promoting regional disparities that continue to affect Sudan's future today. In the North, to ensure that the fanaticism of the Mahdi never returned, the British imported experienced colonial administrators from their famed civil service. Like Major-General Charles George Gordon, the commissioners were incorruptible, but unlike him, they revelled in red tape, a legacy that has survived them in modern-day Sudan. The Khatmia, those tribal families who had resisted the Mahdi, were reinstated and accorded privileged status, but the power of their sheikhs was confined to religious and social matters only. Sharia law was clearly defined even in the distant provinces, and the Grand Qadi, the ultimate judge of all canon law, was always an Egyptian, never a Sudanese. By the 1940s, when the Khatmia increasingly identified themselves with emerging Egyptian nationalism, the colonial authorities switched allegiance and rehabilitated the Mahdi family and the Ansar.

The South was treated differently. To the British, upriver from Malakal and the Sudd, the country was "African" rather than Arab and local law and custom continued with minimal government interference. The xenophobic Southerners held that the British were essentially the Turkiyya and the Mahdiyya in another guise — yet more foreigners from Khartoum exploiting them for slavery, ivory, or military service, or bent on converting them to Christianity. Far from being welcomed as liberators, the British were seen as "Turks" who needed a large military presence in the South to keep the French (and now the Belgians and Germans) out. The South was what it had always been — a treasure house for labour, and now a source of native troops still marked by their slave origins. Soldiers and later police were recruited from warrior tribes such as the Azande and stationed outside their own tribal grounds to pacify other Southerners. As in its other colonies, the British used the diversity of the colonized against themselves, and Equatorian soldiers and clerks were posted in Dinka territory. Uneducated and unrepresented in the colonial government, tribes such as the Dinka resented other Southerners, especially those of Equatoria, and harboured grievances that later surfaced in the 1980s. With the diversity of religions and without the cohesiveness of the sharia code, the South was closer both physically and culturally to the British colonies of Uganda and Kenya, which the British hoped would one day merge with Southern Sudan.

If the British Foreign Office was somewhat cognizant of the challenges in ruling the North and South, the problems of Darfur in the far west were beyond comprehension. As large as the whole of France, Darfur and Kordofan were simply known as the "West." Its border was equidistant between Port Sudan on the Red Sea and Cameroon on the Atlantic. As much a part of Sudan as it was of Nigeria, it incorporated the edges of modern Chad, the Central African Republic, and Libya. The topography was equally diverse: if there were vast stretches of sandy desert and small rust-coloured granite hills, luxuriant pastures, fields of wild grass, irrigated fields, and occasional shady trees were also featured. Its inhospitable landscape has been described thus: "The horizon is never bare, whether there arises from it a long ridge of angular rocks like the bent spine of some prehistoric monster, or a sharp peak pointing skywards like a finger." The monsters that stalked Darfur were environmental degradation and starvation — drought, locusts, and marauding armies. The earliest record of a famine was one that occurred between 1752 and 1787, called the "Karo Tindel," Fur for "eating bones from carcasses." It took such a toll on human life that it is still remembered in oral tradition more than two centuries later.

The colonial maps of Darfur had tribal names written across territories the size of Belgium, incorrectly since they implied that some areas were inhabited exclusively by one of the 30 or more ethnic groups. The boundaries drawn up in London were convenient but false because of internal migration, war, and intermarriage. After conquering a region, the British held that paramount chiefs determined authority over local ethnic groups and the corresponding territory, a policy that allowed London to administer to Darfur with just a handful of colonial officers. The key to making this "native administration" system work was to award a territory, or *dar*, to each group. This was local government that required no funds from Khartoum. The chiefs were paid nothing and received their reward through local despotism. It was the nomadic tribes that were an anomaly: without need of a *dar*, they moved vast distances between dry-season grazing areas in central and southern Darfur and wet-season pastures on the edge of the desert in the north.

Most of Darfur's early history before the 1870s is conjectural. There were a succession of sultanates — Zaghawa, Daju, and Tunjur — until the kingdom of Dar Fur grew up in the area to be discovered when the Turco-Egyptian slavers raided across its borders. The Fur tribe was governed by a permanent court (*fasher*) set up in its capital, now El Fasher. The only trading goods or currencies were grain, which was used as a form of taxation by the sultans, and slaves. In 1874 the slaver king Zobeir Pasha laid waste to Darfur before being called to Cairo, leaving his lieutenants to continue slaving and pillaging in his absence. No better were the Mahdists, the first indigenous Sudanese government. "You are given the choice of treading the path of the garden or the path of fire," the khalifa warned rebellious Darfurians. Presumably, the locals fought back, since years of bloodshed and famine followed until the Mahdists finally enforced a policy of *tajhir*, or forced migration, from El Fasher to Omdurman for the local tribes. Having eaten, drunk, worn, or stolen whatever they could, the Mahdist armies (combined with low rainfall and plagues of locusts) completed the destruction of the rural population. The ensuing famine is still remembered as Karo Fata (White Bone).

If the Arabs and British pushed into Darfur from the east, the French sent punitive expeditions into the region from the west even as famines followed one another with depressing regularity, some commemorated with names such as Dulen Dor (Sun Famine or Cloudless Skies) or Julu (Wandering Famine). To the sultans, and their subjects, there was little that could be done to prevent such catastrophes, since each class was more preoccupied with fighting off invaders than with storing grain. Intelligence reports by British administrators of the region in the 1890s describe it as almost denuded of people, animals, and vegetation. Admirably, the last sultan of Darfur, Ali Dinar, refused to pay tribute to the Condominium, using the outbreak of the First World War (which he saw as God's punishment on Britain and France) to rise up. Making use of bombing aircraft for the first time, the British and French sent a punitive force in 1916 to crush Ali Dinar's army, precipitating a famine in southwest Darfur. During the Condominium, to prevent a resurgence of Ali Dinar's revolt, tribal *dars* (homelands) were created, fiefdoms and slavery were abolished, and tax burdens were kept low. Far from Khartoum, and on a planet not occupied by Cairo and London, Darfur was neglected, unchanging, and forgotten.

Not much changed in Southern Sudan, either. As late as the 1930s, a British officer noted the effects of tribal warfare and slavery, especially on the Dinka, who fought the British and Arab slavers until 1927. The Dinka lost hundreds of thousands of cattle, and thousands of men, women, and children were slaughtered, carried off into slavery, or died of famine. However, the survivors kept themselves alive in the deepest swamps and bravely attacked the raiders when they could, all the while nursing loathing and contempt for the invaders. It was to end the practice of slavery that Britain created the "Closed District Ordinance" in Sudan, which prevented all Northern Sudanese, the traditional slave owners, from entering the South. Arab dress was outlawed, and the missionary activities of the Verona Fathers and Presbyterian churches were encouraged, especially in education. In 1921 the Passport Ordinance Act, like South Africa's apartheid pass system, further enforced this, closing off areas of the South to foreigners and getting Dinka in the North to return home. But while slavery ended, the ivory trade continued, since the selling of licences for big-game hunting was a considerable source of state revenue.

The "Sudanese Policy" was formulated by the British Foreign Office whereby the North was administered along "Arab" patterns with, as in India, an indigenous civil service encouraged at lower levels only and its small business commerce developed by Lebanese and Greeks. Egypt was granted independence in 1922 (except for British military guarding the Suez Canal), and all Egyptian troops were finally withdrawn from Sudan in 1924. This was a signal for Sudanese soldiers stationed in Khartoum led by a Dinka officer named Ali Abd al-Latif to rise against the British. Unfortunately, al-Latif, because of the stigma of his slave origins, had no popular support, and the British easily suppressed the mutiny. The Sudanese elite, particularly the intellectuals, looked down on al-Latif, the son of a black woman and an unknown father, and wouldn't follow him. Far from being hailed as the father of Sudanese nationalism, he later died in an asylum.

The more fertile North lent itself to large-scale crop production, thanks to the Gezira scheme, and it was hoped that Sudan might become the breadbasket of Africa. The old port of Suakin was too small, so the docks at Port Sudan were built for the export trade. Investment in and control of the new industries, as with the remainder of the economy, were concentrated in the hands of a few elite Khartoum families — the Mahdi's posthumous son, Sayyid, being one — who had a stake in the continued existence of such a colonial structure. Ironically, the nationalist movement was split between Ismail al-Azhari, leader of the Khatmia (later called the Democratic Unionist Party or DUP), who looked to Cairo for help and who held that the South still existed to be exploited, and Sadiq al-Mahdi, the grandson of the Mahdi, who maintained Umma, a political party, to further only his family's interests. A third power was the Sudanese Communist Party, which drew its support from the railway workers at Atbara, a group well portrayed in Ahmad Alawad Sikainga's *City of Steel and Fire: A Social History of Sudan's Railway Town.* Organized by and later financed from Moscow, the Communist Party, at its height, had more than a half-million members, most of whom disappeared after the pro-Communist coup in 1971.

During the Second World War, Sudan found itself on the front lines, or more accurately, between them. With the Italians in Ethiopia and Libya and the French African colonies opting to support the pro-Nazi Vichy regime, Sudan became of vital interest to the British, particularly since General Erwin Rommel's tanks threatened Cairo itself. The country was developed as a secure lifeline between East and West Africa, with the terrain mapped and roads, railways, agricultural projects, and airfields built from the Nile to the Marra Plateau. On the unlikely chance that Rommel (or the Luftwaffe at least) would make it as far as Khartoum, an anti-aircraft gun was mounted on the *Melik*, Kitchener's old gunboat, being used then (and today) as a clubhouse for the local yacht club. The British feared not only that the Axis advances would encourage pan-Arab nationalism but that their East African colonies would be isolated and the Suez Canal threatened. Sudan was also used as a base for the invasion of Italian-held Ethiopia, and the Sudanese Defence Forces helped reinstate Emperor Haile Selassie to his throne in 1941.

In the Khartoum War Cemetery on the city's southeast side are 322 Commonwealth graves from the Second World War alone. Mute testimony that "some corner of a foreign field" will forever be Canada's are the gravestones of its military personnel who died far from home. In August 1942, for example, when a United States Army Air Forces aircraft crashed at Wadi Sedina Airfield outside Khartoum, two of the casualties were pilot officers (P/Os) of the Royal Canadian Air Force. The son of John Kirby and Jessie Maude Wyman of Montreal, P/O Peter Hersey Wyman, died on August 19, 1942, and P/O Elroy Fenwick Bent, son of Ernest and Lorna Bent and husband of Frances Evelyn Bent, of Upper Granville, Annapolis County, Nova Scotia, died on August 20.

To bypass the Axis-occupied Mediterranean, the British constructed airports, weather stations, and radio and navigation aids across Sudan. Imperial Airways' flying boats from Cairo had been touching down on the Nile at Khartoum since 1935, the passengers overnighting at the Grand Hotel, which still exists, its shabby gentility evoking those long-ago days of languid air travel. But the airline had also pioneered the overland Takoradi Route, flying across the continent from Lagos to Cairo, with refuelling stops at Fort Lamy in French Equatorial Africa and at Sudanese airfields at El Geneina, El Fasher, El Obeid, Khartoum, Atbara, and Wadi Halfa. When Italy entered the war in 1940, the route's importance increased as an option for supplying aircraft (sometimes flying them off aircraft carriers) to the Royal Air Force squadrons in the Middle East. From Lagos to Alexandria, Egypt, was a journey of 3,850 miles for airmen — safe from the Axis but flown in severely primitive conditions. Of the many Canadians who fought in the region as part of the British military, none were higher in rank than British Columbia–born Air Commodore Raymond Collishaw, who commanded the Desert Air Force, its squadrons responsible for much of the aerial photography and mapping of Sudan.

In 1943 both the Democratic Unionist Party and the Umma Party called for the British to leave and an end to the separate administration of the North and South. The Egyptians had never accepted that Sudan no longer belonged to them — it was, after all, the source of "their Nile" — and that recalcitrance had strategic, if not historic, implications for them. They expected that in the postwar world their ancient colony would be returned. The British forestalled this by arguing that one of the cornerstones of the new United Nations was self-determination of all peoples and that the Sudanese should be allowed to choose their own future.

Two events occurred in 1947 that revealed a lot about British intentions. A new tomb for the Mahdi was built, an exact copy of the old, and the first Sudanese Legislative Council was established in Khartoum, followed by a British-sponsored conference in Juba to bring Southerners in. The disparity between the two sides was very evident in that the Northerners were well acquainted with administrative procedures but had no knowledge of the South, while the Southerners were less educated and mistrustful of their former slave masters. Still, differences were set aside enough for the Legislative Assembly to succeed in passing a statute for self-determination in 1952, a move that angered the Egyptians who still expected Sudan to be returned. As expected, Northerners dominated the assembly so that two years later Southern leaders convened their own conference in Juba. As the British began to withdraw from Sudan in 1955, tensions grew between the Northern and Southern tribes. In Malakal and Torit, when soldiers from Equatoria saw Northerners replacing their British officers, they mutinied. All Northern officers and their families were massacred. Thus, even before independence, Sudan's first civil war became a strange conflict as Egypt's Colonel Nasser supported the Southern rebels, while the departing British brought Northern troops in from the central government to suppress them. London, by now coping with the Suez Crisis, couldn't leave Sudan soon enough, and independence was granted on January 1, 1956, with Ismail al-Azhari becoming the country's first president.

The precedent for self-government in British colonies had been established recently in India, and even earlier among the older dominions of Canada, Australia, and New Zealand. Accordingly, while the British introduced programs of agriculture, transport, education, and health services in Sudan (at independence the University of Khartoum, Gordon Memorial School, and the Sudan Railway Corporation were the best-run in Africa), there were no plans for any political advancement. African colonies were to be given their independence cautiously, possibly not until the end of the twentieth century, with the business of running a government requiring a political apprenticeship. To quit an African colony in haste was, as the senior Labour Party politician Herbert Morrison put it, "like giving a child a latch-key, a bank account, and a shot gun." But the undue rush with which the British departed Sudan, precipitated no doubt by the Suez Crisis, meant that the political apprenticeship never occurred. And that was the linchpin of all other carefully built institutions. When the last Union Jack came down and the last English colonial administrator packed up, the country reverted within a decade to the pre-Kitchener era of the Mahdiyya. In the Sudanese Army the officer corps was so decimated by purges that the Government of Sudan was forced to rely on tribal militias to achieve its aims. Roads, runways, telegraph lines, and water pipes fell apart due to lack of maintenance. So, too, did the educational system, both public and missionary. "To have an intelligent conversation in English with someone of influence in the New Sudan," writes Canadian Nick Coghlan, "I soon learned one must look for grey hair. Almost no one under forty had been to secondary school."

This time, instead of the slave markets being reopened, those carefully husbanded agricultural, health, and transportation services, through corruption and neglect, gradually disintegrated. Percy Girouard's railway system never recovered from the persecution of its Communist Party employees after 1971. The second major casualty of the New Sudan was the new facilities at Port Sudan, the loss of which later impacted famine relief efforts from 1980 to 2007. Sudan Airways, a subsidiary of the railway, took to the air in 1946 as Africa's second-oldest scheduled airline. By 1959 it was flying Vickers Viscounts, christened the "Blue Nile Service," as far as London via Cairo, Athens, and Rome. The airline's upgrade to jet aircraft was spectacularly marked on December 10, 1982, when a flight crew ferrying a Boeing 707 purchased from Ireland (and still in its Aer Lingus livery) mistook the moonlight reflecting off the

Nile for the airport runway lights and made a perfect landing in the river, 15 miles upstream from Khartoum. A team was rushed over from Dublin to scrape the Aer Lingus markings off, and the 707 (ironically registered as ST-AIM) was stripped bare by the locals within three days. During the civil war, when the GOS used the Sudan Airways Boeings to ferry troops and arms into Juba, its aircraft were shot down by the rebels or their pilots crashed while overshooting runways, their hulks becoming Sudan People's Liberation Army barracks at airport edges.

The British had hoped the new country would be secular and federalist, but the Northern politicians rejected both notions and the Southerners sent to Khartoum were too inexperienced to stand up to them. Fear that the Constituent Assembly would move to a federal system of government, seen by Northerners as the first step to Southern independence, caused General Ibrahim Abboud to seize power in 1958. Believing that he could foster national unity, the general promoted Islam and the use of Arabic in the South, making Friday the day of rest instead of Sunday. He also professed contempt for African religions and ordered the construction of mosques and Muslim schools throughout Sudan. His program of Islamization, the expulsion of all Christian missionaries, and the burning of dissident villages forced many Southerners to flee to neighbouring Uganda and the Congo. The exiles called their party the Sudan African Nationalist Union (SANU), colloquially known as Anyanya, a poison concocted by the Mahdi made of snake parts and fermented beans. Ironically, SANU was armed by the Khartoum government itself in 1964 when a weapons cache meant for the Simbas in the Congo fell into its hands. But the rebels were disunited within their own leadership. The better-educated Equatorians alienated the Dinka, who splintered off, as did the Azande, causing the Anyanya to fight one another more than it did Northern troops.

In a move that foretold much, the Foreign Missionary Act was passed in 1962, classifying all Christian missions in the country as foreign institutions rather than domestic ones. Apparently, the GOS had forgotten that Christian kingdoms had prospered in Nubia since the fifth century and that the Catholic Verona Fathers had been in Sudan since 1854. Church property was confiscated, priests and congregation were persecuted, and Muslim converts to Christianity were threatened with the death penalty. Oddly enough, the more than 40 years of Islamist discrimination policies since then have had the opposite effect. Today there are more conversions to Christianity than during British rule.[2]

After a series of strikes, the military stepped down in October 1964, and Sadiq al-Mahdi, the 30-year-old, Oxford-educated great-grandson of the Mahdi, formed a government. At a Round Table Conference held in March 1965, with delegates from both North and South attending, Northern parties refused to allow a plebiscite in the South that would demonstrate any form of self-determination. The British had kept religion and state separate, but after 1956 the Muslim Brotherhood increased the appeal of religion among the Northern population. It advocated a theocratic society, and its followers became the future National Islamic Front (NIF). On the other hand, unlike his great-grandfather, al-Mahdi believed that one day there would be a secular democratic Sudan. He hoped that with modernization his people would agree, but ensuing events showed that he had little support.

There were food shortages and student demonstrations, and news filtered out of the South that massacres of civilians were taking place. The discord came to a head on May 25, 1969, when army officers led by Colonel Jaafar Nimeiri united with Communists to stage a coup. The new government announced that the war in the South would be settled politically rather than by military means, a signal that initiated a jockeying for power among the Southern exiles and the Communists. Sadiq al-Mahdi went into the first of many exiles as the country lurched into civil war.

On the international scene the GOS joined the Arab cause immediately after independence. After all, the ruling elite considered itself more a part of the Middle East than of Africa. Sudan also joined in condemning Israel after that country's 1967 war with Egypt, Syria, and Jordan; broke off relations with the United States; and aligned itself with the Soviet Union. It paid dearly for all of these actions: Israel now armed the guerrillas, the pro-Western governments of Uganda and Ethiopia sheltered them, and the United States ended all aid. Rather ungratefully, the local Communists, with Soviet support, attempted a coup against

Major-General Charles George "Chinese" Gordon poses in full regalia as "pasha" and governor general of Sudan in 1884. (Library and Archives Canada C-009992)

General (later Field Marshal) Garnet Joseph Wolseley in 1884 when he was chosen to command the Nile Expedition to relieve Major-General Gordon in Khartoum. (Library and Archives Canada C-009993)

In 1884–85, Lieutenant-Colonel Frederick Charles Denison commanded the Canadian voyageurs in the failed attempt to save General Gordon in Khartoum. (Library and Archives Canada C-009997)

Lieutenant-Colonel William Nassau Kennedy of Winnipeg served as quartermaster and paymaster for the Nile Expedition and brought 92 Manitobans into the voyageur contingent of the Gordon relief effort. (Library and Archives Canada C-009985)

Sir Édouard Percy Girouard was in charge of railways in Sudan from 1896 to 1898 and contributed greatly to Major-General Herbert Kitchener's victory at Omdurman. (Library and Archives Canada C-5800)

The steamboat captains from the Ottawa River who served with the Canadian contingent of the Nile Expedition in 1884–85. (Library and Archives Canada C-009986)

Top: The Canadian voyageurs gather in Ottawa in 1884 before heading to Egypt to be part of the Nile Expedition. (Library and Archives Canada C-009990)
Bottom: To keep law and order in distant parts of Sudan between world wars, the British used Fairey "Gordon" aircraft, as seen here with No. 5 Wing of the Royal Air Force over the Nile River, circa 1935. (Library and Archives Canada PA-118318)

Top: The ancient city of Meroe has more pyramids, albeit smaller, than Egypt. Canadian archaeologists Peter Shinnie, Krzysztof Grzymski, and Adam Giambrone have contributed much to its excavation. (Photo courtesy Fellowship for African Relief) **Bottom:** A *haboob*, or dust storm, approaches Khartoum like a giant wall of sand. (Photo by Miriam Booy)

Top: For Sudan veterans such as World Vision Canada's Emmanuel Isch (far right), Sudan is an enigma — hospitable people, with a great history and culture and much potential, but a country subject to conflicts at various levels and unable to deal with them. (Photo courtesy World Vision Canada) **Bottom:** Major Gilles Legacy (left), officer commanding the Canadian Training Cadre in Thiès, Senegal, greets the Senegal Commandos Battalion commander Samba Tall. (Photo by Combat Camera)

At Camp Um Kadada, Master Warrant Officer Dan Boivin inspects an armoured vehicle general purpose (AVGP) loaned by Canada to the African Union Mission in Sudan (AMIS). (Photo by Lieutenant-Commander Nicholas Smith)

Top: SkyLink helicopters provide vital air mobility to AMIS, so much so that the company was nicknamed "Canada's air force in Darfur." (Photo by Lieutenant-Commander Nicholas Smith) **Bottom:** A Grizzly AVGP is unloaded from a Russian Antonov An-124-100 at Dakar International Airport in Senegal. (Photo by Combat Camera)

At AMIS Camp Zam Zam in Darfur, green-bereted African Union (AU) troops guard the main gate. (Photo by Lieutenant-Commander Nicholas Smith)

Emmanuel Isch (wearing a ball cap), now with World Vision Canada, first came to Sudan in 1991 as part of Serving in Mission (SIM) Canada. (Photo courtesy World Vision Canada)

In 2007 Major Sandi Banerjee of The Queen's Own Rifles finds a tranquil moment during his stint as deputy commander of the Canadian Task Force, Operation Safari. (Photo by Ingrid Schmidt, UNMIS)

In Thiès, Senegal, Master Corporal Rock Bourdeau, a Canadian Forces vehicle technician from CFB Valcartier in Quebec, instructs an AU soldier about the start-up procedure for the Grizzly AVGP. (Photo by Combat Camera)

On November 25, 2004, Prime Minister Paul Martin visits a school at Camp Mayo in Khartoum. (Photos by Dave Chan, courtesy of the Office of the Right Honourable Paul Martin)

Nimeiri. By 1971 the rebels, called the Southern Sudan Liberation Movement (SSLM), were a united, potent force under Joseph Lagu. The overthrow of Milton Obote in Uganda the previous year and the coming to power of Idi Amin, who was from the border region (and an ally of the Israelis), meant that the SSLM could regroup in bases across the border beyond Khartoum's reach. Chastened, Nimeiri opened a dialogue with the SSLM, and both sides met in neutral Ethiopia to hammer out the Addis Ababa Agreement.

Limited regional self-government was grudgingly granted to the South. For example, the Southern Regional Government could now raise local taxes for local expenditures. Thorny problems such as borders and mineral rights were left unsettled, but integration of the armed forces on both sides did begin, with ex-Anyanya being accepted into the police, the prison system, and wildlife protection. In fact, the president's own bodyguards were ex-Anyanya. A new constitution was chartered, establishing the country as a secular state and giving freedom of worship not only to Christians and Jews (officially designated as "people of the book") but to the animists of the South, as well.[3]

The Western world applauded all of these measures, though diplomatic ties with the United States were set back when on March 1, 1973, Palestinian terrorists of the Black September organization murdered the U.S. ambassador and deputy chief of mission in Khartoum. Sudanese officials arrested the terrorists and tried them on murder charges, but in June 1974 they were released into the custody of the Egyptian government. U.S. relations with Sudan remained static until early 1976 when President Nimeiri redeemed himself by mediating the release of 10 American hostages being held by Eritrean insurgents in northern Ethiopia. Grateful, the United States decided to resume economic and military assistance to Sudan.

In a continent of dictators, Nimeiri was commended for loosening the strings of power and rebuilding Sudan. For the first time since independence, the country was at peace, and aid and investment from both Western and Arab governments flowed in, thanks to Bona Malwal, the minister for industry and mining. Heavy investment in ambitious projects such as mechanized farming, irrigation schemes, and the Kenana

Sugar refinery were begun. The government's plan was to make Sudan the breadbasket of the Middle East. What happened in reality was that small farmers and cattle herders were destroyed when they lost their lands in courts that were biased in favour of the government's mega-schemes.

These developments coincided with droughts in Kordofan and Darfur that further dispossessed the inhabitants. After independence in 1956, Khartoum attempted to correct the colonial system in Darfur and introduced local services such as police, schools, and clinics. The positions of sheikhs and nazirs were formally abolished, and "people's councils" were put in place to do the same job. But the GOS never delivered the funds for regional administration, and soon the local government was bankrupt. If the police chief of Darfur wanted to mount an operation against bandits, he had to commandeer vehicles and fuel from NGOs. Khartoum then studiously ignored Darfur Arabs and non-Arabs equally, allocating fewer funds for education, health care, and development assistance. Even Southerners were better treated.

Nothing was more contentious for Nimeiri than the building of the Jonglei Canal. As far back as 1901, there had been plans to divert the water from the Upper Nile, before it vanished into the Sudd, to the cash-crop-growing areas of the North. The Southerners were suspicious of what they saw as yet another hijacking of their resources by the central government but allowed planning of the canal to take place. Khartoum thought that it had mollified local concerns by building a few schools, roads, and hospitals along the proposed route to allay Southern fears. It didn't take Southerners long to realize that all the essentials for Sudan's growth — water, oil, and fertile land — lay in their neighbourhood and in their control. But projects like the canal proved to be too ambitious for the economy, and the large-scale "breadbasket" farming faltered due to poor planning, corruption, and distrust. For example, all mechanized pump schemes in the Upper Nile were owned by Northerners and were financed by Islamic banks. The country had borrowed heavily to underwrite Nimeiri's grand schemes, and Sudan's annual balance of payments deficit inflated from S£30.5 million in 1973–74 to S£310.6 million in 1983–84. The International Monetary Fund, controlled by the United States, managed to reschedule Sudan's debt of $6.3 billion, while the

United States Agency for International Development (USAID) pumped another $1.4 billion into the economy. This money was conditional on the Sudanese government reducing expenditures on lavish projects, a stipulation that affected the South drastically. To stem rising solidarity there in 1981, the Southern Assembly in Juba was suspended and the Southern region was broken up into three provinces.

With the overthrow of Emperor Haile Selassie in Ethiopia and the installation of a Marxist regime there allied to the Soviet Union, as well as the growing hostility of Libya, Sudan looked to the United States for both economic and military aid. In return Sudan allowed U.S. troops and naval units to use Sudanese bases. The United States also armed Nimeiri, turning a blind eye when those arms were used against his own people. Nimeiri then supplied the Eritreans with weapons against the Mengistu regime in Ethiopia. He also put down two coups in 1975 and 1976, both from hard-line Muslims and both backed by Libya. As the Sudanese economy floundered, radical Islamic parties such as the Muslim Brotherhood, led by the Sorbonne-educated Dr. Hassan Abdullah al-Turabi, Nimeiri's brother-in-law, grew in popularity. They wanted the Addis Ababa Agreement torn up, Southern regional power reduced, and the boundaries between the North and South redrawn so that the newly discovered oil fields would now be in the North.

In the twentieth century, oil had become for Sudan what slaves had been previously. Chevron had spent four years exploring for oil in the Muglad basin in South Sudan before striking it rich in 1978 near the town of Bentiu on the Southern Kordofan border. The two American exploration companies, Chevron and Total, estimated that there were 10 billion barrels of reserves, but unfortunately for Khartoum the deposits were all in the Southern Upper Nile and Jonglei Provinces. Without consulting the regions the central government reconfigured the old provincial boundaries laid down by the British so that the oil was now in a special Northern state, ironically called "Unity." Then Khartoum sold Chevron the concession to exploit the Unity fields. Chevron wanted to keep its oil production in reserve, producing when international military prices were high. There were questions as to where the refinery and pipelines would be located — in the South, which would then benefit from the taxes, or in the North? It was no surprise where al-Turabi and the hard-line Muslim Brotherhood wanted it. Under pressure from the latter, Nimeiri reconciled with al-Turabi and made him attorney general.

These developments were the beginning of the unravelling of the careful balance that Nimeiri had achieved in 1973. By his third re-election in April 1983, he had become corrupt, cruel, and paranoid, his Al Amen al Goumi thugs (the State Security Force) keeping him in power with torture, disappearances and, it was rumoured, the operation of more than 400 "safe houses." Declaring an Islamic Revolution and that Sudan was an Islamic republic, Nimeiri unsuccessfully attempted to give himself the title of "imam" and required that all government officials and military officers pledge allegiance to him as a Muslim ruler. Sharia law was enforced across the country, multiple amputations were meted out for real and imagined adultery, Western-style dancing was banned, and in a well-publicized ceremony Nimeiri personally emptied the whole liquor supply of Khartoum, valued at $11 million, into the Nile.

Foreign correspondents reported that there were even more disturbing aspects to Nimeiri's fanaticism. Petty thieves, they said, began losing limbs in public executions, and a special arena was built in Khobar Prison to view the amputations. In September 1983 a state of emergency, known as the September Laws, was declared, the constitution was suspended, and all strikes, public demonstrations, and gatherings were banned, with sharia law forcibly applied throughout the South. In a typical Sudanese scenario, Omdurman was bombed by an aircraft of unknown origin, for which the authorities initially blamed the opposition. But since it was the home of the leader of the opposition, Sadiq al-Mahdi, that had been targeted and damaged while he was under house arrest, they switched tactics and accused the Libyans. Many saw the government's hand in the bombing and believed Nimeiri had staged this "Libyan attack" to secure a renewal of the $287 million aid package that Washington seemed reluctant to hand over.

Colonel Muammar al-Gaddafi was the perfect scapegoat for Nimeiri even before 1975 when the latter executed 98 mercenaries who had allegedly been paid by the Libyans to depose him. "Libya, in every sense," writes Robert D. Kaplan, "acted according to an understanding that Sudan was a country in name only, whose politicians could be bought for a price which was best paid in military assistance to fight southern rebels, rather than in food for drought victims. The United States, which saw Sudan in more charitable terms, was no match for that strategy."[4] Gaddafi dreamed of an "Arab belt" across Sahelian Africa, the key to which was control of Chad, Sudan's neighbour. But Chad was a former French colony, and Paris still maintained a military presence in the country. (Idriss Déby, Chadian President Hissène Habré's chief of staff and heir apparent, had trained as a helicopter pilot at a French military college.)

However, the three Sudanese states of Darfur were another matter. Ignored by Cairo, London, and now Khartoum, they were closer to Tripoli physically, socially, and economically. Goods on sale at the border town of El Geneina came from Libya, as did the remittances sent home by locals working in Libyan oil fields. In August 1985, in response to the famine, food convoys escorted by Libyan soldiers started arriving in the Darfurian capital of El Fasher, and local tribal chiefs were invited to Tripoli to meet Gaddafi. Armed by Libya, Chadian rebels soon used Darfur as a base, helping themselves freely to the crops and cattle of local villagers. Most of the automatic weapons in use in Darfur in 2008 originated with those rebels.

Gaddafi also gathered discontented Sahelian Arabs and Tuaregs and formed them into an Islamic Legion that was to be the vanguard of his offensives. Among the "legionnaires" were Arabs from Western Sudan, many of them of the Mahdist Ansar sect who had been persecuted by Nimeiri. When, just as their ancestors had fallen to Kitchener's machine guns, the Ansar were soundly routed at Ouadi Doum in 1988 by French Air Force Jaguar fighter aircraft and the Chadian army, Gaddafi lost interest in them. But the Ansar no longer needed him. Already possessed of an Arab supremacism and now well armed and mobile, they crossed over to Sudan and found new employment as Janjaweed in Darfur.

Here, by the end of the 1980s, diminishing land and water resources had pitted the locals against one another. Since both sides were Muslim, it wasn't a religious or ethnic war. As in much of Sudan, this war was fought for access to water and grazing rights. The nomadic Arab herders whose herds grew more numerous every year were forced by desertification to migrate farther and farther into traditional Fur lands where the farmers, also with burgeoning families, resented their invasion. Organized into a political bloc called the Arab Alliance and now sanctioned by the GOS, the Mahdist Ansar wedded their racist ideology with a desire to ethnically cleanse Darfur of black farmers. The legacy of Gaddafi's Islamic Legion was to haunt Darfur. Ali Muhammad Ali Abd-al-Rahman, wanted in 2007 by the International Criminal Court in The Hague for planning and participating in massacres, had like other Janjaweed leaders been armed and trained in Libya.

Coverage of the famine in Darfur was eclipsed in October 1984 by a historic television news report. The power of the media was demonstrated by BBC reporter Michael Buerk's coverage of the Ethiopian famine, which inspired worldwide relief and British pop singer Bob Geldof's Band Aid. By the time Nimeiri acknowledged the crisis at home in December, the United States had already unilaterally committed emergency food aid to the region. The delivery of food to Western Sudan in 1984–85 was one of the world's largest relief operations since the Second World War and went almost unnoticed by Western media. USAID alone sent 125,000 tons of sorghum in two batches, all of it consigned to the rural areas. Less than a third was distributed to the north and south of Darfur, delays not only because of the rains.

If the relief attempts were hopelessly inadequate, it was because the Darfur regional government had been so long starved of funding and had no means of transport for the food. Based entirely in towns, Khartoum's representatives in the west of the country, the Sudan Socialist Union (SSU), had a strong urban bias. Consequently, most of the sorghum ended up in the towns where it remained to be sold off to government employees. The priority of the relief agencies was to feed the people in greatest need — the farmers and herders. If they abandoned their farms and headed for the towns to be fed, they festered in what were called "famine camps," which the relief agencies were anxious to avoid because of the very high death rates that occurred in them. But since it was the first time that the rural people of Darfur had ever seen any aid at all, they were delighted. The USAID food, known as "Reagan" after the man who authorized it, surprised communities that had always relied on themselves. "Who is this Reagan?" asked one farmer. "He ought to be promoted."

"By March 1985, the epicentre of the famine in Africa had shifted westward from Ethiopia to Sudan," recalls Nova Scotia lawyer Peter Dalglish. In areas north of El Geneina, Oxfam reported that up to 77 percent of all children between the ages of one and five were suffering from malnutrition. Moved by scenes of the Ethiopian famine on television, Dalglish organized an airlift of relief supplies consisting of powdered milk, tents, drugs, and Canadian Food Supplement. On Christmas Eve 1984, in two chartered Air Canada aircraft (christened *Donner* and *Blitzen*), he left Halifax with the relief supplies for Addis Ababa. In the two weeks that followed, while feeding starving children in Ethiopia's Ogaden, Dalglish discovered his calling. "I realized that my place on earth was with desperately poor kids who had few friends or allies," he says. "I had no idea what I had to offer, or exactly what my contribution would be … but I knew at that moment that these girls and boys of the desert, with whom I had virtually nothing in common, were now my life." Once back home in Halifax, he gathered up his law textbooks, sold them to the university's second-hand bookstore, bought a pair of hiking books and a Silva compass with the proceeds, and returned to Africa — this time to Sudan.

"The Nile flood waters were at their lowest level in 350 years," remembers Dalglish. "Ships carrying grain had arrived at Port Sudan … but the country's antiquated railway system had collapsed and little grain was getting through. Millions of lives were at risk." World University Service of Canada (WUSC) had been awarded the contract by the United Nations' World Food Programme (WFP) to set up a transportation system between Khartoum and Darfur. Dalglish decided to sign on with WUSC and take a job as a fieldworker in Darfur. After 15 days, 21 flat tires, and 1,000 miles of desert travel, he arrived in El Geneina, the westernmost point of the air bridge, which because of the flooded wadis between Khartoum and Darfur had become the lifeline for the famine victims. From the holds of C-130s the sacks of sorghum were transferred by chanting labourers to the waiting trucks that took them into the town centre where they were loaded onto the backs of camels for transportation to isolated villages. For Dalglish no two days were the same. He supervised the drivers, arranged for warehouse space, maintained an inventory of spare parts, and wrote field reports. "On several occasions," he writes in his book *The Courage of Children: My Life with the World's Poorest Kids*, "we went to villages where we found nobody — they were ghost towns ... my drivers would shake their heads and mutter prayers under their breath. This was the heartland of their country and it was dying before their eyes."[5]

Western pressure forced Nimeiri to abolish the SSU in April 1985, by which time the relief agencies had bypassed the regional government and taken all aspects of grain distribution into their own hands. The drought and famine of 1984–85 set the nomads against the farmers in a struggle for diminishing resources. Alex de Waal, the author with Julie Flint of *Darfur: A Short History of a Long War*, notes that since the GOS couldn't intervene effectively, each side armed itself. De Waal and Flint go on to write that "A herd of a thousand camels represents more than a million dollars on the hoof: only the most naive herd-owner would not buy automatic rifles to arm his herders." Thus, the villagers armed themselves in response.

The September Laws united all Southerners — Dinka, Nuer, and Equatorians — against the GOS, and once more mutinies flared up in Southern army units that joined with the remnants of the Anyanya now gaining popular support. For months Khartoum lost all control of the South. The railway was sabotaged, the Kosti-Juba Nile ferry was blown up, and the main roads were mined. This time it was the Dinka that took the initiative. Khartoum sent Colonel John Garang, a Dinka officer, to quell a mutiny of 500 Southern troops who were resisting orders to be shipped to the North. Instead of doing so, he encouraged them and other Southern units to rebel, forming the nucleus of his Sudan People's Liberation Movement/Army (SPLM/A).

"The first time I met John Garang was at the Presbyterian mission printing press in Southern Sudan," recalled a Canadian missionary in 1965. "A tall, lanky young man, he was pedalling a stationary bicycle that powered a small press. His gangly height and piercing eyes set in a jet-black face instantly revealed he was a Dinka, Sudan's largest ethnic group. His Presbyterian mentors, Reverend and Mrs. Lowery Anderson, had led him to Christ and taught him the operation of the press, which turned out Gospel pamphlets, Bible studies, and teaching materials." Schooled by missionaries in East Africa, Garang was sent as a promising young officer in the Sudanese Army (he was in the same class as Omar al-Bashir, Sudan's current president) to the United States for military training at Fort Benning, Georgia, before completing his education with a Ph.D. in cultural economics at Iowa State University. For his doctoral thesis, Garang chose the Jonglei Canal, criticizing the lack of developmental planning in the project. With his beard and heavy physique and the dark skin of his ethnic group, Garang was one of the most complicated rebels in African history, and despite his being at the centre of the Sudanese conflict for 22 years, little was known about him.

Marxist to the Ethiopians, Christian fundamentalist to the Americans, what is known about Garang is that he was an expert in survival — someone who knew how to bend with the wind and be all things to all men. While many of his SPLM/A colleagues urged a separate state for Southern Sudan, Garang claimed not to be a separatist himself, believing that if the non-Arab population in Sudan — all the Southerners and marginalized groups in Northern Sudan, like the Fur — could form a numerical majority, they would dominate a secular, pluralist, and united Sudan. He wanted a "New Sudan," he espoused, where there would be more autonomy and equal development for the various regions and a restructuring away from the central authority. But implicit in Garang's rhetoric was the threat that if Nimeiri didn't acquiesce, he would take the South out of the country altogether. Western observers suspected that his "New Sudan" speech was mouthed to get the support of Arab tribes in the North. As it had with Ali al-Latif in 1924, Garang's ancestry worked against him as the SPLM/A was seen more as a Dinka army than truly representative of the whole South, and other Southern tribes such as the Murle and Nuer resented this. Taking advantage of the tribalism, the central government offered to supply any anti-Dinka faction with weapons to fight Garang.

Initially, the rebels had little international support. The United States was allied with Nimeiri, ensuring that Israel would no longer sustain the Southerners. Other African states, fearing that separatism would spread to their own countries, ignored all requests for aid from Garang. Only the Ethiopian dictator Mengistu Haile Mariam was happy to provide bases, airdropped weapons, a radio station — and Marxist rhetoric. Thanks to Mengistu, the SPLM/A transformed itself from what Garang called a mob into an army. But it also picked up some of the Ethiopian bad habits that prevented it from ever gaining popular support. For one thing, Garang's Dinka tribe ensured its superiority over all potential rivals. Taught to live through the barrels of their guns and to be as Mao had advocated for all successful guerrilla groups "as fish swimming in a friendly sea," i.e., raiding refugee camps for food, SPLM/A recruits chorused the following on graduation:

> Even your mother, give her a bullet!
> Even your father, give him a bullet!
> Your gun is your food; your gun is your wife.

To explain its aims and attract friends, the SPLM/A issued its first manifesto in July 1983, listing its grievances and noting the failures of the Addis Ababa Agreement. The language about blaming tribalism and colonialism for Sudan's ills could have been lifted entirely from Marxist cells in Ethiopia. It was all the proof the United States and the GOS needed that the SPLM/A was allied with Mengistu and Colonel Gaddafi of Libya, both enemies of President Ronald Reagan's administration.

The outbreak of civil war allowed age-old enemies to reassert themselves and rearm (sometimes with government help) and take up the profession of their ancestors — slave raiding. During the drought in Kordofan and Darfur when tribes had lost much of their livestock, the Baggara raided non-Muslim tribes, abducted women and children for labour, gave them Arab names, and forcibly converted them to Islam. If the government didn't encourage such actions, it turned a blind eye and used the slave raiders as proxy forces against rebellious minorities such as the Dinka.

While the GOS was slaughtering rural populations it considered sympathetic to the rebels, the SPLM/A was starving out government-held towns in the South. By 1986 the SPLM/A was estimated to have 12,500 armed men organized into 12 battalions equipped with small arms and mortars, according to Sudan specialists who monitored the war. It ambushed World Food Programme convoys, murdering the drivers and refusing to negotiate with church and humanitarian groups to allow the food through. On August 15, 1986, Garang banned all Red Cross flights over Southern Sudan, claiming they were a cover to resupply GOS army units. To emphasize his point, on August 16, on taking off from Malakal, a Sudanese Airways airliner was shot down by a SAM-7 missile and the GOS retaliated by banning all further humanitarian flights into the region. "We are not repentant," Garang told the *Washington Post*. "We warned that the airspace is closed."

Neither the 1926 Slavery Convention, nor the 1956 Supplementary Convention on the Abolition of Slavery and the Slave Trade — both of which the GOS had signed and ratified — required countries to report on measures taken against slavery, nor had the United Nations established any form of permanent treaty-monitoring committee. But slavery practised in this age gained a very high profile, particularly in the United States among church groups who "redeemed" the abducted by buying them and returning them home. The freeing of slaves by purchasing them, as Major-General Gordon had once done, from Baggara abductors soon became a mini-industry, with the middlemen reaping sizable profits by driving up the price of the captors to arrange the sale and frequently "selling" children who hadn't been abducted. The highly controversial program received so much publicity that in 1999, supported by the United Nations Children's Fund (UNICEF) and Save the Children, it forced the GOS into action. The Committee for the Eradication of Abduction of Women and Children (CEAWC) was launched, and some of the kidnapped people were returned home. That didn't satisfy Anti-Slavery International, the British group working to end slavery since Gordon's day, which pointed out that the root problems were the government's proxy raiders and the diminishing of pasture land due to the encroaching desert. Mike Dottridge, the director of Anti-Slavery International, appealed to President al-Bashir that "the reality is that people being abducted from communities in northern Bahr al-Ghazal by government-backed militias are being exploited as slaves in the households of militiamen and others."

Since Sudan was a base for the destabilization of Marxist Ethiopia and pariah Libya, the United States desperately wanted to shore up its ally, so in 1984 it sent Vice-President George H.W. Bush on a high-profile visit and defended the use of its military aid in the United Nations. The SPLM/A struck back at what it considered a legitimate U.S. government target. In March 1984 three Chevron oil fieldworkers were kidnapped from Bentiu and executed, and the company shut down its facilities in Sudan. By 1985 the country was bankrupt and dependent on foreign aid, which now accounted for 80 percent of the national budget. When Nimeiri left for Washington on March 27, 1985, to ask President Reagan for $60 million in aid, there were bread riots in the streets. But with the collapse of Mengistu in Ethiopia and the end of the Cold War, the United States was less interested in Sudan and Nimeiri found himself without a country. He was deposed in a bloodless coup on April 6, 1985, by a group of army officers. Calling themselves the Transitional Military Council (TMC), they said they would run the government until elections could be held. They also immediately appealed to the Arab states for financial support and got Gaddafi to cut aid to the SPLM/A.

The general election in April 1986, sanctioned by the TMC, soon to be called the Revolutionary Command Council (RCC), brought Sadiq al-Mahdi and his Umma Party in to run the country. Forced to share power with the Democratic Unionist Party, al-Mahdi once more presided over a Cabinet composed of sworn enemies such as Foreign Minister Hassan al-Turabi and his National Islamic Front (NIF). Not surprisingly, the Islamic legal code, which included *hadud* or flogging, stoning, and amputations for offences, was soon tabled in the Legislative Assembly, a move that prompted all Southern Region members to quit and relief agencies to protest by ending developmental aid to Sudan. On the advice of the more moderate members of the Cabinet, al-Mahdi opened negotiations with the SPLM/A and repealed Arabization in the South, which made al-Turabi and his hard-liners leave the government in retaliation.

* * *

Peter Dalglish had been reassigned from Darfur in December 1986 to manage the World Food Programme Road Transportation Operation in Khartoum. Now desk-bound, he coordinated the transport and distribution of relief supplies, the sheer drudgery of which was, he felt, "coming dangerously close to that of my lawyer friends back in Canada." His redemption occurred in the alley next to the Acropole Hotel where he caught a child jimmying the lock on the door of his Land Rover with a nail. The boy he grabbed was tiny and frail and wore only a pair of blue shorts. The youth started whimpering, then buried his head in his arms as if expecting to be hit. Dalglish had seen Khartoum's street children before. The civil war, drought, and famine in the South had forced an estimated 10,000 such boys to migrate to Khartoum where they lived on the streets, begging and eating out of dumpsters. They were organized gangs of thieves, he had been told, and were not to be trusted. When Dalglish brought the boy food from the hotel, he watched it disappear down the child's throat. The aid worker felt that "at last he had done something good for someone in Sudan's miserable capital city." The next morning his Land Rover was spotless. The child had somehow found a rag and a bucket and had scrubbed the vehicle clean.

The street kids had no friends among the police who periodically rounded them up to interrogate, imprison and sexually abuse them. Middle-class Sudanese called them monkeys and slaves, and relief agencies whose air-conditioned SUVs were familiar to the children, only prompted them to ask, "If they call themselves Save the Children, then why won't they save us?" Accompanied by a UNICEF representative, Dalglish met with the government minister responsible for the kids only to be told by her of the government's plans: "We are going to take the children far from the city and dump them. Then we are going to build impenetrable barriers to keep them out." With funding from Bob Geldof, Dalglish convinced the staff of an underused technical training school donated by the Belgians to take in street children and train them as auto mechanics. But Dalglish wanted to do more. His goal was to set up a small business that would get the kids out of the garbage dump and launch them into self-sufficiency. The enterprise had to be simple so that when he returned home the children could run it themselves.

In the 1980s, decades after the departure of the British, Khartoum had an almost non-existent postal system and its land-line telephones served only as decorative paperweights on people's desks so that U.N. agencies had resorted to using satellite phones to communicate with one another locally. So, Dalglish thought, why not set up a bicycle courier service for profit? The kids knew the streets — and the value of making money. Unlike China or India, Sudan wasn't a bicycle culture. It was a matter of pride for the Sudanese not to be seen pedalling in public; they would rather take an overcrowded bus to commute. But the street kids were hungry enough do anything.

Going door to door, Dalglish drummed up support for the project. The embassies and aid agencies were intrigued but warned that once given bikes the kids would steal them. However, the editor of the *Sudan Times* agreed to a tentative contract if Dalglish's neophyte couriers could deliver copies of his newspaper to all subscribers by 10:00 a.m. On September 18, 1986, the Canadian lawyer turned entrepreneur initiated Street Kids International (SKI) with half a dozen clients and three borrowed bikes. "When I sent the kids out that first morning," he recalls, "I didn't know if I would ever see them again." But they returned, having delivered every copy of the newspaper by 10:00 a.m. Two weeks later there were enough profits to buy three new bicycles — sturdy, bone-jarring, Chinese-made "Flying Pigeons."

SKI quickly became famous. Orders came in, the French embassy donated money for uniforms, the BBC did a documentary film, and the British newspaper *The Guardian* sent out fluorescent newspaper bags printed with SKI COURIER, NOT TOMORROW — TODAY. As for dealing with the kids stealing the bikes, Dalglish writes in *The Courage of Children*: "Sister Ann in my London, Ontario, grade two class was the inspiration — whenever one child acted up, we were all forced to stay behind after school. With SKI, if a bike was stolen, lost, or sold — the cost of a new one came out of all the kids' wages."

Two years later, after bailing kids out of prison, cleaning their wounds, and dispensing anti-malaria tablets and lice-prevention shampoo, Peter Dalglish left Sudan with an idea. If SKI worked for the street kids in Khartoum, why wouldn't it in other Third World cities? Back in Canada in a renovated warehouse on Toronto's Front Street, he drafted a plan to make Street Kids really international. Dalglish left SKI in June 1994 to become director of Canada's national youth service corps. In 2002 he served as the chief technical adviser on child labour to the United Nations in Nepal. He never returned to Khartoum, but its street kids were never far from his thoughts. "I went to Africa to rescue destitute children, but they ended up rescuing me," Dalglish writes in *The Courage of Children*. "The world's poorest kids taught me that my life is worth far more than the clothes on my back or the car in my garage."[6]

* * *

Unlike his illustrious ancestor, Sadiq al-Mahdi had no popular support in the hinterlands. So, to pacify the South, since he couldn't rely on the military, he employed tribal "friendlies." He attempted to put the SPLM/A down by arming the Baggara tribes and letting them raid into Dinka territory, burning villages and raping and killing the inhabitants, especially in the Bahr al-Ghazal area. It became a war by proxy as armed tribal militias called *murahleen*, with the government's encouragement, attacked Dinka strongholds such as Southern Kordofan, dispossessed the locals of their land and cattle, burned villages, and abducted women and children into slavery. Just as their ancestors had co-operated with Arab slave dealers against their own people, so now did tribes such as the Rufa'a in the Southern Blue Nile area, the Fartit in western Bahr al-Ghazal, and the Acholi in Equatoria prey on the civilian population in the Dinka regions.

The level of brutality at which the "friendlies" operated, slaughtering any non-Muslim blacks, only gave the SPLM/A new converts. The atrocities of government-sanctioned thugs coupled with the SPLM/A's radio publicity campaign beamed in from Ethiopia allowed the rebels to take much of Southern Sudan. By June 1989, the SPLM/A held three large towns — Torit, Boor, and Nasir. Now controlling much of the oil-rich South, the rebels were able to attract wealthy entrepreneurs from the commercial world, the most prominent being the British financier Roland "Tiny" Rowland, who wanted the oil pumped south through

Kenya and away from Port Sudan. Khartoum's fortunes were on the decline everywhere. At home currency devaluation and the lifting of price controls on food and fuel led to riots in the streets. Abroad, having backed Saddam Hussein in the First Gulf War, Sudan lost both Arab and Western support.

The devastating famine of 1988, caused by a severe drought, brought unwelcome (to the GOS at least) Western attention, and Operation Lifeline Sudan (OLS) was established, but not before a quarter-million Sudanese had perished. In March 1989, Sadiq al-Mahdi announced that he intended to restart the peace process with the SPLM/A and negotiated a temporary ceasefire that allowed the return of relief agencies to resume development aid. While this action is sometimes viewed as a last-ditch attempt by al-Mahdi to curry favour with the West, it was a historic humanitarian intervention. The OLS would be the official umbrella for some 35 relief agencies that would distribute food through negotiated "corridors of tranquility" to all sides. After the 1986 Malakal incident, however, pilots were cautious about flying into either government- or rebel-held areas.

The brainchild of James Grant, the head of UNICEF, Operation Lifeline Sudan was designed to be neutral. Its main purpose was to negotiate with the warring parties the establishment of safe areas in which humanitarian organizations could distribute food to the war-affected populations on the government's side as well as on the rebels'. OLS was hailed as a major diplomatic breakthrough, especially so for Sudan since it was the first time that a government had agreed on a violation of its own national sovereignty by accepting that humanitarian organizations could aid rebel-held areas — in effect, feeding enemies of the state that it was trying to destroy. However, Khartoum wasn't above manipulating access to certain rebel-held areas by enforcing flight bans meant to starve out the rebels and the civilian population. The Nuba Mountains were a major target during the war, and consequently a permanent flight ban was in force from 1994 to 1999. Aid workers complained that the GOS would deny food deliveries to an airstrip under rebel control "for security reasons" but speedily divert it to one of its own. Neither did the SPLM/A do itself any favours when it shot down a well-marked

Médecins sans Frontières (MSF) aircraft, killing three of the French doctors onboard.[7]

But OLS and the truce were too late to save al-Mahdi. The Sudanese military knew that many of those being fed were rebel combatants and arrived at the same conclusion as MSF, which noted that OLS had become an instrument of war rather than a force for peace. When al-Mahdi also suspended Islamic law in the South, it served to combine the dissatisfaction of the military with the displeasure of the Islamic hard-liners. On June 30, 1989, units commanded by Colonel Omar al-Bashir overthrew the government and imposed a state of emergency on the country. Inconspicuous until the coup and stationed in the Muglad basin protecting the Chevron oil fields, al-Bashir had been implicated in "cleansing" the Nuer and Dinka villages around them. In 1988 he had gathered a group of middle-ranking officers around him to form the Islamist National Salvation Revolution. Although they pretended that a 15-member Revolutionary Command Council had taken over the reins of power, it was no secret that the éminence grise behind the coup was Hassan al-Turabi and his National Islamic Front (NIF).

With buck teeth and a girlish giggle, al-Turabi was initially ignored by Western intelligence agencies to their great cost. The son of an Islamic judge, he had founded, as a young man, the Sudanese branch of the Muslim Brotherhood. Educated at the University of Khartoum, the University of London, and the Sorbonne in the 1970s, al-Turabi had moved to Saudi Arabia where, with the blind Egyptian cleric Sheikh Omar Abdel-Rahman (now imprisoned in the United States for his role in the 1993 bombing of New York's World Trade Center), he had set up the Islamist International, a global force of jihadists dedicated to combatting what they saw as the Zionist-Crusader conspiracy.[8]

Using the army and the Brotherhood, the new Islamist government in Sudan suspended the constitution, dissolved Parliament, abrogated the negotiated OLS ceasefire, and banned the media, trade unions, and all strikes. Periodically, it rounded up street kids and conscripted them into the army where they were certain to be cannon fodder against the SPLM/A — ironically fighting their own people. The NIF continued the policy of legitimizing "friendlies" like the Baggara and Miseriya militias to massacre SPLM/A supporters such as the Nuba in Southern Kordofan and the Southern Sudanese in Jabalain. For the first time, too, the Sudanese Air Force (SAF) ventured across the Ugandan border to bomb SPLM/A camps. Al-Bashir was also quick to purge his own circle of potential rivals, and in April 1990 he executed 28 high-ranking RCC army officers, 4,000 lower officers, and 11,000 soldiers whom he accused of attempting a countercoup. The Ministry of Justice promulgated the Criminal Act of 1991 in which robbery was punishable by crucifixion and adultery by public stoning. Universities were scoured clean of professors and students suspected of being liberal. All Christian churches were closed, the Anglican bishop of Sudan was sentenced to be publicly flogged in 1993, and ridiculously the director of the government antiquities department was imprisoned for excavating more Christian than Islamic ruins. "Whoever thinks of subjugating us," al-Bashir warned, "they will find a nation that loves martyrdom."

The institutionalized cruelty of the government was closely rivalled by the savagery of the SPLM/A. Neither side respected the neutrality of civilians or relief agencies. Amnesty International had troubling questions about the SPLM/A's recruiting methods. For one thing, thousands of young boys known as "unaccompanied minors" were disappearing into recruiting camps. Far from being the Che Guevara of the rebellion, John Garang became increasingly aloof and intellectually arrogant and was criticized as a stooge of Ethiopia's Mengistu. To the disappointment of many of its supporters, the SPLM/A hadn't opted for full independence of the South from the GOS, and there seemed to be an absence of any political agenda outside the battlefield. In the liberated areas of the South, no shadow governments were set up. Instead, the freed regions were returned to the former colonial structure whereby old chieftaincies and traditional tribal customs were reinstated, especially in the courts. Neglect by the GOS had destroyed the old British infrastructure of civil administration in the South, and roads, medical facilities, and government services no longer existed. The locals looked in vain to the SPLM/A to provide them, but for someone schooled in graduate economics, Garang was oddly uninterested, relying on local chiefs to do what they could.

Garang was particularly preoccupied with extending the rebellion, and in 1991 he overreached himself by sending a small SPLM/A force into Darfur to begin an insurrection. It evolved into a cruel tragedy. Led by Darfurian Duad Bolad, the rebels had to cross a vast distance in the dry season with the only available water in carefully guarded boreholes. Moreover, the territory was occupied by cattle-herding Arab groups who betrayed them to the GOS. The Sudanese military quickly tracked Bolad's men and hunted them down, using both the regular army and the local Beni Halba Arabs. A few rebels escaped and walked for months through the Central African Republic back to Southern Sudan. Bolad was captured and tortured by the local governor, Colonel al-Tayeb Ibrahim, and was never seen again. Unfortunately, his diary was found, with the names of every member of the clandestine network, all of whom disappeared into prisons and/or the GOS's "ghost houses."

John Garang had other problems by then. Haphazard guerrilla strategy and a lack of any political or social platform caused two of his officers, Reik Machar and Lam Akol, to consider removing him. The careers of both had been sidetracked, and in 1991 they were commanding SPLM/A units in Nasir on the Ethiopian border. With Mengistu's days in Ethiopia numbered, Garang became increasingly preoccupied with taking the Southern city of Juba as soon as he could; it would be a bargaining chip in future negotiations. The ambitious pair waited in the wings as local bad harvests caused refugees to flood into Nasir, closely followed by the international aid agencies and Western media networks scenting a "disaster story." As the only authorities in the town, Machar and Akol sprang to international prominence. Soon both commanders were doing media interviews and negotiating with the GOS to allow aid to be barged in. With Garang marginalized and the relief agencies, media, and Khartoum recognizing their legitimacy, Machar and Akol staged a coup on August 28, 1991.

The overthrow of Garang was announced on local radio and then to the world on the BBC. Unfortunately, this proved premature as the rebels didn't have the necessary support from rank-and-file SPLM/A. Garang had learned the cardinal rule of political longevity in Africa: keep your friends close but your enemies closer. He proved more decisive than either Machar or Akol. Stripping his remaining commanders of rank, he took control of the Torit garrison, then moved loyal troops to surround the Nasir region, destroying supplies and villages that might aid the mutineers.

It soon became evident to the watching media and aid agencies that the GOS was backing the anti-Garang forces with weapons and food. Machar admitted to this, explaining that the alliance with the government was temporary and tactical, but his name was now tarnished. The Sudanese military took advantage of the dissension within the SPLM/A to send army units far into the South, its proxy forces raiding in Garang's territory. They also sealed off the Sudanese-Ugandan border to the rebels. This was accomplished by entering into an alliance with the distasteful Lord's Resistance Army (LRA), a move universally condemned. Formed in 1987 to fight the government of Uganda, the LRA had abducted thousands of children, looted and victimized the population of northern Uganda, and displaced 1.7 million Ugandans, who fled to internally displaced person (IDP) camps. While remaining uncompromising on sharia law and Islamization, Khartoum then began a propaganda campaign, holding out the possibility that it would grant the South independence and taking some of the wind out of the SPLM/A's sails. But the Western media discovered that what the GOS considered the "South" was a region with a redrawn border that put the precious oil fields in the North's Unity Province.

As mentioned earlier, the first foreign oil company to seek oil in the Muglad basin of Southern Sudan was Chevron, which was granted a concession in 1974. Four years later it made its first discovery, and in 1980 followed that with a significant strike in the Unity/Talih area north of Bentiu in the Western Upper Nile. By May 1982, Chevron had found substantial oil reserves in Heglig, just inside South Kordofan. After the SPLM/A murdered three of Chevron's workers in 1984, the company stopped drilling, resuming only in 1988 to recoup some of its investment. But with the military coup and the coming to power of al-Turabi and the hard-line NIF the following year, the company had second thoughts. Promised a huge tax write-off by the Bush administration on June 15, 1992, Chevron sold its 42-million-acre concession for an estimated

US$23 million to Concorp International, a private multinational company registered in Sudan, Uganda, and India. Concorp then sold blocks of the concession to various buyers, one of which was Vancouver-based State Petroleum Corporation, by some reports a dummy corporation formed by Canadian Muslims with good GOS connections who wanted to buy former Chevron concessions at fire-sale prices. With Chevron's exit the U.S. State Department, conveniently forgetting years of military aid, declared Sudan a country that sponsored terrorism and forbade American companies from doing business there. But the United States couldn't prevent Canadian companies from doing so.

Owned by Pakistani-Canadian Lutfur Rahman Khan, State Petroleum Corporation bought Blocks 1, 2, and 4 of the Chevron concession.[9] Khan told the *Globe and Mail* that he had heard from his father, a Pakistani military officer, and his uncle, who was a Pakistani diplomat in Washington, that Chevron was about to retreat from Sudan. Khan went to Khartoum and met al-Turabi, who despite the Canadian's lack of cash or oil exploration expertise, gave him access to Chevron's seismic data, showing the extent of the wealth of the Heglig and Unity Fields. The Pakistani-Canadian returned to Vancouver and then founded State Petroleum with Pakistani businessmen Dr. Asif Syed and Nadeem Khan.

In June 1992, Arakis Energy Corporation, also Vancouver-based, acquired five million shares from State Petroleum. Its wunderkind CEO James Terence Alexander announced on December 7 that his company had formed a partnership with State Petroleum. Alexander called the project "the opportunity of a lifetime" for a company like Arakis (which until then had operated primarily in the Appalachian Mountains) because it could bring about its transformation from a small to a midsize independent oil company.

Sudan wasn't the Appalachians, however, and the country's unique problems called for a larger oil company with deeper pockets, which Arakis wasn't. Still, in July 1993, Arakis announced that it would assume full ownership over the project, buying out State Petroleum, and concentrate on raising the estimated US$750 million to $1 billion needed to finance its Sudan project. But although it made new discoveries at Toma South and El Toor (Athonj) oil fields in Block 1, the Canadian upstart couldn't raise enough capital to complete the project. Nevertheless, it pressed ahead and built roads north of Bentiu in 1996 in preparation for moving in heavy equipment. That year Arakis also brought eight wells on stream at Heglig, subsequently shipping low levels of crude oil to a small refinery at El Obeid in Northern Kordofan for domestic consumption.

A journalist who visited the Arakis drilling site wrote: "The relationship between Arakis and its Sudanese hosts is self-evidently symbiotic…. The oil camp opens its doors to military men as well as nomads. Arakis services broken military trucks, provides electricity lines to their barracks and even pipes in water to army camps." But not all Sudanese were as close to Arakis. "The oil is taken from here and the cash goes to Khartoum to buy bombs that then kill our people," Salva Mathoc, a local SPLM/A commander, told the *Toronto Star*. "They [Arakis] are our next target." Using a defence later repeated by Talisman Energy, Arakis claimed that it was politically neutral and only interested in a "completely commercial project."

By January 1994, Arakis's Sudanese project was spending millions of dollars that Alexander didn't have, so he launched a selling blitz, getting Anthem International in the British Virgin Islands to buy one million Arakis shares. That September he reeled in Hatfield Investments Limited, which agreed to buy 500,000 Arakis shares at $5.10 each for $2.55 million. On November 1, 1994, Alexander coaxed Verwaltungs-und-Privat Bank Aktiengesellschaft into buying one million shares for $6.37 million. By now the Vancouver Stock Exchange (VSE) was becoming inquisitive. It wondered if Hatfield and Verwaltungs had put any money down at all.

Alexander's desperate need to pour even more money into Sudan grew daily: he had to raise cash to finance a refinery and the 900-mile pipeline to Port Sudan. By July 1995, it looked as if he had pulled it off. He announced that Arab Group International for Investment and Acquisition (AGI) would provide US$750 million in financing. With that news, Arakis's share value leaped from $5.10 to $26 on the VSE. Had its shareholders sold then, they might have done well. But the bubble burst on August 22 when, in a news release, Arakis admitted that AGI wouldn't be contributing its originally announced investment. On the VSE, Arakis stock fell $15.50 after heavy trading, and two days later the company voluntarily delisted itself from the VSE and Alexander resigned.[10]

Arakis sold 75 percent of its stake in the Sudanese project on December 6, 1996, to three other companies, all of which were state-owned, forming a consortium called the Greater Nile Petroleum Operating Company (GNPOC), valued at approximately US$1 billion. The Canadian firm gave itself a 25 percent share, with the China National Petroleum Corporation taking 40 percent, the Malaysian Petronius Carigali Overseas Sdn Bhd acquiring 30 percent, and the Sudanese state oil company Sudapet assuming 5 percent.

On March 1, 1997, in the Crude Oil Pipeline Agreement (COPA), the Arakis-led GNPOC consortium found the financing to build a pipeline from the oil fields north to a new port for supertankers on the Red Sea. But by now, with the United States imposing economic sanctions on Sudan, Arakis had had enough. In late 1997 the company started searching for a way to exit. Finally, in August 1998, it sold its interest in GNPOC to Calgary-based Talisman Energy. (Before investing in Sudan, Talisman's executives met with Canada's Foreign Affairs Africa Desk to be briefed about the volatility of the region. In light of subsequent events, the company's shareholders should have been made aware of that.)

Talisman issued one of its $33 shares for every 10 Arakis shares, buying up 8.92 million shares in a transaction worth CDN$295 million. Oxford-educated and a former astrophysicist, James Buckee, president and CEO of Talisman, told the media: "This is a rare opportunity with spectacular potential." In October, with an immediate advance of CDN$46.5 million to meet its debt, Talisman bought up Arakis and its share in GNPOC for CDN$277 million. Talisman also took the precaution to register its Sudanese operation in the Netherlands, where the Dutch-owned Trafigura Beheer BV had obtained the right to sell Sudanese oil internationally.

The largest independent oil and gas company in Canada, Talisman Energy was the fourth largest in the world. Created in 1992 as part of a management buyout of the assets of BP Canada, Talisman (the good-luck-charm name was chosen through an employee competition) had never been risk-averse, and while its Canadian operations accounted for most of its income, it was active in the North Sea, Algeria, Indonesia — and now Sudan. While its ownership base was in Alberta, it was also the largest oil and gas producer in Ontario — two politically sensitive provinces for the Liberal government then in power in Ottawa.

Talisman's decision to invest in Sudanese oil was the reason why its 1999 revenues climbed to CDN$2.3 billion, a 51 percent increase over the company's 1998 earnings. This spectacular jump in earnings would later explain why Talisman's management was so committed to Sudan despite the ethical questions involved. Talisman now owned 25 percent of five oil blocks (three exploration and two development) in the Heglig, Unity, and Kaikang Fields, operating in the Heglig-Pariang area of South Kordofan and the Western Upper Nile, locations whose problems the company's shareholders, human-rights activists, and the Canadian government certainly knew about.

The partners restarted Chevron's operations in the Unity and Heglig Fields on the Upper Nile–Kordofan border. The following year other foreign companies entered Sudan: the Qatari Gulf Petroleum Corporation became active in the Adar Yal Field in the Upper Nile; the Swedish International Petroleum Company teamed up with Petronius Carigali; and the Austrian OMV (Sudan) Exploration Gmbh set up shop in the Adok-Ler area. The news that the Swedish company found oil deposits estimated at 300 million barrels at Thar Jiath made Sudan an oil exporter on the world stage.

Human-rights groups had long since claimed that the oil concessions were only possible through the wholesale clearances of the civilian populations from the areas. The pattern was for local "friendlies" to sweep down on horseback or camel on the sleeping village, kill the men, round up the cattle, and kidnap the women and children. Then, protected by the Sudanese military, the oil companies would move in and build camps, roads, and airfields that could be used by the government to further widen the circle.

From November 1992 to April 1993, the GOS and Arab *murahleen* began a five-month offensive of looting, burning, and abduction. That same month Islamic jurists in El Obeid, the capital of Kordofan State, issued an edict referring to members of the Nuba ethnic group as infidels and to the war against them as a jihad. They called upon all Muslims to kill Nuba and take over their land out of religious duty. It was the start of the ethnic-cleansing campaign that between April and November 1993 led to the forcible removal of "tens of thousands" of people from the Nuba Mountains to "peace camps" in the north of the state, while thousands more were killed and thousands of women and children were taken as slaves.[11]

A second offensive began in December 1993 when 26 people were killed in hamlets near Heglig. After that the area was deserted except for GOS forces. The Dinka village of Athonj was ethnically cleansed and renamed El Toor, while the GOS deployed troops in Maper and changed its name to Munga. Over the years the attacks and displacements led to a gradual Dinka depopulation of the oil-rich area, since few of the original inhabitants returned after each displacement.

The U.N. Commission on Human Rights established the post of special rapporteur on human rights in Sudan in 1993, appointing Gaspar Biro of Hungary to the position. After visiting Northern and Southern Sudan in September and December 1993, Biro issued a report detailing human-rights violations committed by the GOS, including extrajudicial and summary killings, disappearance, torture, arbitrary arrest and detention, slavery, and the abduction of children. He also detailed human-rights violations committed by both SPLM/A factions, including the killing of civilians on the basis of ethnicity.

President al-Bashir not only rejected the U.N. report but accused Biro of "insulting Islam" and committing heresy, warning him that Sudan would withdraw its membership if the United Nations didn't stop condemning "Allah's laws." Biro was succeeded by the equally tough Leonardo Franco of Argentina, who in his April 1999 report stressed Sudan's obligations under international human-rights and humanitarian law, citing the Geneva Conventions and warning that a "swath of scorched earth/cleared territory" was being created around the new oil fields.

None of this slowed the pace of construction on the Unity–Port Sudan pipeline, and uncharacteristically for Sudan, it was completed by

April 1999. That was because all labour, engineering, and materials were provided by the China National Petroleum Corporation, and there were rumours that Chinese convicts had been used. With China, the GOS had found a country where human-rights violations weren't a problem. In May a new offensive was launched from the Nuba Mountains, with Antonov bombers and helicopter gunships supporting government troops using armoured personnel carriers. It wasn't lost on observers that because of the roads and airfields built by the oil companies, military forces were able to reach their destinations more easily than before. The offensive lasted two months, the movement slowed by the rains, and by July, aid agencies discovered that more than half the population in Ruweng County had disappeared. Villages east of Heglig didn't escape, either, and were also subjected to periodic attack, bombing, looting, killing, and abduction.

It is said that every child in Darfur soon learns to distinguish between the sound of a Lockheed Martin C-130's Allison engine and the noise of an Antonov's Kuznetsov engine: the former means life, the latter signifies death. Based in Lokichokkio (Loki), Kenya, the C-130s are used by the World Food Programme to drop food, and the starving multitudes attracted to the drops have been dubbed "C-130 invitees." In contrast with the Afghan war and its surgically targeted Predator Hellfire strikes, the conflict in Sudan is a low-tech affair in which bombs are rolled out of the rear of Sudanese Air Force Antonov aircraft that are indistinguishable from those also used by the WFP to drop sacks of grain. Sometimes the operations follow each other, the bringers of destruction and the saviours taking off from the same airfield at the same time. The bombs "were just oil drums packed with explosives and scrap metal," observed Canadian diplomat Nick Coghlan. "I was told that the Antonovs bombed in exactly the same manner as their UN counterparts dropped food: the rear door was opened, the aircraft went into a steep climb, and the load rolled out of the back and into the void."[12]

Built in the former Soviet Union from 1957 to 1973, the Antonov An-12 features in the Sudanese civil war as a crude but effective bomber. The worldwide availability of the turboprop medium transport after the collapse of the Soviet Union has made it a fixture in Hollywood movies and real-life drama, and the more modern Chinese version, the Yun-8 (now upgraded by Pratt & Whitney Canada), will ensure its longevity in Africa well into this century. Neither is Sudan the first to employ Antonov freighters as bombers. An-12s in the Indian Air Force were utilized for the same reason in that country's 1971 war with Pakistan.

The history of the Sudanese Air Force reflects that of the country's shifting allegiances. It began in 1956 with ex–Royal Air Force Hunting Provost trainers (similar to the Canadair CL-41 "Snowbirds"), and in 1960, Pembroke C Mk. 54s and Fokker F27s were acquired for light transport. Four years later all the Provosts had crashed, either because of poor maintenance or pilot error, ending the monopoly of British equipment. In 1969, after Jaafar Nimeiri's coup, the Communist Bloc equipped the SAF with Shenyang F-4 (the Chinese version of the MiG-17F) fighters, An-12 and An-24 transports, and Mil Mi-4 and Mi-8 helicopters, along with the requisite Russian military advisers and technicians to keep them in the air.

All Soviet personnel were sent home in July 1971 after the failed Communist coup, and during the rest of the 1970s, the United States took over, supplying six C-130H Hercules transports, while Canada sold the country four de Havilland Canada DHC-5 Buffaloes, one of which in 2008 was still said to be operational. But when Nimeiri wanted fighter capability, Washington refused. Adept at playing Western nations off on one another, Nimeiri turned to France in April 1977 to negotiate the purchase of 14 Mirage fighters and two Puma helicopters. The United States changed its policy in 1978 and supplied 10 F-5E fighters and two F-5F trainers. The SAF's first helicopters were 20 MBB Bo-105s from Germany for communication purposes. Later, in order to ingratiate himself with the GOS, Libya's Colonel Gaddafi donated a squadron of MiG-23 "Floggers." But by the early 1990s, attrition, pilot error, and the U.S. arms embargo took their toll on the SAF, and none of the C-130Hs, F-5s, or "Floggers" were operational. The Chinese era began in 1996, with Iranian funding, and 10 years later the SAF inventory consisted of Chinese F-7 fighter bombers (Fishbed), NAMC Q-5 (Fantan) ground-attack aircraft, and the omnipresent Antonov bomber/transports.

Oil revenues allowed Khartoum to purchase 12 MiG-29 (Fulcrum) fighters for US$400 million directly from Russia in 2002. These sophisticated fourth-generation fighters are said to be based at El Obeid and are reportedly flown by mercenaries. As feared as Stuka dive bombers were to defenceless refugee columns in the Second World War are the eight Mi-24 (Hind) helicopter gunships bought in 1995 and reportedly flown and serviced by Libyan and Iraqi crews.[13] It was these aircraft that featured in the Harker Report as being operating from the Talisman-built airstrip at Heglig and that Nick Coghlan would later see at Unity Field "taking on large amounts of ammunition and unloading none." In 2006 the SAF acquired its most lethal weapons ever — the Russian-made Mi-24 assault helicopters with remote control under-nose gun turrets.

On August 27, 1999, oil began to flow, with the first shipload of 300,000 barrels exported to Singapore from Port Sudan. The ceremony was keenly watched by representatives of Western oil companies (and the pardoned former Sudanese President Nimeiri) as well as government representatives from Chad where oil had also been discovered. This shipment alone, bound for Singapore, brought US$2.2 million to the Sudanese treasury. That year production from the Heglig and Unity sites accounted for US$480 million of the government's annual budget of $1.2 billion, allowing for the first repayment of international loans. The country now an oil exporter, the International Monetary Fund reinstated Sudan for future credits. Sudan's oil reserves were soon revised far above expectations: the GNPOC holdings alone were estimated to be 800 million barrels, with Swedish Lundin's at 300 million barrels. The GOS's future revenues were estimated at $3 to $5 billion. With U.S. companies banned, other national oil companies, particularly from the European Union (EU), began to court Khartoum. European developmental aid had ended in 1990, but with the prospect of so much oil, the EU opened a dialogue with the GOS.

Sudan may have entered the new century as an oil exporter, but the flow of petrodollars had no effect on a certain segment of Khartoum — those Sudanese who lived in Mayo, Jebel Atulia, Wad El Bashir, and Dar es Salaam, the four camps that ringed the capital. The United Nations had a vague idea that there were as many as 1.5 million IDPs eking out an existence around the capital city, which had a minimal infrastructure to begin with. When Nick Coghlan saw them, they housed 250,000 people. "A vast poverty belt on the fringes of the city," he writes in *Far in the Waste Sudan*, "where the families survived by drastically reducing their food consumption (usually to one meal a day), by looking for work in the informal sector, and by putting the entire family (including young children) to work."

In truth, no agency, government or foreign, knew how many IDPs there really were, for the numbers varied day by day. All wars have their refugees. Those who escape by crossing a border are legally so, but these people were all Sudanese nationals, from the North, South, and West, who had been driven out of their homes by the fighting and now survived in camps, dependent on the United Nations and various relief agencies for aid and protection. Up to 4.5 million people had been displaced in Sudan since the beginning of the last phase of civil war in 1983, estimated U.N. Special Rapporteur Leonardo Franco. In his report to the U.N. General Assembly, he reiterated his concern at the continuous war that "has affected mainly the civilian population, whose plight should be regarded as one of the most pressing human-rights concerns facing the international community." Every large Sudanese city now had its IDP camp, the government allowing such shantytowns to proliferate while pretending they didn't exist.

The camps had some water, sparse medical services, no public transport, and minimal electrical power. The GOS reasoned that if it ignored the IDPs they would give up and return home as soon as the war ended and no longer strain the North's resources. Most of the IDPs had moved around the country for so long that whole generations had been born in the camps, the young had lost their tribal language, and few remembered where their homes had once been. But even with the minimal services grudgingly provided by the GOS (the only schools available taught in Islamic) the IDPs knew the camps were far safer than their isolated villages, if only because the Western media based in Khartoum gave protection from GOS helicopter gunships and the SPLM/A.

Some relief agencies operated programs for the IDPs, and Nick Coghlan was impressed by the Canadian Fellowship for African Relief

(FAR) in Wad El Bashir, which ran a child-to-child educational campaign where young children instructed one another in basic health and hygiene practices. Coghlan writes: "Then with the help of two successive Canadian interns — the appropriately and biblically named Rachel and Rebecca — the organization had grafted onto this program an entire peace-building curriculum: how and why you should get on with people from different ethnic groups, how to deal with bullying on the playground … the program was an inspiring one, and the kids loved the performing that it involved."[14]

The Canadian Assessment Team had visited Wad El Bashir in 2000 and was told that it alone "housed" about 50,000 people, some of whom had been there for as many as seven years. Most IDP households were run by women who to feed their families in circumstances where there were no jobs or financial support from the GOS did what they could. "When they turn to producing alcohol, as many do, the results are catastrophic," the Harker Report noted. "The activity is illegal in Sudan, though it does earn the women a subsistence income. Perhaps the authorities are against it as much for this reason as any other. In any event, the result is often heavy fines and very hard imprisonment, sometimes children incarcerated along with mothers, further family breakup and destitution all round."[15] At that time the United Nations estimated that the camps in Khartoum and other cities held barely 20 percent of the IDPs roaming the country, but with thousands arriving daily no accurate count could be kept.

Population displacement had been practised by government forces and the SPLM/A from the very earliest days for similar reasons. The more popular term was *asset stripping* — the driving of people away from their traditional homes, their houses burned, crops destroyed, and cattle seized. Both sides justified this by claiming that the victims were traditionally nomadic and had stolen their present locations, anyway. The reasons were common to any war — a scorched-earth policy to deny the enemy resources — but it was also typically Sudanese. The stolen land, with wells, was redistributed among allied tribes (or oil exploration companies), the cattle were seized by Arab "friendlies" and sold in the Omdurman market, and the women and children were kidnapped and used as labour in a modern form of slavery. Nor was the SPLM/A innocent, either. The guerrillas exchanged stolen cattle and women with government garrisons for ammunition and food. Tribal areas that were known to have provided the SPLM/A or government militias with recruits were attacked and looted to forestall potential recruitment.

Mediation talks between the SPLM/A and the GOS had been suggested by the Kenyan and Nigerian governments and various church groups and were finally convened in Abuja, Nairobi, and Washington. The Nigerian government warned Khartoum that if it remained intransigent the United States would intervene on the side of the SPLM/A. The GOS needn't have worried. In March 1993, when the U.S. ambassador to Sudan, Donald Petterson, met surreptitiously with John Garang and Reik Machar in the rebel-held South, the complete indifference the well-fed soldiers had for the starving civilians around them so disgusted the Americans that Petterson recommended holding off support. Inevitably, the meetings proved inconclusive, and Hassan al-Turabi exploited the dissatisfaction within the SPLM/A ranks skilfully, seducing both Machar and Lam Akol into negotiating separately with the central government, each thinking that his platform would prove to be the most acceptable. In January 1992, Akol met with the central government in Frankfurt, Germany. The meeting produced a vague assurance from both sides on Southern self-determination, but it did obtain safe passage for the GOS's troops through Akol's territory to fight the SPLM/A in Equatoria.

Increasingly, the fratricide between the Machar/Akol faction and Garang's people descended into a tribal war, especially since the former were mainly Nuer and the latter were Dinka. With famine caused by the war, the SPLM/A commanders weren't averse to diverting relief supplies to feed their troops, something the agencies and the Sudanese government strove to prevent. Because of this, Khartoum insisted that all NGOs that wanted to operate in the South had to be based in the capital under its scrutiny and that no Southern sector relief workers could enter SPLM/A-held territories without a visa from the government.

The front lines in the Nuer-Dinka war were in Jonglei Province, running along the towns of Kongor and Ayod. In Ayod the unfortunate

Nuer population had not only suffered floods and trypanosomiasis (a cattle-killing disease) but the Machar/Akol rebels had eaten what remained of their livestock. When Emma McCune, Machar's photogenic British wife, began harassing the United Nations to open relief centres in neighbouring Kongor, the reason became clear when her husband moved troops into the Dinka area (and Garang's hometown) and occupied the United Nations Development Programme compound in Panyagor.[16] The SPLM/A then pushed the displaced into what aid workers called the "hunger triangle" between the towns of Ayod, Yuai, and Kongor, knowing that relief agencies would be forced to air-drop food into it and thus feed their own soldiers. The U.N. relief agencies knew they were now feeding the Machar/Akol army and not the refugees it had displaced. It was the most blatant manipulation of relief needs in a war that saw such tactics repeated continuously.

The objectives of commanders during the Sudanese civil war was not to gain strategic towns or routes but to receive the manna that dropped out of World Food Programme C-130s and garner the attention of Western media camera teams. These were the prizes that all parties wanted to capture. Waging a war is an expensive proposition with regard to food, arms, and medical equipment, and historically rebel groups have relied on a diaspora (as did the Irish Republican Army), have tapped into local wealth such as oil fields (as in Angola), or have begged from sympathetic states (as did Ethiopia). With none of these options now available to the SPLM/A, foreign aid was blatantly diverted to military commanders, clan leaders, and local chiefs.

In the 1998 famine, for example, DANIDA, a Danish relief agency, recorded that 80 percent of its aid went to soldiers, 15 percent to "administration," and the remaining 5 percent to the intended victims. In this war both the rebels and the GOS routinely hijacked "humanitarian infrastructures" such as roads, airstrips, SUVs, helicopters, and radios put in to facilitate food distribution, using even ceasefires (like the one negotiated in 1995 by former President Jimmy Carter) as a cover to move troops about. No wonder Garang, Machar, and Akol had no need for a social agenda for the areas under their control. All they had to do was parade the starving before media cameras and wait for the relief agencies to respond with food, medical care, seeds, et cetera, while they concentrated on waging war against the GOS and each other. A lesser-known consequence of the aid pipeline was that in an agricultural society like Sudan its continuous flow transformed what had been seasonal soldiers (who previously had stopped fighting to return home and grow crops) into permanent ones.

Negotiations between the GOS and the SPLM/A were initiated on January 4, 1994, in Nairobi under supervision of the Intergovernmental Authority on Drought and Desertification (IGADD). An African regional response to environment, food security, and humanitarian affairs and composed of six East African countries (Djibouti, Ethiopia, Kenya, Somalia, Sudan, and Uganda), IGADD was supported financially by Canada and other Western countries. Renamed the Intergovernmental Authority on Development (IGAD), it would claim some success in getting the GOS and the SPLM/A to accept a Declaration of Principles, giving the unity of Sudan a chance as well as allowing the people of the South to opt for independence if need be. At the Foreign Ministers' Standing Committee on the Sudan Peace Talks, Machar and Garang agreed on a common agenda, including a negotiated ceasefire by all sides in the conflict to be monitored by neutral parties; the right of self-determination for the people of Southern Sudan, the Nuba Mountains, and "other marginalized areas," to be decided by referendum; and detailed arrangements between the South and the North for the transition period leading up to self-determination.

By 1989 the SPLM/A's strength had reached 20,000 to 30,000 men and would rise to between 50,000 and 60,000 in 1991. But as a popular alternative it had lost its early momentum: the South was no closer to secularized self-determination than it had been in 1956. The SPLM/A had missed opportunities at brokering settlements acceptable to the GOS, its own supporters, and the international community, and its leaders had time and again demonstrated that they had their own agendas. Furthermore, the end of the Ethiopian wars and the closure of the Ugandan border stripped the SPLM/A of its safe havens.

Khartoum had fared no better. The end of the Cold War, the election of Bill Clinton as president, and pressure in the U.S. Congress by church and anti-slavery groups to disengage from supporting the Sudanese central government allowed the United States to change tack, publicly criticize the GOS, and even put Sudan on its list of State Sponsors of Terrorism. Watching U.S. military activity in nearby Somalia, the GOS feared that the Clinton administration would begin supplying the SPLM/A with sophisticated weapons. Playing into Washington's paranoia at a conference on April 15, 1991, al-Turabi invited Islamists from around the world to join him in attacking the "Zionist-Crusader" conspiracy by forming a permanent council and working out a "global action plan to defy the tyrannical West."

Then largely unknown in the West, Osama bin Laden had just been exiled from his native Saudi Arabia, and it came as no surprise to the CIA when he and his family showed up in Khartoum, his Gulfstream G-8 executive jet and other aircraft prominent on the airport tarmac. To reward al-Turabi beyond a US$5 million donation to the NIF, bin Laden invested heavily in Sudanese businesses, and his family construction firm was given a contract to build highways. Large tracts of agricultural land on the Red Sea coast, traditionally belonging to the Beja nomads were sold by the GOS to bin Laden and other Gulf Arabs. These actions only intensified guerrilla activity by the Beja, to which the GOS responded by banning the Beja Congress in 1997.

In his weekly diatribes at the Al Qaeda guest house in Khartoum, bin Laden warned that not only was the United States using its military bases in his homeland to keep down the price of "Muslim oil" but with so many troops in Somalia, Washington was next going to crush the Islamist resurgence in Sudan. In April 1993 he began providing arms to General Mohamed Aideed's ragtag militia to take Mogadishu while at the same time encouraging Sudanese clerics to issue a fatwa against all Americans in Somalia. Using his own fortune and buying Iranian military equipment, bin Laden also operated training camps for Al Qaeda at Hamesh Koraib near Kassala, activities that didn't go unnoticed by American spy satellites. Al-Turabi's support of Saddam Hussein during the First Gulf War also caused an economic crisis at home when all Sudanese workers were expelled from the Persian Gulf, ending their remittance dollars being sent home. Bin Laden's old friend from his

Saudi Arabian days, the blind cleric Sheikh Omar Abdel-Rahman, had moved to New Jersey in 1990, there to plot blowing up New York City landmarks. After six Americans were killed by a car bomb detonated in the World Trade Center on February 26, 1993, along with the sheikh, six of those convicted were Sudanese nationals, with two Sudanese diplomats sent home for aiding the conspirators.

Three years after eliminating all opposition within the military the ruling NIF then wiped out its civilian rivals. When Sadiq al-Mahdi, the former prime minister and leader of the Ansar Islamic sect and opposition Umma Party, was imprisoned on April 5, 1993, for criticizing the NIF in a speech at a religious feast in Omdurman, the action inaugurated the government's crackdown against the Ansar sect, Umma, and the Democratic Unionist Party, in other words, anyone critical of government policies. Police raided the Ansar's holiest shrine in Omdurman on May 22 and expropriated all mosques of the Khatmiya and Ansar al-Sunna orders. Worse was to come when gunmen attacked worshippers in the Sheikh al-Hadiya Mosque (also belonging to the Ansar al-Sunna sect) in Omdurman on February 4, 1994, killing 28 and injuring 16. Initially claiming that foreigners were involved, the police then issued a general security alert and accused the Jama'at al-Muslimeen, another Sudanese Islamic group, of responsibility and publicly executed one of its members.

The Revolutionary Command Council dissolved itself on October 16, 1993, only to reappear in civilian clothes. Lieutenant-General Omar al-Bashir was made president until the as-yet-unscheduled general and presidential elections. Al-Bashir had the same powers he held as RCC chairman and chairman of the Council of Ministers, and the ministers of the former Council of Ministers retained their positions. Accused of plotting with Egypt to assassinate Hassan al-Turabi and other NIF leaders, Sadiq al-Mahdi and three other leading Umma Party members were arrested in June 1994. Al-Mahdi denied the charges and eventually fled Sudan in 1996 "by night on camel, clad in a women's dress."[17] He would return on November 23, 2000, arriving at Khartoum Airport in triumph in a scene that his great-grandfather would have appreciated, his cavalcade mobbed by the faithful upon entering Omdurman.

In the west of the country, Darfur claimed al-Bashir's attention — briefly. Khartoum brought back the old British native administration council in 1994 and allocated territories to chiefs of the 90 tribes in the region. Like London, it attempted to rule on the cheap, providing no funds for services, and the tribal chiefs, suddenly elevated to the authority their fathers once had to distribute land, now increasingly scarce, descended into local ethnic cleansing. Where once the African farming tribes — the Fur, the Zaghawa, and the Masalit — had coexisted with the Arab camel nomads of northern Darfur and the cattle herdsmen of southern Darfur, even intermarrying with them, the competition for land and water coupled with Khartoum's neglect now polarized both sides. As Alex de Waal and Julie Flint note in *Darfur: A Short History of a Long War*, since the GOS couldn't intervene effectively, each side armed itself: "A herd of a thousand camels represents more than a million dollars on the hoof: only the most naive herd-owner would not buy automatic rifles to arm his herders." Where tribal mediation had settled disputes, now Kalashnikovs did.

Based in Darfur's Jebel Marra, the Sudan Liberation Army (SLA), made up of the Fur, Zaghawa, and Masalit, attacked GOS facilities and opted for independence from a regime that had not only neglected them for decades but now openly supported a scorched-earth policy against them. Thus desertification apart, the Darfur conflict originated in land rights and the faults of the Khartoum administration. With much of the Sudanese Army's lower ranks "press-ganged" from Dinka and Darfuri villages, Khartoum resorted to its proxy militias to manipulate local tensions, easily attracting men like Musa Hilal, the sheikh of the Um Jalloul tribe, to run a Janjaweed training camp from his base at Mistiriyah.

The ruling NIF's mad-dog tactics climaxed on June 26, 1995, when the Sudanese government was implicated in the assassination attempt against Egyptian President Hosni Mubarak in Addis Ababa. First, the Organization of African Unity (OAU) condemned the act on September 11, 1995, and then the U.N. Security Council pronounced it a "crime against an internationally protected person." On January 31, 1996, Security Council Resolution 1044 stated that the attack was "aimed, not only at the President of the Arab Republic of Egypt, and not only at the sovereignty, integrity and stability of Ethiopia, but also at Africa as a whole." The Security Council called upon the Sudanese government to extradite to Ethiopia for prosecution the three suspects sheltering in Sudan and "to desist from engaging in activities of assisting, supporting and facilitating terrorist activities and from giving shelter and sanctuaries to terrorist elements and act in its relations with its neighbours."

When U.S. Secretary of State Madeleine Albright met officially with John Garang in Kampala, Uganda, in 1997, the Sudanese government knew that the United States had come to terms with the SPLM/A's miserable human-rights record and was on the verge of recognizing the rebel group. Repeatedly losing battles with the now well-armed rebels, the GOS then signed several peace agreements under the banner "peace from within" that year. Next, Khartoum suddenly accepted the IGAD Declaration of Principles and agreed to discuss self-determination for the South.

The GOS already had a government-in-waiting. After it pacified the South, it set up the Southern States Coordinating Council (SSCC). The SSCC had its own army, the South Sudan Defence Force (SSDF), which was commanded by the Nuer warlord Paulino Matiep, "a singularly sinister figure," writes Nick Coghlan in *Far in the Waste Sudan*, "who some compared with the Marlon Brando character in *Apocalypse Now*." As the guardian of the Talisman Heglig and Unity Oil Fields, Matiep had orchestrated so many successful Dinka massacres with Khartoum's approval that he could even call on the Sudanese Air Force to provide bombing runs when needed.

The GOS effectively exploited tribal divisions in the South: the Equatorians, Nuer, and Dinka all jockeyed for prominence, fighting one another more than they did the government in Khartoum. In a bewildering turn of events, part of the South Sudan Defence Force was the Equatoria Defence Force, a pro-Khartoum Southern militia that fought against the SPLM/A. Now tentatively aligned, Machar's Nuer-dominated South Sudan Independence Movement/Army (SSIM/A) and Akol's SPLA United Movement of the West-Central Upper Nile signed the Khartoum Peace Agreement in April 1997. Five months later they did the same with the follow-up Fashoda Agreement. Both called for self-determination for Southerners and for a future referendum on self-government. But ever suspicious of Khartoum's hand in the negotiations, the mainstream SPLM/A guerrillas rejected both agreements and remained in the bush to fight on.

By 1998 the Dinka and the Nuer realized that peace between their tribes was within reach, and in February/March 1999 they sat down at the Peace and Reconciliation Conference held at Wunlit. The agreement promised that border grazing lands and fishing grounds would become shared resources and that all hostile acts would cease between the two tribes. A second meeting between Madeleine Albright and the SPLM/A and the National Democratic Alliance leaders (a coalition of national opposition groups) took place in 1999. This time Albright officially promised Washington's full support. But proving that old habits die hard, the following year Reik Machar put together the Nuer-run Sudan People's Defence Force (SPDF).

On the international scene the only ally the GOS had was Iran, which it was rumoured had flown Scud missiles with chemical warfare warheads into Juba and was supplying the Sudanese with the technology to build their own. Although there was no evidence of this, the suspicion that Sudan was manufacturing chemical weapons persisted, at least for the Clinton administration. With al-Turabi's acquiescence, Carlos the Jackal, one of the world's most notorious terrorists, was kidnapped by the French Secret Service on August 13, 1994, on the promise that Paris would use its influence with the International Monetary Fund for a Sudanese loan. Two years later international lobbying forced al-Bashir to end his protection of Osama bin Laden. On May 16, 1996, the most infamous terrorist in history left for Afghanistan to plan his campaign against the United States.[18] The terrorist's handiwork was becoming well-known to the West, and in retaliation for the bombings of its embassies in East Africa, on August 20, 1998, the United States launched Tomahawk cruise missiles against the al-Shifa pharmaceutical plant in Khartoum, designating it a chemical warfare factory. When it turned out that all the target did was manufacture veterinary drugs and that its main customer was UNICEF, the U.S. government quietly compensated the owner. Meanwhile, the Sudanese maintained that

President Clinton had taken the action to divert the media spotlight from the Monica Lewinsky affair. Nonetheless, Sudan's leaders were awed at what the Americans could do with impunity.

By the 1990s, the differences between President al-Bashir and Hassan al-Turabi, sometimes compared with that of Joseph Stalin and Leon Trotsky, were ever more apparent. Simply put, al-Turabi wanted a jihad throughout Africa and the Middle East, while al-Bashir held the traditional view of Sudan as the possession of a tiny Arabized elite, as it historically had been. The pair struggled over ideology, foreign policy, and power, with other African leaders warning al-Bashir that he risked Western intervention if he didn't drop the old jihadist.

Al-Bashir's opportunity came from an unlikely place — Darfur. The Justice and Equality Movement (JEM), founded by Darfuri Muslims loyal to al-Turabi, was led by the intellectual Khalil Ibrahim Muhammad, author of *The Black Book: Imbalance of Power and Wealth in the Sudan*, about the disproportionate numbers of Arabs in powerful positions. The JEM eventually fragmented into several tribal groups, the most dangerous of which was the National Movement for Reform and Development (NMRD), commanded by Jibril Abdel Karim Bari from the Zaghawa tribe. Known as "Tek" and a former colonel in Chadian President Idriss Déby's murderous republican guard, he was on the U.N. list for war crimes. Khartoum knew that the NMRD was supported by Chad — Déby was also from the Zaghawa and had even been born on the Darfur border. Al-Bashir already blamed Déby for instigating the war in Darfur, since his tribe had provided many of the fighters. With such a history, al-Turabi was too dangerous to be free.

Al-Bashir declared a state of emergency in 1999, which he said would last three months and which allowed him to dissolve Parliament and remove al-Turabi. The ruling Islamist coalition was split: the administration, the military, and all of the security force were loyal to al-Bashir. The students, the clerics, and the regional Islamist party cells went into opposition with al-Turabi, who then formed his own Popular National Congress Party (PNCP), which he claimed was secretly supported by much of al-Bashir's government. Over the next few years al-Turabi would be let out and then rearrested three more times, the last on May 11, 2008, when the JEM stormed Khartoum ostensibly to link up with him. But like that of Sadiq al-Mahdi, al-Turabi's time seems to have passed and he is no longer a serious danger to al-Bashir. Without his embarrassment the GOS could approach the United States and engage in a more serious peace process with the SPLM/A.[19]

Khartoum's problems in the immediate future are numerous. While obstructing the deployment of UNAMID, al-Bashir has been trying to orchestrate a coup against Chad's Déby so that a more malleable regime can be installed in N'Djamena. Such a regime would abandon the Sudanese rebels in Darfur and prevent the deployment of European Union forces in Chad, which so close to Sudan's western border would be witness to the atrocities taking place in Darfur.

And even if by some miracle the Khartoum regime were to meet all the aspirations of all the rebel groups in Darfur, that would spark fighting on a third front — Sudan's eastern Red Sea Province. Here the local Beja Congress and other organizations in eastern Sudan, while receiving arms from Eritrea, also agitate for autonomy from Khartoum. Both the Beja and Darfuris know that the Comprehensive Peace Agreement (CPA), South Sudan's power-sharing agreement with Khartoum, only came about through decades of prolonged violence — that guerrilla warfare is the only means of loosening the GOS's iron grip on the hinterlands.

Even as its armies thrashed about to put down separatist movements and its president faced international isolation, Sudan was in the throes of an exercise with biblical connotations. The signing of the CPA signalled a shift in population from North to South, and as in the reign of Caesar Augustus, all Sudanese were called to return to their hometowns to be counted. Constituency boundaries were drawn up for the national elections in 2009 and ultimately the referendum in 2011 when the South's secession would be decided. The last national census had been in 1993, and the logistical and technical challenges of carrying one out in Africa's largest country were immense. The census had been delayed three times, but both the North and South understood that a population count would determine power- and wealth-sharing in a future Sudan, especially in the oil-rich Abyei region. The stakes were high, particularly for the Government of South Sudan (GOSS), since the larger the number of Southerners who returned home to be counted, the greater its representation in the 2009 National Assembly would be. The international community might focus on the Darfur conflict, but it was the results of the polls that would create the new Sudan.

Of the four million IDPs in the country, approximately half lived in squatter areas on the outskirts of Khartoum, the remainder in camps across the Uganda and Chad borders. Repatriating all of them by April 15, 2008, when the count was to begin, was impossible, so claimed the GOSS, which lobbied to postpone any census until January 2009, even accusing Khartoum of preventing Southerners from returning home. Pressured by the international community, the government did initiate the census in April. However, it wasn't only traditional mistrust that hampered the exercise. Away from the populous river corridor, the nomadic population, estimated at about five million, was impossible to count, and many of the minorities — Darfuris, Equatorians, and Beja — feared the census results would be used against them, so they refused to participate. All the rebel groups were united in their opposition. In fact, the JEM threatened to attack anyone conducting it.

For Southerners who chose to return home, the journey was fraught with hardship, disease, bandits, and land mines. With no North-South railway and few roads, they relied on the Nile, the river that Arab slavers had once used to penetrate their homelands and kidnap their ancestors. For the Khartoum IDPs, the trip began with a 200-mile ride by truck to Kosti. Once there they waited for up to a month for a barge to take them upriver to Renk, living on the barge (depending on where they got off) from five to 25 days. The Canadian humanitarian organization, Fellowship for African Relief, was heavily engaged at strategic points along the return route, its program covering areas of displacement, transition, and final destination. FAR provided the returnees with clean water, sanitation (latrines), health facilities, nutrition, and shelter materials. At the wharf at Kosti where hundreds (an average of 400 to 500 IDPs weekly) waited for the barges to their areas of origin, the returnees risked contracting diseases such as respiratory infections and diarrhea due to overcrowding. When they arrived at Renk, FAR ensured they were given basic medical drugs and resettlement kits of plastic shelter, cookware, mosquito nets, seeds, blankets, and plates and cups.

To have two million people streaming into a South wracked with poverty, little infrastructure, and communities traumatized by six decades of war was bound to lead to local tensions, especially over land ownership. Properties abandoned by the returnees have been developed by more recent settlers, causing years of litigation. Then there are thousands of rusting land mines and unexploded ordnance that cripple any possible development. Regions changed hands many times during the civil war, with each group planting its own mines. Development donors refuse to begin providing aid for crops, cattle, or schools until de-mining has been completed.

Those that return home, particularly to the South's cities of Malakal and Bor, discover a country now run by the former rebel SPLM/A. Here Arabic and sharia law no longer apply, and neither do strict Islamic prohibitions on alcohol and entertainment, which makes for a thriving nightclub and rock music scene, to say nothing of a building boom in Juba.

While the African, animist, and Christian South has always differed markedly from the Muslim, Arabic-speaking North, post-CPA it has come into its own. Phone connections symbolize everything: calls to neighbouring Uganda are considered local, while those to the North are international, if they work at all. Although no international border is crossed, visitors now need a separate visa to move between the two Sudans, as well as a permit from the Sudan Relief and Rehabilitation Commission, issued from the "New Sudan" offices in Kampala and Nairobi. Along with U.S. dollars, Ugandan and Kenyan shillings are accepted as currency, but not the Sudanese dinar. There is even talk that should the SPLM/A win a nationwide majority in 2009, its leader, Salva Kiir, though not as iconic as his predecessor John Garang, would definitely be more acceptable than Omar al-Bashir domestically and internationally.

When Somali pirates seized the MV *Faia*, a Ukrainian cargo ship carrying 33 tanks and assorted weaponry, in late September 2008, it was no surprise that the cargo was destined for Southern Sudan via Kenya. This was the third shipment of tanks to the South — the first came from Ethiopia — and diplomatic sources say the South is arming itself because it knows the North is, too. The rules of the CPA ban either side from replenishing arms or ammunition without approval of the Joint Defence Board, but like most other agreements in Sudan, this, too, has been flouted. There is no global embargo to prevent either the North or the South from acquiring arms — the only arms embargo enforced in Sudan covers armed groups in Darfur. Khartoum signed two military co-operation agreements with Iran in 2007, and a rise in oil prices allowed it to purchase sophisticated military equipment, including fighter aircraft from Ukraine and Russia. The Sudanese Army is said to be self-sufficient in conventional weapons, even building its own unmanned surveillance planes for use in Darfur. While there were no signs that a North-South conflict was imminent in 2008, the long-term prospects post-2011 are gloomy.

Whatever happens, the ancient country is on the verge of significant political and social change. Rather than applying short-term Band-Aid solutions, concentrated attention by the international community, especially Arab, Chinese, and Indian, could make a decisive difference. That the South will go its own way seems likely. How that will play out in Khartoum is anyone's guess, but Southerners firmly believe the North will employ force to prevent them from separating because it wants the oil fields. After decades of being instructed by government-controlled media, Northerners would find the decreased revenue that inevitably would follow the sharing of oil wealth and the loss of political power from an integrated government difficult to adapt to. In the wake of centuries of treating all Southerners, Dafurians, and Beja as backward children, little more than slaves, how will Northerners adapt? Will the Khartoum elite, which has exploited the hinterland since its city was a slave market, live up to the terms of whatever agreement or protocol it signs? Truly, when Allah created Sudan, he laughed.

6

ENTER TALISMAN

For Canada, Sudan was a backwater, overshadowed by the cultural wealth of Egypt, its downriver neighbour. Not part of the Commonwealth or francophone Africa, with negligible immigration, trade, or cultural ties, Sudan warranted some developmental aid but no permanent Canadian presence. It was, as a British Prime Minister Neville Chamberlain said of Czechoslovakia in 1938: "that faraway country of which we know little."

Bilateral diplomatic relations weren't even contemplated until May 1961 when Abd Alaziz Elnasry Hamza, the Sudanese ambassador resident in Washington, was accredited to Ottawa, while Robert Ford, the Canadian ambassador resident in Cairo, was accredited to Khartoum. It was Sudan that took the initiative to open its first embassy in Ottawa on December 27, 1978, sending the great Dinka chief Francis Mading Deng as its first ambassador. The Canadian government was pleased that Sudan bought four de Havilland Canada DHC-5H Buffalo aircraft in May 1978, the transports leaving Toronto throughout the summer for an epic 30-hour flight to Khartoum. By April 1986, three of the Buffaloes had been destroyed by the hostilities, but one (CN 85) would return to Canada, ending up at the Canadian Warplane Heritage Museum in Mount Hope, Ontario, in January 2003, where it is painted in the markings of the Canadian Forces Buffalo shot down over Syria on August 9, 1974.[1]

But Canada continued to keep its diplomatic distance from the GOS, leaving the Canadian ambassador resident in Addis Ababa to be accredited to Khartoum. It was diplomatic representation from afar,

since the Canadian immigration, commercial, and development coun-
sellors accredited to the GOS would reside in Cairo, with at one time
two accredited attachés as far away as Amman, Jordan, and Rome.
From Ottawa's point of view there was little need to do more. The few
Canadians who might visit Sudan on business or pleasure had access
to the consular facilities at the British embassy or in case of emergency
were to be evacuated by the U.S. embassy.[2]

There had been a single bilateral visit on February 19, 1979, when
the Sudanese presidential envoy came to Ottawa and met with the
prime minister and provincial officials. Looking for a photo opportunity to mark the visit, the two countries drew up and signed three
treaties. These allowed for the establishment of a Joint Businessmen
Union, opened "a discussion" to loan money to Sudan, and explored "the
avenues for co-operation" between the University of Alberta and the
University of Khartoum.

But it was the non-legally-binding Memorandum of Understanding
signed in October 1980 that really made a difference. There are those
at the Canadian International Development Agency who say the idea
originated with Canadians stationed with the British Army in Sudan
during the Second World War who noticed the similarities in climate
and soil between the eastern Sudanese province of Gedaref and the
Canadian Prairies. The project was "to establish the economic viability
of medium- and large-scale mechanized farming in Sudan; to develop
improved agronomic practices; and to effect a transfer of technology to
farmers in the Sudanese private sector."

The Canadian taxpayer contributed CDN$23.14 million toward
this scheme, and a model farm was set up near Sim-Sim (Sesame)
Mountain. Canadian farm machinery was sent out and Canadian agron-
omists advised the locals on various techniques for growing sorghum,
sesame, sunflower, and cotton crops. "The farm was really a small village," remembers Nick Coghlan, who drove five hours from Khartoum
after hearing from everyone about the Canadian project. Coghlan writes
in *Far in the Waste Sudan* that the project was "complete with prefabri-
cated houses — originally imported for Canadians; the walls were still
adorned with calendar pictures of icebergs, polar bears, and now-retired

National Hockey League stars — at the centre of ten thousand hectares of prime agricultural land.... It conducted weed control research and developed new strains of seed ... the development of four new strains of sorghum, and four of sesame."[3]

Coghlan saw that with the fields around Gedaref, Sudan had the capacity to be self-sufficient in food — indeed, it could be a regional exporter. But although heroically maintained by the locals, the 1980s Canadian farm equipment, 20 years later, was at the end of its useful life and there was no longer a budget for fertilizer or road improvements. When Coghlan tried to interest Ottawa in reinvesting in its most successful project, he was told: "Don't you know that those mega-projects are out of fashion these days?" Canadians could take some comfort in knowing that because of the development of mechanized grain production at the Sim-Sim project in the 1980s, the availability of food allowed the people of Darfur to escape the worst of the Sahelian famine in that decade. Another factor was the flow of remittances sent back by Darfuris working in Gedaref.

Budgetary restraints at home were blamed for the closure of the Sudanese embassy in Ottawa in June 1983, a move the embassy linked to the reduction in developmental aid from CIDA. Perhaps the loss spurred the reopening of the embassy two years later when Canadian aid increased in 1985. But although Canada didn't have an embassy in Khartoum, its diplomats based in Addis Ababa were still committed to reminding the GOS of basic humanitarian principles. Marc Perron, the Canadian ambassador to Ethiopia (1985–87), was one such man, working out of a single room in the Khartoum Hilton. "Most ambassadors travel around the city in limousines or the latest-model Mercedes-Benz with tinted windows," remembers Peter Dalglish. "Ambassador Perron broke all the rules. He didn't consider it appropriate for Canada's representative to be chauffeured around Khartoum in a $60,000 vehicle. He began each morning on the steps of the Hilton, bargaining with taxicab drivers for the best fare of the day, saving Canadian taxpayers money."

Dalglish often accompanied Perron to the IDP camps outside the city: "He asked all the right questions and made no idle promises that could never be kept." Perron was outraged at the Sudanese government for prohibiting UNICEF from drilling boreholes to provide safe drinking water for the IDPs. The Canadian diplomat heard that the commissioner of Khartoum was sending in bulldozers to level the camps and that the police were arbitrarily arresting young men. After mornings with the IDPs, the ambassador returned to the Hilton, had a quick shower, and then attended meetings with Sudanese government officials. "With crocodile tears," Dalglish relates, "they would tell him how concerned they were about the plight of the Nuer and Dinka newly arrived in the city and the generous provisions they were making to ensure the displaceds' well-being. Perron would keep silent, let them talk themselves into a corner, and then he would clobber them." Why was the GOS doing everything in its power to make the lives of the IDPs so miserable? Who had ordered in the bulldozers to destroy their dwellings? "If countries such as the United Kingdom, France, and Germany," Dalglish concludes, "had men and women of Marc Perron's calibre as their representatives in Sudan, Khartoum would never be able to run roughshod over the rights if its own citizens. Perron did his best, but Canada could achieve very little acting alone."[4]

Hassan al-Turabi came to Canada in May 1992 for a three-day visit, meeting with Foreign Affairs officials, Members of Parliament, and the editors of two Toronto newspapers. Because he was travelling on a visitor's visa and not an official visa, no Canadian security agency was informed of his visit in advance and no protection was afforded to him. Bizarrely, al-Turabi came to the attention of the Canadian public on May 25 when he was attacked at Ottawa's airport by an exiled Sudanese who also happened to be a martial-arts expert. Although hospitalized for several weeks, al-Turabi said he bore Canada no ill will and believed the attack on him had been organized by the CIA.

With the exception of missionaries, aid workers, and archaeologists, few Canadians knew much about Sudan until 1998 when Talisman Energy entered the country and the protests began. At that time labour unions, faith groups, student associations, and Sudanese living in Canada campaigned persistently for the Canadian company to leave. They found a receptive ear with Foreign Affairs Minister Lloyd Axworthy who had frequently spoken out against the impact of the civil war on human security in that country. In September 1999 he met with the Sudanese minister of foreign affairs at the U.N. General Assembly in New York to reiterate his concerns. The two ministers discussed Talisman's role in the Sudanese oil sector, with Axworthy's greatest coup occurring when he convinced the GOS to agree to a Canadian Assessment Team to tour the country. The mission would be mandated to: a) independently investigate human-rights violations, specifically in reference to allegations of slavery and slavery-like practices in Sudan, and b) investigate and report on the alleged link between oil development and human-rights violations, particularly in respect of the forced removal of populations around the oil fields and oil-related development.

Taking on Talisman, a star in Alberta, was courageous, and Axworthy faced considerable resistance in caucus, especially from his own party's colleagues. Canada's strengths overseas were in the resource-based industries: hydroelectric power, mining, and oil. And for Canadian investments to be pulled back from countries "just because they might not be the flavour of the month at Foreign Affairs"[5] was sure to make Axworthy unpopular — with his own party, his government, and the oil industry.

In 1997 Talisman, just listed on the New York Stock Exchange, was then raising capital for what was to be the largest energy investment by a Canadian company in Southeast Asia, a US$1.3 billion operation straddling Malaysia and Vietnam. It was prestigious, both for Canadian expertise in oil exploration and for Ottawa. Nor could the Liberals afford to lose what little support they had in the West. To boost its case in Ottawa, Talisman also took the precaution of hiring the "strategic communications consultancy" of Hill and Knowlton as lobbyists.

"You suddenly had an influx of Canadians at the airport," Sudan veteran Emmanuel Isch, then with Fellowship for African Relief, says. "At that time the Lufthansa flight was the most efficient way out. You would recognize those from the oil fields and from the Talisman office in Khartoum." Isch was even asked by Talisman to do an orientation for the company's employees going out to Sudan. "They had a naive approach," recalls Isch, "to what they were getting into. Essentially, they went in with their eyes somewhat shut. With Oxfam, FAR had already come out with a statement critical of Talisman, and they knew that. Although there was a clear boycotting of the oil company by NGOs, they invited everyone to their receptions. I went and met them, and basically, they were reading from a prepared script. The Canadian workers were told that Talisman was doing social work in Sudan like building schools and hospitals in the oil fields — in the sense they were given the party line, well, let's say it was a certain perspective in reality.

"Who did these hospitals benefit? The original people around the oil fields had already been displaced, so the social impact was limited. Talisman, willingly or not, played into the hands of the GOS, and that was an issue for us from a Canadian NGO perspective. Especially for those operating in SPLM/A areas because the rebels were saying that any oil revenue generated by Talisman would be used against them. Talisman clearly didn't anticipate the backlash from Canadians. The eternal question is: Can you be more effective in country or out? Talisman said if they weren't there, the Chinese and Indians would be, and their track record was worse than theirs."

The first Canadian government initiatives on Sudan were announced on October 26, 1999, to bolster international efforts backing a negotiated settlement to the 43-year civil war, including the announcement of an assessment mission to Sudan to examine allegations about human-rights abuses and the resurgence of slavery. The statement stressed that Canada was deeply concerned that oil extraction by the GOS and its partners, including Talisman, might be contributing to the forced relocation of civilian populations residing in the vicinity of the oil fields. The assessment mission would "help inform the Government of Canada in their examination of such options." If it became evident that oil extraction was exacerbating the conflict, or resulting in violations of human rights, the Canadian government would consider applying economic and trade restrictions to Sudan. But when organizations like the Federation of Sudanese Canadian Associations wrote to Foreign Minister Axworthy to argue for Talisman's forced withdrawal from Sudan by government action, they didn't realize there was little the Canadian government could do legally or financially to force the company to quit Sudan.

Still, even if Khartoum was impervious to pressure, a Canadian oil company wasn't. Talisman, with its outspoken CEO Jim Buckee, made itself into a perfect target. By 1999 American and European humanitarian and church group heavyweights such as Amnesty International, Project Ploughshares, the U.S. Steelworkers' Humanity Fund, and Christian Solidarity International were adding their considerable clout to the "Get Talisman Out" movement. With more than 40 percent of Talisman's shareholders residing in the United States, protests were especially virulent from that country's South where slavery was an emotionally charged issue. The annual Talisman shareholders' meeting at Calgary's Hyatt Hotel erupted into a forum for dissent, with church groups, students, and even the "raging grannies" outside the doors chanting, drumming, and singing, "We will never say never. We must be free."

Buckee, now seen as the face of Canada in Sudan, initially challenged many of the allegations of human-rights violations, denouncing reports of atrocities as being "very partisan reporting of an issue which doesn't necessarily represent the truth." Sudan and Talisman were unfairly targeted for criticism, he maintained. "Sudan is not the most perfect place, but geez, look at Angola. There are lots of other nasty places. Why us? Why Sudan?" He asserted that "we are not supposed to be defending Sudanese history or the Sudanese government or anything else. We're just a business." Appearing on the CBS television program *MarketWatch*, he insisted that allegations of genocide were "wrong" and that it wasn't "true the government of Sudan is deliberately, systematically, committing genocide."

The assessment mission team toured Sudan for three weeks. Its members were:

- Mission Leader H. John Harker, who had served as a special adviser in the Office of the Deputy President of South Africa and had counselled various Canadian prime ministers on African issues. As a former representative in Canada of the U.N. International Labour Organization, he was familiar with labour and human-rights issues.
- Georgette Gagnon had extensive field experience in the area of human-rights investigations. She

had served with the United Nations in Rwanda
and Bosnia-Herzegovina as a field investigator and
legal adviser in international human-rights and
humanitarian law.[6]

- Audrey Macklin, an associate professor from
  Dalhousie University Law School and a U.N.
  expert on "Gender Persecution in Armed Conflict:
  Refugee and Displaced Women." She had expertise
  in immigration/refugee law, forced migration, and
  international and domestic human rights.

- Ernie Regehr, an associate professor of peace and
  conflict studies at the University of Waterloo. He
  was director of Project Ploughshares and coordinator of the International Resource Group on
  Disarmament and Security in the Horn of Africa.

- Dr. Penelope Simons, with a doctorate in international law, was a vice-president of the Simons
  Foundation, an organization promoting education
  in peace, disarmament, and global co-operation.
  She had worked in the area of international human-
  rights and humanitarian law, international criminal
  responsibility, and humanitarian intervention.

- Hamouda Soubhi from the University of Quebec was
  fluent in Arabic and French and had extensive field
  experience in North African and Middle Eastern
  development work. At that time he was the coordinator for the Centre for Arabic Studies in Montreal.

The above were also accompanied, at different times, by three
Canadian foreign service officers: Kerry Buck, deputy director, human
rights and humanitarian affairs, Foreign Affairs, Ottawa; C. Senay, political officer, Canadian High Commission, Nairobi; and Hugh Adsett,
political officer, Canadian embassy, Addis Ababa.

In Khartoum these people met with GOS officials, leaders of opposition parties, human-rights groups, and diplomatic representatives, as

well as with displaced Southern Sudanese and the U.N. officials trying to help them. Talisman co-operated fully, even putting its helicopter at the team's disposal. Visits were made to oil pipeline sites north and south of Khartoum, and to Dilling in the lower reaches of the Nuba Mountains. Three days were also spent at Talisman's Heglig operating base.

The central question to which the assessment mission turned was whether the GOS had been "sponsoring" the raids against the Dinka and others through the practice of "hiring" Baggara tribesmen, the *murahleen*, as a protection force, which the Canadians were told took its payment not in cash or kind from the GOS but as booty — "the goods and people they can make off with." GOS officials "strongly" informed the assessment team that "slavery does not and could not exist" in Sudan. Foreign Minister Osman Ismail assured Harker that he would personally intervene in any case of slavery brought to his attention. Earnestly attempting to explain local tradition, a Sudanese Foreign Affairs official told the incredulous Canadians: "The Baggara don't kill women and children. They just take them as war booty."

The team saw different phenomena in the slavery/abductions issue:

- There was armed and organized raiding in which the role of the GOS wasn't clear. "Sometimes," the team reported, "we were informed the GOS provides arms, sometimes the groups of *murahleen* go off on their own. Tribal groups have been known to organize raids with 'representatives' from other Arab groups, returning with children, women, and cattle taken in these raids."
- The team was also told about joint punitive raids carried out by the GOS and the *murahleen* who, under the Popular Defence Act, enjoyed status as state-sponsored militias — the Popular Defence Forces (PDFs).

The creation of the Committee for the Eradication of Abduction of Women and Children (CEAWC) was a first step, but up to that point Harker felt it was still insufficient "toward ending a practice, the abduction into a condition of being owned by another person, which must be stopped. At this time perhaps 15,000 Sudanese women and children live in such a terrible status. The GOS, focusing on the visible absence of classical slave markets, bridled at the use of the term *slavery* more than at the plight of these women and children, and for this absolute misplacement of moral indignation there can be no sympathy whatsoever. Certainly, all our sympathy is with the women and children and their devastated communities. The CEAWC was now receiving funds from the European Union, channelled through UNICEF, and the EU maintains that it will be monitoring the progress." Field monitoring would be greatly assisted, it was suggested, if Canada helped provide affected communities with training and equipment to record any *murahleen* raids.

The assessment team, as its members said, was "naturally interested in people moving or being moved because of oil development," so it travelled outside Khartoum, once to the north, along part of the pipeline route to the new refinery being built by Chinese contractors, and to Dilling in the Nuba Mountains to the site of a pumping station on the pipeline. On each occasion the team was assured that local people who had to be moved because of the pipeline were given compensation. Talisman officials told them that the oil field area had never known permanent habitation, had always been the scene of widespread flooding in the rainy season, and was always subject to cattle drives and nomad camps in the dry season. "For Talisman," the team reported, "so very much seems to be explained as 'merely an inter-tribal problem,' but displacement has gone on, and is still going on, and in Ruweng County, it is hard to deny that displacement is [happening] now, and has been for some time, because of oil."

The team met with al-Turabi, who more than once mentioned that the people of Southern Sudan had "voted with their feet," by which he meant they had left the South voluntarily and moved northward, with many settling in the Khartoum area. At the team members' insistence Dr. Sharaf Eddin Ibrahim Bannaga, minister of housing for Khartoum State, drove them to Wad El Bashir, one of the smaller camps for IDPs. They were told that it "housed" about 50,000 people, some of whom had been there for as many as seven years.

The team also met with Reik Machar, chairman of the South Sudan Coordinating Council. Even if there was no oil, Machar said, there would still be war. He insisted that the political objectives weren't oil but instead were at the heart of the "nature of the state of Sudan: is it to be multiracial, multi-ethnic, and multicultural?" He maintained that the "South has been fighting for a federal system, democracy, power sharing, and development, which can be achieved with oil, but not without it." Dissenting from the party line, John Garang wanted Talisman's operations in Sudan to continue. With oil revenues, it was felt, his supporters could correct developmental imbalances and end the war.

However, it was the evidence collected from ordinary Sudanese such as surviving village chiefs and the elderly that was most effective and heartbreaking.

HEAD CHIEF

"All of us are civilians here. We are going to lose our lives for oil. We know the Arabs will kill us. We are waiting for our deaths because the Arabs are chasing us, burning our villages, bombing us, and killing us. Aren't we included in the human rights of the world? Don't we have human rights? This is the first human-rights team to visit us, and we have been dying since 1984. If we are included in the human rights of the world, why are the Arabs killing us? The population here is displaced, there are many diseases, water is polluted, and women are giving out children early [miscarriages and still births]. Civilians, cattle, and children have been killed, and our *tukuls* [huts] are burnt. The discovery of oil has caused these problems. Before, in the 1970s and 1980s, the Arabs weren't able to exploit the oil, but now they can with the help of the West. The Arabs are united against us and want to push us out. We blame the Christian community because the war is being made a religious war. Why is the Christian world not helping us? The shells you saw are being used to kill us. The shells are manufactured by Russians, not Arabs." [Mission members were shown parts of shells, an unexploded bomb, and shrapnel that were among those dropped in the Nhialdiu area.]

HEAD CHIEF

"All villages north, south, east, and west of here, about 50 villages, were burned and bombed by the GOS. Most of our children are scattered by bombardment because we can only take a few of them when we are escaping. Most of them are in the forest, and we don't know exactly where. Eight hundred children are lost — we don't know if they were killed or what happened. We can do nothing to defend ourselves. The GOS keeps coming with Antonovs, and we are running away. Our Nuer area borders with the Arabs, so we have nowhere to run. We need a resettlement process."

HEAD CHIEF

"We are having problems. They bomb us during the day, so we usually hide in the forest, but we came out to meet you. There is often bombing in the day. We are afraid when we see a plane coming, because of the bombing. Bombing made us run away from our villages. We are dying in the face of oil. Isn't the oil company Christian? Most of our population has died. We are blaming the world for co-operating with the Arabs to clear us from our land and take our oil. We have been suffering since 1983 when the first shot was fired. By the time your report is out, we will be dead. The GOS will kill us because you visited us."

ELDERLY MAN

"We are happy that we are not forgotten by the world. We are not happy seeing our children dying before us — most of our leaders have died from Antonovs and fighting. We know all of us will die before the year 2000."

* * *

"It is certainly fair to acknowledge that the durable civil war in Sudan is not fundamentally about oil," the assessment team concluded, "but oil has become a key factor. Ordinary people in the South, even their leaders, can confuse Talisman ... with other oil companies which hold the concession, known as 5A, around which war is raging south of these rivers. But two things are certain. First, the gunships and Antonovs which have attacked villages south of the rivers flew to their targets from the Heglig airstrip in the Talisman concession. Second, it is a prominent perception of Southern Sudanese that Talisman, 'the Canadian oil firm,' is in active collaboration with the GOS economically, politically, and militarily. It is also the perception of these Southerners that the government of Canada is either supportive of or indifferent to that collaboration. In short, they identify oil extraction not as a positive development but as a major grievance with a Canadian label and say it must be stopped."

The Harker Report recommended a step-by-step approach:

> It is clear that many Canadians, not to mention Sudanese, want Talisman either out of Sudan now or at least to have halted production of oil. But we have been reluctant to advocate immediate application of the Special Economic Measures Act (SEMA)[7] because of our strong desire to have Talisman meet its responsibilities in full [and] not be allowed to slip away from them. There is a measured approach requiring action by the Minister of Foreign Affairs. He could, in a public statement expressing grave concern about Sudan and the mounting evidence that Canadian oil extraction activity is exacerbating the Sudan crisis, announce that certain exports to Sudan will be subjected to scrutiny under the Export and Import Controls Act. If Talisman's operations in Sudan are not brought to comply with human rights and humanitarian law, consideration should be given to placing Sudan on the Area Control List (ACL). Placing certain exports under Export Controls List scrutiny, and, if necessary, putting a country on

the ACL, would provide Canada with leverage over Talisman to encourage monitored compliance with the ethical approach the company says it adheres to.[8]

Delivered to Foreign Affairs Minister Lloyd Axworthy on January 26, 2000, the Harker Report, in effect, recommended that no sanctions be placed on Talisman if it agreed to actively police the GOS, its business partner. The report disappointed many people such as Mel Middleton, director of the Calgary-based Freedom Quest International, which thought that both Axworthy and Buckee had seized upon Harker's counsel against sanctions to ignore "Talisman's complicity with the GOS against non-Islamic civilians." The consensus among the media was that the report permitted Axworthy to back away from his threat to impose sanctions if the Harker probe found that Talisman's oil project actively contributed to the country's long-running civil war.

Axworthy agreed that a policy of engagement would provide more benefits for Sudanese people and promised to establish a Canadian "office" in Khartoum. He also raised the possibility of discussing economic sanctions against Sudan when Canada assumed the presidency of the U.N. Security Council in April 2000. But here, too, Axworthy's initiative was less than successful.

The Security Council's five permanent members were indifferent to Canadian concerns. The Russians and Chinese had their own agenda with regard to Sudan. The Stockholm International Peace Research Institute (SIPRI) noted that the former supplied 80 percent of the arms to Sudan and that the latter was a major oil buyer.[9] As for the United States, increasingly worried about Al Qaeda, it was looking for Sudanese co-operation in intelligence gathering, so in May 2000 it entered into "a bilateral dialogue on counter-terrorism" with the GOS. That summer a team of FBI and CIA agents arrived in Khartoum to begin combing government files for terrorist networks. Evidence of the new U.S./GOS co-operation was seen in the expulsion that year of the collaborators in the Hosni Mubarak attack. Still, aware of its religious and humanitarian lobbies, Washington's shift to a new friendship with the GOS had to be done discreetly.

Talisman's president, Jim Buckee, was alone in welcoming the government's decision not to impose sanctions. He credited his company with having drawn the attention of North America to the problems of Sudan and wrote to Axworthy to assure him that corporate ethics was always a strong internal priority at Talisman. With respect to encouraging the GOS to allow for independent experts to examine allegations of forced removals, Buckee said that he had raised this point with the Sudanese ministers for energy and foreign affairs and also with al-Turabi and had received "positive assurances." No Talisman executive or worker had ever seen any evidence of forced removals in and around the oil fields, he claimed. Having dug wells, built roads, and run medical clinics for the locals, he thought Talisman was acting in a responsible manner in the country.

The architect of Canadian policy toward Sudan, Lloyd Axworthy left politics in the fall of 2000 (his exit hastened, it was rumoured, because of disillusionment with his caucus colleagues over Talisman and Sudan). Later, as president of the University of Winnipeg, he recalled his efforts to introduce mechanisms for monitoring operations of Canadian companies working in conflict zones: "We tried to use the findings of the Harker mission to bridge the governance gap with a strong, legislative framework."

But the church coalitions couldn't find forgiveness in their hearts for Talisman. It was a replay of the falling-out between Major-General Gordon and the London Anti-Slavery Society. All the venom that the religious establishment had aimed at communism during the Cold War was now reserved for rogue regimes — and their Canadian collaborator. A delegation from the Interchurch Coalition on Africa, including representatives from the Anglican Church, the United Church, the Canadian Council of Churches, the Canadian Catholic Bishops, and the Presbyterian Church, visited Sudan from April 1 to 7, 2001, touring refugee camps and bombed-out villages south of the oil fields. At the obligatory Parliament Hill press conference on April 10, they called for a moratorium on oil development in Sudan, especially by Talisman.

"The church groups don't want to hear that Talisman is putting roads in, allowing everybody to use its hospital, and is building schools," Fraser

Institute researcher Lydia Miljan commented. "They just want to score points by standing up at the annual meeting with simplistic solutions." Miljan thought that Talisman offered real hope to the Sudanese people. "You only get sustainable freedoms where you have a strong economic base," she said. "Which is better, to get Talisman out of Sudan, or to make sure the right people get access to economic benefits?" Miljan explained by saying that investments from companies such as Talisman were helping Sudan and other countries create the economic infrastructure necessary for the growth of democracy and that the GNPOC project had created 2,000 jobs, 90 percent of which were with local people. "Even if you could argue that the easiest thing Talisman could do was abandon its Sudanese property, in the long run it wouldn't really solve anything. Most of the world's oil is in places where you have civil unrest." In her view, "it took a lot of strength for Talisman to stay. It will do good in the long run."

Mathew Ingram of the *Globe and Mail* pointed out that if Talisman was forced to leave Sudan, the human-rights situation could easily get worse, with the GOS being pushed toward Muammar Gaddafi's Libya or Saddam Hussein's Iraq. The more cynical were of the opinion that if Talisman withdrew and another, non-Canadian company took its place, Canada could return to its high moral principles on the international stage. And if the Sudanese people continued to be crushed by oil-revenue-generated tyranny, at least it wouldn't be stamped with a maple leaf.

With Axworthy out, it should have been plain sailing for Talisman. Producing 225,000 barrels of crude oil daily, the Talisman oil field was the primary source of revenue for the Khartoum government — an estimated annual CDN$767 million. The SPLM/A launched what it said would be its first attack on the Heglig facilities on August 5, 2001. Previous attacks had been confined to the Heglig-to-Port-Sudan pipeline, but this marked the first time the SPLM/A actually targeted the production site. It was hardly a Stinger missile strike — a shed housing a computer was hit by small-arms fire. "There were no injuries to staff or security personnel and no damage to production facilities," a Talisman spokesman said. "As a routine planned response to such an incident, production was briefly suspended, but has been restored."

SPLM/A spokesman Samson Kwaje told media from Nairobi: "Since 1999, we have been attacking the pipeline ... now we are shifting to the real oil area." From now on oil company operations would be considered legitimate military targets, and Kwaje urged Talisman to withdraw its personnel. Yet on the Toronto Stock Exchange, the day after the attack, Talisman shares actually rose 25 cents to $60.35. (Talisman had traded as high as $65.77 and as low as $43.80 in 2000).

"There's a little bit of negative news from Sudan, but the overriding factor [on the share price] is Talisman's financial performance is looking up based on oil prices," said Steve Calderwood, an analyst with the investment firm Salman Partners in Calgary, "and the fact they are growing their North Sea oil production substantially." Sudan only accounted for about 10 percent of Talisman's total production, he added.

Talisman might have been able to withstand the SPLM/A, church groups, and Lloyd Axworthy, but it met its match with American lawyers. On November 8, 2001, in the wake of his nation's coping with the tragedy of 9/11, U.S. attorney Carey D'Avino, suddenly known as "an avid supporter of compensation" for the Nuer tribe living near the Talisman oil concession, filed a class-action complaint in the U.S. District Court against the Canadian oil company on behalf of the Presbyterian Church of Sudan and other plaintiffs. On the evidence of a scribbled note, D'Avino alleged that Talisman was engaged in "an unholy alliance with the government of Sudan by knowingly participating in the government's campaign of ethnic cleansing to create a 'cordon sanitaire' around Talisman's oil infrastructure."[10]

Buckee's nemesis had been working its way inexorably through numerous Washington committees since 2000. Born during the Clinton administration and aimed at punishing companies such as Talisman that operated in the war-torn African country, the Sudan Peace Act included an amendment that would bar all non-U.S. companies involved in oil development in Sudan from being listed on U.S. stock exchanges or raising capital on Wall Street to do so. The legislation suffered several near-death experiences but always survived until, helped no doubt by the events of 9/11, it passed through the U.S. House of Representatives on October 7, 2002, by a vote of 359–8. When the act received unanimous consent in the U.S. Senate on October 9, 2002, President George W. Bush signed it into law.

The act condemned the GOS's human-rights record, the slave trade, government use of militia and other forces to support slave raiding, and aerial bombardment of civilian targets. It authorized funding of up to US$100 million for each of the fiscal years 2003, 2004, and 2005 for assistance to areas outside government control to prepare the population for peace and democratic governance, including support for civil administration, communications infrastructure, education, health, and agriculture. The act also sought a U.N. Security Council resolution for an arms embargo on the Sudanese government. But most pertinent to Talisman, the act instructed U.S. executive directors to vote against and actively oppose loans, credits, and guarantees by international financial institutions for investment in Sudan. As far as Talisman was concerned, the act would not only force a full disclosure of company practices but make it impossible while it was in Sudan from securing capital on Wall Street ever again. Even before the legislation passed, Buckee admitted that his company would rather get out of Sudan than lose its coveted spot on the New York Stock Exchange.

All these were good enough reasons why despite impressive production and remarkable profits, by late 2002, the Canadian company planned to quit Sudan. In October 2002, Buckee commented: "Shareholders have told me they were tired of continually having to monitor and analyze events relating to Sudan." In Talisman's Corporate Responsibility Report for that year, its CEO acknowledged that "it was time to turn the page on this controversial asset for a number of reasons." He was just waiting to be offered the right price.

This turned out to be CDN$1.2 billion, paid by ONGC Videsh Limited, a subsidiary of India's national oil company. "As a business, they were in Sudan to make a profit," said World Vision's Emmanuel Isch, "and they did, using the money to expand to other areas." But when the deal was formally completed on March 12, 2003, it was a sad day at the Calgary head office. It was the first time Talisman had walked away from a core investment. "Talisman may have walked away from operations," a company spokesman said, "but not from the people of Sudan. We are committed to maintaining a presence in Sudan until 2005 and will have invested an additional US$2 million in community projects by the time we leave. One such project is a 50-acre model farm in Rubkona, which trains local Sudanese villagers in farming techniques, crop selection, and marketing to increase agricultural yields."[11]

The departure of the Canadian company was a relief for Khartoum. With the announcement the Sudanese government made it clear that it preferred companies to invest in oil exploration that were unlikely to bow to criticism from human-rights groups. "We prefer the Indian company," Foreign Minister Mustafa Osman Ismail said, "because it is government-owned and pressures of non-government organizations on it are less than they are on private companies."

When Georgette Gagnon, one of the assessment team members responsible for the Harker Report, heard of Talisman's departure, her "initial surge of jubilation quickly faded to feelings of profound sadness for the Sudanese people. They remain the human cost of oil." Gagnon took solace in knowing that the lessons of Talisman's controversial four years in Sudan had not gone unnoticed. "I recently heard that several Canadian corporations passed up lucrative contracts in Iraq for fear of becoming 'Talismanized.' This is a somewhat positive sign that some Canadian companies are looking at both the reputational and human-rights implications of doing business in a conflict zone."[12]

The Harker Report had demonstrated the need to increase Canada's profile in Sudan, or at any rate put a more humanitarian spin on its tarnished image. Besides making the problems of Africa, and particularly Sudan, the focus at the 2002 G-8 summit in Kananaskis, Alberta, before he left the Liberal government, Lloyd Axworthy appointed Senator Lois Wilson as Canada's special envoy to Sudan, specifying that her job would be to increase Canadian leverage in IGAD. Long before her appointment to the Senate in 1998, the Winnipeg-born, the Very Reverend Wilson, the first female moderator of the United Church of Canada, had actively defended human rights, co-chairing, with Senator Mobina Jaffer, the Canadian Committee on Women, Peace, and Security and leading delegations to China and North Korea.

When Wilson retired, on August 9, 2002, Minister for Foreign Affairs Bill Graham appointed Senator Jaffer to take her place. "Sudan is very complicated," Jaffer said. "There are layers and layers. There is no one sound bite to sum it up. Basically, the envoy's role is to speak to the other envoys and push the issue and bring it to the parties around the table." Initially, Sudanese Foreign Minister Mustafa Ismail wasn't pleased at the appointment, saying that Senator Jaffer hadn't been approved by his government, but when he visited Ottawa in May 2003, Jaffer won him over, hosting and introducing him to the prime minister and colleagues in Parliament and discussing at length Canada's role in the peace process.

The first Muslim to sit in the Senate and the first African-born senator, Mobina Jaffer visited Sudan many times — with Prime Minister Paul Martin, Senator Roméo Dallaire, and Minister for International Co-operation Aileen Carroll, meeting with GOS leaders and John Garang and representing Canada at the Naivasha Peace Agreement. Originally appointed to deal with the North/South conflict, she saw the problems in Darfur arise in June 2004 and toured the IDP camps near Nyala and El Jemina. She warned also of further trouble in the eastern part of the country. "Canada had a very special role in Sudan — an example was the training of parliamentarians in which fellow MP, Jean Augustine, played an important role. We have special expertise in, for example, the empowerment of women, rule of law, the training of judges, training of the civil service, conflict resolution, in effect, bringing the various communities together."

Sadly, in January 2006, after Senator Jaffer forged precious links with rebel groups and the GOS, the incoming Conservative government decided a Special Envoy to Sudan was unnecessary. "When my role ended, I did speak to the prime minister and urged him to appoint someone he could trust as an envoy as I believe that this was an important role. Unfortunately, he did not see it the way I did." Her Sudan Task Force colleague, Senator Dallaire, was even blunter about the Tories ignoring Darfur: "Nobody's picked up on the ball, except they've thrown some cash, hoping that it will go away and they can 'Pontius Pilate' their way out of this exercise."[13]

With other countries, the Canadian government had applied the terms of Security Council Resolution 1054 in 1996 to reduce the size of the Sudanese embassy in Ottawa, trimming the number of diplomats and ordering Sudanese representation be lowered to the level of chargé d'affaires. It was still better than Canada's presence in Sudan, which was in Addis Ababa. The first mention of a Canadian "office" in Khartoum was on February 14, 2000, when a press release from Lloyd Axworthy's office announced further Canadian initiatives on Sudan. It added that "discussions were under way to locate the office within the British embassy in Khartoum."

In 1990 the Canadian Foreign Service Officer Awards were instituted by the Professional Association of Foreign Service Officers to provide recognition by one's peers for exceptional achievement by an individual officer. The criteria were initiative and creativity; dedication to serving Canada and Canadians; effectiveness in interacting with cultures in which the officer has worked; and ability to inspire colleagues and professional contacts. It came as no surprise in 1995 when Nick Coghlan was recognized by his peers for possessing all of those attributes.

In June 2000 Foreign Affairs appointed Coghlan, currently posted to Bogotá, Colombia, to be "our man in Khartoum." Coghlan holds a master degree in modern languages from Oxford University and while in the Lester B. Pearson Building in Ottawa had toiled in the Middle East Division, the South America Relations Division, and the Mexico Division. Before Bogotá he had served in Mexico (1995–97) during the Chiapas uprising. "Mr. Coghlan has worked tirelessly over the past years to protect villagers in conflict zones in Colombia," the accompanying press release noted, "by supporting a strategy of 'accompaniment' to remind guerillas and paramilitary groups that the outside world is watching."[14] Although he spoke no Arabic, Coghlan had some qualifications in "reporting from conflictive situations where there was a Canadian stake." With such experience he was ideal for Sudan.

Coghlan wouldn't present his credentials to the president of Sudan as protocol demanded because the "office" was an extension of the Canadian embassy in Addis Ababa and the Canadian ambassador in Ethiopia was already accredited to Sudan. For despite the publicity created by Talisman, Canada still kept Sudan at arm's length. Still, as the Harker Report had demonstrated, Canada needed someone on the ground in Khartoum. The idea, Coghlan later wrote, "was not to spy on what was going on in the oil concession — but rather to give us eyes and ears in this, the largest country in Africa." Unusually for a foreign service officer being sent abroad, he was told to: "Do nothing whatsoever to encourage further trade or investment."

On arrival in Khartoum the Coghlans put up at the Hilton Hotel (built by a Canadian construction company) for seven weeks while their house in the suburb of Amarat was readied for habitation, relatively speaking. This they discovered was a local interpretation of that condition. In an experience that most Canada-based staff would recognize, the Coghlans discovered that "the finishing was poor and few items … ever worked reliably. There were upside-down door handles, and doors that didn't close or that left inch-wide gaps at their foot; there were burned-out lights in totally inaccessible locations and inexplicable wires hanging out of the walls. It was a given that in the summer the power would go off for eight or ten hours at a time which meant cranking up the giant generator hidden behind bushes by our front gate. If the power went out at night, there was usually a sickening whirring as every piece of machinery in the house wound down, a pause, then a noise from the neighborhood like a tank regiment warming up, as generator after generator cranked up. Then the lights would come on with temporarily blinding brightness."[15] As for the "office," three adjoining rooms on the ground floor of the British embassy were made available for the first representative of the Canadian government in Sudan and his three local staff. Inside the main reception area and at the entrance to the Canadian suite, Coghlan put up the Canadian coat of arms in standard sober mock-silver alloy.

In Khartoum the war and the South were a universe away. The cocktails and canapés diplomatic circuit that proliferates in every capital was reinforced here with that of the aid world (composed of organizations with a baffling number of acronyms). Both kept the lone Canadian representative moving from meeting to meeting. To justify their existence, it seemed that every aid group in the city competed for the same pool of cash controlled by Western governments. And to pry some of those dollars away for pet projects, they kept themselves busy presenting proposals that duplicated one another's work. For example, Coghlan discovered that there were endless "needs assessments" conferences — "to the point at which one of the main findings started to be that the poor and needy found themselves to be over-assessed and over-researched."

In the South, once behind rebel lines, Coghlan found that because of Talisman, "going around as a Canadian at this time was like wearing a KICK ME sign on your back." But he did tour the region several times, each trip beginning with catching the 3:35 a.m. flight to Nairobi to get a permit from the SPLM/A office there. Then Coghlan would take the many-storied 748 Services — "Proud to be the most trusted bird in the African Sky" — to Loki and hook up with a U.N. Cessna Caravan onward.

The SPLM/A officials Coghlan met appeared naive and myopic. They didn't realize that the political agenda of the Western donor nations didn't necessarily correspond with their own. "When I concluded [a discussion with them] by asking whether it really was justified for Canada to invest large resources here, given ... limited prospects for lasting peace, more than once the question provoked the comment: 'Maybe you'd better chose somewhere else.'" When he asked how Canada could contribute to the peace process, "the most often stated serious suggestion was ... that we lean heavily on Talisman to leave Sudan." Other requests ranged from "Give us Stingers" to "Bomb Khartoum like you bombed Belgrade." The common refrain was: "The best thing you could and should have done is support us with weapons." Coghlan wondered what CIDA would have made of that request.

After extensive inspection tours, he concluded that the South was really no worse off than large areas of the North — and in some places better off. The lush Equatorias, especially, were lands of plenty when compared with the deserts of Northern and Western Sudan. What infrastructure there was had been neglected and abandoned by the locals themselves. And while the often-heard mantra that "the North never did anything for us" had some validity, the Southerners didn't know that Khartoum never did much for the North, either, or the East or West.

The SPLM/A people Coghlan met all wanted Talisman out and the oil flow to end, despite the Canadian company's community-friendly programs that would definitely end when the Chinese and Indians took over. Couldn't we phase out the endless food runs, he wondered, by doing what all the aid manuals said: build roads, schools, hospitals ... as the old truism goes, give people fishing rods rather than fish? This smacked too much of helping build a new country, he was told, and no Western donor nation was ready to go that far in defying Khartoum. Doing such would also be more costly and less visible than the airdrops of food and consequently difficult to sell to skeptical Western taxpayers with short attention spans.

The United Nations, Coghlan saw, was (in early 2003) spectacularly uncoordinated between its own agencies in Khartoum and those like UNICEF and WFP that operated in the South. When a food assessment by the U.N.'s Food and Agricultural Organization said there was a surplus, for reasons of its own, the WFP projected a deficit. In mid-2002, when the United Nations appointed "an energetic, no-nonsense" Australian as its resident coordinator in Sudan, he made the mistake of criticizing Khartoum's flight bans. The GOS retaliated by objected to his remaining in the country, and to its shame, U.N. Headquarters in New York meekly acquiesced and pulled the man out, leaving its entire system in Sudan leaderless. The United Nations' member nations themselves were selfish and vain and pursued their own agendas first. For example, in the Nuba Mountains ceasefire arrangement the United States contracted with its favourite company, Lockheed Martin–owned Pacific Architects and Engineers, to run the logistics (the same company that in 2008 serviced the Canadian armoured personnel carriers in Darfur), then paid part of the bill and presented outstanding accounts to the other countries for settlement. When Norway, the co-host of long-running IGAD, pushed its way into the Machakos Peace talks in Kenya, it "conveniently forgot about the group of countries (including Canada) that it was supposed to be representing."

In late 2002 the British embassy advised Coghlan that with a possible peace agreement near, they planned to expand and needed the "Canadian office" space back. He had until the end of April 2003 to vacate. If the problems of finding a suitable property in Sudan weren't bad enough — there is no advertised property market and realtors operated on an informal and cutthroat basis — dealing with Ottawa was worse. The attitude of Foreign Affairs could be summed up as incoherence, inattention, and indecision. "My first instructions," Coghlan writes in *Far in the Waste Sudan*, "were to 'Find a modest place that would allow for some expansion, maybe from three to five staff,' which evolved to 'No, go the whole hog and get a big place that would eventually allow us to expand to full embassy status,' then — once a lease had been signed on a large property — devolved back to 'Actually, we've cut our original budget by 90 percent, and you'll have to make do with fitting up less space than you have now; and by the way you'll have to stick with that antiquated communications platform, even though no one here knows how to fix it anymore.'"[16]

A large yellow villa was located on Airport Road, a quarter of which was to be the (still diplomatically obscure) "office" and the remainder the residence of his successor. Despite 50-degree heat, Ottawa refused to pay for air conditioning or renovate the swimming pool on the grounds and even squeezed the two Sudanese support staff into a tiny room as their workspace. But at least Canada finally had its own *sifaara* (embassy) in Sudan.

"They say on the diplomatic circuit that you cry when you learn you have been posted to Sudan, but you cry even harder when the time comes to leave," Coghlan comments. In his three years he was fortunate to have met two of the players in the country's drama — Hassan al-Turabi, who had told him that coups were the way they did things in Sudan (and he should know), and Sadiq al-Mahdi, who thought that Canada was a country with all of the natural resources of the United States and none of its hegemonic intentions. Coghlan had also met cooperative Talisman officials and a Canadian oil worker who had said to him: "Yeah, we're economic prostitutes.... So what's your point?" The ordinary Sudanese that Coghlan had come to know, he thought, were the most hospitable people in Africa, ground down between the callousness of their despotic government and equally ruthless rebels. And then there were the selfless Canadian aid workers, mainly female, in a myriad of humanitarian organizations, including FAR, War Child, World Vision, CARE, and MSF.

At the Blue Nile Sailing Club, which had as its headquarters Her Majesty's gunboat *Melik*, Coghlan had raced "Khartoum One" sailing dinghies. In criss-crossing a country the size of Ontario and Quebec combined, he had feared for his life in venerable Russian aircraft. He had alerted Ottawa to the Hind gunships and had escorted Senator Mobina Jaffer, Canada's Special Envoy, about. And he had stood at Fashoda where Captain Marchand once claimed Sudan for the French empire.

In late 2003 Nick Coghlan left Sudan to take up a position as consul general at the Canadian embassy in Cape Town, South Africa. Two years later, far from the Nile and Sudan, he and his wife sailed the South Atlantic and South Pacific on their 24-foot sloop. Not only Canada's eyes, ears, and voice at a time when so little was known about Sudan, Coghlan was also the conscience of his country. "These are days of hope for Sudan," he concludes in *Far in the Waste Sudan*, paying tribute to the enterprising and resilient people he had lived among who were, above all, survivors.

Ottawa raised Coghlan's position to that of chargé d'affaires, and he was followed by David Hutchings in February 2003 and then Alan Bones in September 2005. The best-known of Canada's chargé d'affaires in Sudan was Nuala Lawlor, expelled on August 27, 2007. Foreign diplomats have been declared *persona non grata* by Ottawa for any number of reasons — industrial espionage during the Cold War, trying to lure young girls into a car (Ukrainian diplomat Olexander Yushko), or calling Canada "a pig country" and joking about a bomb at Vancouver's airport (Italian diplomat Giorgio Copello). Lawlor, together with European Union envoy Kent Degerfelt and Paul Barker, country director of CARE, were expelled for "interfering in the internal affairs of Sudan."

Sudanese Foreign Minister Ali Ahmed Karti[17] said that both diplomats had been thrown out for seeking the release of opposition leader Mahmoud Hassanein and that they had been warned twice before. The European Union quickly apologized for Degerfelt, who was on holiday in Italy at the time of the announcement, and said it must be "some sort of misunderstanding somewhere." But just appointed to the position of minister of foreign affairs, Maxime Bernier called Lawlor's expulsion unjustified and said that Canada wouldn't apologize. "The diplomat was acting in the finest traditions of Canadian diplomacy and was standing up for our values of freedom, democracy, human rights, and the rule of law in Sudan," he said.

In retaliation his department ordered the Sudanese diplomat Mwada Omar booted out of Canada. Faiza Hassan Taha, Sudan's ambassador, thought Lawlor's expulsion had nothing to do with meeting with the opposition leader. "The real cause has been stated clearly that the two diplomats ignored the diplomatic protocol in conveying their messages to the director of national intelligence and security services. These kinds of mistakes will not be accepted in any country, even in Canada." But Lawlor was in good company. The year before the GOS had expelled U.N. envoy Jan Pronk for using his blog to criticize its activities in Darfur. There were some who saw the Canadian diplomat's expulsion as an attempt on Khartoum's part to distract the world from its complicity with the atrocities in Darfur. That same week Amnesty International released photographs it claimed proved the government had been deploying military equipment to the region, despite a U.N. arms embargo. It was a charge that the GOS vehemently denied.

Two days later, on August 29, during a memorial celebration at St. Paul University in Ottawa to mark the second anniversary of the death of John Garang, Sam Hanson was introduced as the new Canadian chargé d'affaires to Sudan. Hanson had been ambassador to Bosnia-Herzegovina in 2000 and policy coordinator in the Foreign Affairs Middle East and North Africa Bureau. When the then Liberal Member of Parliament Wajid Khan toured the Middle East, Hanson assisted "in organizing and synthesizing the themes that emerged from the series of meetings" Khan participated in.

During the Second World War, Vincent Massey, the Canadian High Commissioner to London, opened Canada House to the hundreds of homesick Canadian Army personnel in the United Kingdom. At Christmas he and Alice Massey, his wife, personally served them dinner at the Beaver Club within. With so many Canadian Forces members rotating through Khartoum, the embassy premises inevitably became known as Canada House. "The staff at the Canadian embassy were amazing and very much part of our extended CF family here," Major Sandi Banerjee, deputy commander of the Canadian Task Force, remembers. "What was critical to our collective morale there were their support and that of our various regiments, ships, air wings, and the Royal Canadian Legion [RCL]. The Legion, along with the Canadian Forces Personnel Support Agency, saved Christmas for us in Sudan as theirs were the only packages that got through before the local authorities shut down the flow of anything labelled 'Christmas.' The HQ staff split all of our CARE packages in three ways: some items went to other soldiers who may have run out while in the field, other items like candies, pens, and toys were given to local orphanages and schools, and a few reminders from home were kept for Canada House. The beautiful RCL tree ornament was front and centre at Canada House. So, too, were little things like red licorice, pepperoni sticks, and even Handi-Wipes, all perfect for patrols in the desert and jungle. The Tim Hortons coffee was much in demand, and I am sure is still being hoarded for a rainy day."

The new chargé's own time in the media spotlight began at precisely 10:40 a.m. on April 29, 2008, when Abousfian Abdelrazik, a Sudanese-born Canadian citizen walked into the embassy. A frequent visitor already (where he collected his $100 monthly from the "distressed citizens" account that every Canadian embassy has), he had also been given access to the embassy phone to call his family in Montreal. But this time he told the staff: "I don't intend to leave." U.S. authorities considered Abdelrazik a key figure in a Montreal Al Qaeda cell and an acquaintance of Ahmed Ressam, the former Montrealer known as "the millennium bomber." The Canadian Security Intelligence Service (CSIS) connected him with Adil Charkaoui, a non-citizen that the Federal Court of Canada had identified as a national security risk.

In 2003, complaining that CSIS was harassing him, Abdelrazik returned to Sudan, ostensibly to visit his mother. The Sudanese authorities arrested him twice (at the request of U.S. and Canadian security agencies) and held him for a year the first time and seven months the second. The Canadian citizen later complained that he had been beaten and ill-treated in prison, entirely plausible given that the U.S. State

Department's 2007 Country Reports on Human Rights Practices cited Sudan for torture, harsh prison conditions, arbitrary detention, and denial of due process. Then the GOS, perhaps realizing it could make more capital out of his release, freed Abdelrazik, saying the accusation that he was a terrorist was groundless. But since he had been put on the U.N. no-fly list at the request of CSIS (which prevents repatriation of terrorist suspects by commercial aircraft), and since he no longer had a Canadian passport, Abdelrazik was marooned in Sudan.

"A citizen, whether we like it or not," editorialized the *Globe and Mail* of April 30, 2008. "It has been convenient for Canada to leave Mr. Abdelrazik stranded in Sudan. A potentially dangerous person was left far from Canadian soil; a person who could expose possible Canadian complicity in human-rights abuses was left far from the media glare. Canada granted Mr. Abdelrazik citizenship and at this point must face the consequences."

Nothing in the U.N. sanctions precluded the repatriation of terrorist suspects, nor do commercial no-fly lists apply to government or military aircraft.[18] Foreign Affairs did grant Abdelrazik "temporary safe haven" and allowed embassy staff to feed him. While the burden on the chargé's hospitality might not have been as onerous as that of his colleagues at the Canadian embassy in Beijing (where, in 2004, 44 North Korean defectors camped out for three months), getting Abdelrazik out of Sudan remained a contentious bilateral issue.

When Foreign Affairs Minister Maxime Bernier and parliamentary secretary Deepak Obhrai visited Sudan from March 25 to 28, 2008, Abdelrazik's supporters hoped for a breakthrough. Even Sudanese Ambassador Faiza Hassan Taha hoped it would begin an era of "government-to-government dialogue" after the tit-for-tat diplomatic expulsion the previous year. But she knew the Canadian government had set a precondition for rapprochement: Sudan would have to make significant efforts to resolve the crisis in Darfur.

"Are you asking for 100 percent perfection?" Ms. Taha demanded when interviewed by journalist Lee Berthiaume (*Embassy*, April 2, 2008). "It depends on how you measure progress." The ambassador was correct. There had been progress of a macabre sort. The situation in

Darfur was improving — the number of civilians being raped, tortured, and/or slaughtered by her government and its militia proxies was down. For while the ethnic cleansing continued unabated, 90 percent of the deaths had occurred four to five years earlier, and it was becoming more difficult to make a clear distinction between President Omar al-Bashir's Janjaweed and the rebel groups.

In the four days Bernier was in Sudan, he promised that Canada would invest CDN$275 million in the country in 2008–09, including $84 million in mandatory support for peacekeeping missions. He met with Foreign Minister Deng Alor Kuol, the veteran SPLM/A spokesman and former Garang lieutenant, and with presidential adviser Mustafa Osman Ismail, who had recently achieved a measure of notoriety when he disputed U.N. Undersecretary-General John Holmes's claim that 300,000 civilians had been killed in Darfur. Bernier presented Canada's views to each of them, emphasizing that Khartoum had to allow the hybrid African Union–United Nations peacekeeping force the help it required and had to seek a non-military solution to the Darfur conflict. "We are just telling them what to do," Obhrai said. "Now we will wait and see."

The pair's wait would be long, for Khartoum had heard it all many times before. More hopeful than anything Bernier and Obhrai said were the peace initiatives then being quietly introduced by the tiny Persian Gulf state of Qatar, the chair of the Arab League. Obhrai did meet with the embassy's long-staying guest, the unfortunate Abdelrazik but, loath to defy the U.S. terrorism no-fly list, did not guarantee him an emergency passport (a fundamental entitlement of Canadian citizenship) or hold out any hope of bringing him home in the government Challenger. Instead, Abdelrazik told his lawyer he was "quizzed" about why he had come to Canada and was asked his views on Israel. Significantly, Bernier flew to Juba, where it was expected he would announce that Canada would soon open a consulate in the future capital of the Government of Southern Sudan. That didn't happen, however, and the minister cautiously called for only "full implementation" of the terms of the CPA.

Security Council Resolution 1706, the doctrine of Responsibility to Protect adopted by the United Nations, had been Canadian-initiated, and Canada's moral dilemma concerning a government that ignored the responsibility to protect its civilians was shared by many other countries. But how do you influence a regime when the opposition is non-existent and the human-rights records of the rebel groups are as bad? Al-Bashir, who had served in the Egyptian army during the 1973 war with Israel, believed that the West's interest in Darfur was part of a Western-Zionist agenda and wasn't motivated by genuine humanitarian concerns. And at what it would regard as the first sign of interference in its domestic affairs the Sudanese government would instantly close down all aid operations as it did with missionaries in the 1950s and expel all Westerners. Given that the many Canadian aid organizations in Sudan already suffered interminable delays getting their visas and vehicles through the country's Byzantine bureaucracy, one can only imagine (if the teddy bear riots were an indication) what their fates would be.

The genocide in Darfur has been called Rwanda in slow motion, and who better to recognize that than Senator Roméo Dallaire? He wrote in the *Globe and Mail* on September 14, 2006, that history would judge Canada, not Sudan, on the fate of Darfur. Those who call for simplistic military intervention (Canadian- or U.N.-led) or a Kosovo-type bombing campaign believe that such tactics would scare Khartoum into granting Darfur its independence. But a gamble like that would only make al-Bashir fight harder while he gained even more support and popularity at home and abroad. In July 2008, when the International Criminal Court called for al-Bashir's arrest for committing genocide and crimes against humanity, the first ever in the history of the court for a sitting head of state, it only strengthened his hand domestically and abroad in the African and Arab world. If Canada were to intervene militarily in Darfur, it would be alone. The European powers already in neighbouring Chad have no stomach to be vilified as "neo-colonists," and the United States is too bogged down in Iraq and Afghanistan for direct "boots on the ground" involvement.

There is too much at stake for such precipitate action. In 2008 the massive aid effort finally brought the death rates among Darfur's children down to pre-2000 levels — and that aid effort has to be kept going at all costs, even if it means appeasing those in power and the rebel factions. Perhaps author A.E.W. Mason had it right. In his *The Four*

Feathers, a British officer leans over the rail of the upper deck of a steamer as he travels down the Nile and thinks: "The narrow meagre strip of green close by the water's edge upon each bank was the only response which the Soudan made to Spring and Summer and the beneficent rain. [It was, he thought], a callous country inhabited by a callous people." Whatever happens, relations between Canada and Sudan are guaranteed to be contentious for years to come.

7

MISSIONARIES, AID WORKERS, AND NGOs

"We all admire those who dedicate their time, money, and energy to helping those less fortunate than themselves. When that helping hand stretches from London, Ontario, all the way to the impoverished and often brutalized people of southern Sudan — an area so remote and isolated that just getting there is a daunting challenge — then our respect quickly turns to admiration, as well." Speaking to the Canadian Economic Development Assistance for Southern Sudan (CEDASS) group in March 2007, Peter MacKay, the minister for foreign affairs at the time, paid tribute to the hundreds of Canadians who have sought to make a difference in Sudan.

The earliest Canadian humanitarian workers in Sudan were missionaries. Canada was the historical base for the Soudan Interior Mission (SIM) when Canadians Walter Gowans and Rowland Bingham, with American Thomas Kent, envisioned bringing Christianity to Sudan in 1893. Unable to interest the established missions to do so, the three set out for the country alone, with malaria killing Gowans and Kent and Bingham returning alone to Canada. He went back, caught malaria once more, and was forced to return home permanently. Bingham sent out a third team in 1902, this time to Nigeria, where the first SIM base was successfully established at Patigi. In 1909 SIM was incorporated in Canada, and as its first general director, Bingham had originally thought of making the mission part of his Canadian Baptist denomination but later opened it up as an interdenominational mission that would, he hoped, "come together for one important task — the giving of the Gospel to every soul in the Sudan."

The Sudanese government expelled all missionaries from the South during the1960s, forcing them to evacuate at short notice.[1] After 1973, missionaries of all agencies were allowed to return to the South, but in 1984 they were once more banished, the remaining few moving to Khartoum. SIM joined a coalition of humanitarian agencies, some of which were World Relief Canada, Emmanuel International (Canadian), and the Fellowship for African Relief, the last the only Canadian development agency that had been operating in Sudan since 1984 and originally run by Marv Koop from Manitoba. The agencies pooled their resources for humanitarian purposes, focusing on activities designed to address the root causes of poverty and providing relief, rehabilitation, and development assistance within Sudan.

"What was it like for our daughters when we went to Sudan?" teacher Don McPhee asks rhetorically. "Both were born in St Paul's Hospital, Vancouver, and Siobhan was four years old and Dara was two when we went to Sudan to work for APSO [Agency for Personnel Services Overseas]. We decided to put them in a Sudanese primary school in Wad Medani. The building was in poor repair with holes in the floor and walls and almost no teaching materials. But it had very capable, highly motivated teachers as the school was also a teacher training college. Wad Medani provided an excellent environment for our daughters to grow up in as they were always with many friends and with people who were interested in them and in their development. It was an environment focusing on family relationships, love, friendship, and the relationship with God — whatever your religion. Now in their twenties, our daughters remain in close contact with their Sudanese friends and are fluent in Arabic."

McPhee taught English to classes of about 60 teenagers, a daunting challenge anywhere. "I co-managed the Irish-Sudanese teaching project with my wife, and in addition travelled to various schools in Gezira Province to coach and help the young Irish teachers in the various schools. We regularly had young teachers come to Wad Medani to stay with us for a weekend or a few days or a week. As young, single people, they found staying with us and our two daughters a refuge from the challenges of living in Africa and in a conservative Muslim culture.

"In 1984, together with some British teachers, we put on a production of George Bernard Shaw's *Arms and the Man* as students had to study the play for their high-school certificate. Until our incredibly popular production, for the Sudanese, it had only been words in a book. The props were begged and borrowed from a myriad of sources, and the play ran for three days to a packed theatre. Dizzy with this success, the next year we mounted a production of South African Alan Paton's novel *Cry, the Beloved Country*, adapted for the theatre by my wife. It, too, was a huge success.

"I left APSO in February 1985 to join Plan International [formerly known as Foster Parents Plan International], a child-centred community development organization, as assistant director, and later became field director for the program in East Gezira. I led a child development program in 50 communities in East Gezira, an arid Sahelian area east of the Blue Nile. We worked together with community leaders, teachers, women's groups, and children to help them ensure the well-being of their children and the sustainable development of their communities. Our projects included water systems, school construction, teacher training, and provision of school books, equipment, and teaching aids. We set up more than 30 small co-operatives and developed one of the first Women's Development Centres in rural Sudan." Don McPhee left Sudan in January 2000 for Haiti to be one of Plan International's field directors there but returned to Khartoum in November 2007 as the country director.

Emmanuel Isch first came to Sudan in 1991 as part of SIM Canada and remained when the next year it joined FAR. "In the 1990s, CIDA had a considerable budget for food aid for NGOs, so FAR had programs on food aid in Northern Sudan. I was based only in certain areas. My job at this end was to ensure compliance in reporting — food aid had to be shipped out from Canada, so you had to have agents at ports, transportation, and distribution. The overall food package was 4,000 tons of food, oil, and pulses shipped from Montreal to Port Sudan, and the beneficiaries were over 100,000 in rations in two areas in North Kordofan.

"FAR had a main office in El Obeid. Later FAR would start working in the Nuba, but at that time you could only drive as far as Dilling.

With regard to food aid being used as a weapon in the war, well, we were working only in GOS-controlled areas, but we insisted that we control its distribution through our own monitors. We registered people on the basis of nutritional assessments and needs for the food. We would be told you should give to certain people and not others, but this wasn't the politics of North/South but more localized tribal issues. We knew we couldn't do this forever and began looking at development.

"Seed distributions, health needs, and access to water became our priorities — this is desert area — and we did some small irrigation schemes to allow them to sustain growth. Twenty years ago you had drought cycles every six or seven years. Now it's every year, and not just in Sudan. At a macro level the desert keeps encroaching annually. When I first came, I thought, *Why do people even bother living here?* But it's their tribal home and they've adapted. In the 1990s the traditional coping mechanisms had been eroded."

FAR began working in the post-conflict areas of the Nuba Mountains in January 2002 when the GOS and the SPLM/A signed the Burgenstock (Switzerland) Agreement that allowed for humanitarian aid during a ceasefire monitored by the multinational Joint Military Commission (JMC). "At that time," Isch says, "we were based in El Obeid, but as you moved into Dilling, you crossed the battle lines, so we were able to get an initial grant from the EU that allowed FAR to work in both GOS and rebel areas. Since then it has received CIDA funding to do so. So FAR became the first agency to work in both the SPLM/A and the GOS areas of South Kordofan. I was doing quite a number of 'back and forths' through the mountains and remember meeting some Canadians as JMC advisers, but it was mostly Americans, South Africans, and EU [people]. Nick Coghlan was in Khartoum, and he became the Canadian reference point. The Nuba Ceasefire Agreement, I think, was a good model for the CPA [Comprehensive Peace Agreement] and Darfur Peace Agreement [DPA]."

When the CPA was achieved, FAR was in a good position to support it by rebuilding the health, water, and sanitation resources that had been destroyed in the devastated areas. In both the North and South, Nick Coghlan noticed, the principal challenge to day-to-day survival for ordinary people wasn't fatal diseases or being killed by the enemy, but the scarcity of pure water — for themselves and their cattle. "Anyone looking to spend some spare development dollars in Sudan," Coghlan says, "could never go wrong by investing it in the drilling of boreholes or the supply of hand pumps." To increase the local capacity to manage water resources and health services for the expected 45,000 returnees and host populations in communities, FAR was involved in well drilling (equipping the wells with hand pumps) and constructing eight sub-surface dams to capture scarce rainfall. To address the health concerns of people in Nuba, FAR outfitted bicycles with medical equipment so health practitioners could reach previously inaccessible villages. Additionally, health-centre and first-aid stations were being installed in 20 schools.

Miriam Booy grew up in Tanzania where her father worked for World Vision. "We returned to Canada," she says, "where I attended Trinity Western University in British Columbia and graduated in May 2006 with an honours degree in international studies. In July 2006 I came to Sudan to start a six-month internship with FAR, based in the Nuba Mountains. After six months, I moved to a full contract and worked in Nuba for the next year and a half. I usually travel by bus from Khartoum to Dilling in Nuba, which takes about nine hours. It is amazingly flat the entire way. Crossing over the White Nile, south of Khartoum, you pass through Kosti, where thanks to the ready supply of water and to its strategic location at the junction of rail, road, and river routes to Darfur, Eastern Sudan, and Southern Sudan, there are a number of settlements for IDPs. FAR runs projects in Kosti that assist IDPs and the returnees who are heading back to the South on the barge. The barge leaves Kosti and travels upriver along the Nile, taking up to three weeks to reach Juba. People are normally crammed on in the open air with all their belongings. FAR provides medical care for returnees as they wait for the barge to depart and also on the barge as they travel.

"The empty paved road climbs slowly away from the Nile west across the desert toward Darfur, and as it approaches the Mahdist capital of El Obeid, which boasts one of Africa's largest cathedrals, and Dilling, the *jebels* start to appear. These are small granite hilly outcrops, which make up what are known as the Nuba Mountains, known locally simply as

Nuba. Nuba is much more beautiful than Khartoum in my biased opinion! There are supposedly ninety-nine rocky *jebels*, each corresponding with its own tribe, and they are great fun to climb. Nuba looks like an area that should have lions lying in wait for passing gazelles, but the only animals you will see are the hundreds of cows, goats, sheep, and chickens that are kept by many households.

"Everyone in Nuba speaks Arabic as well as his or her own tribal language. Tribal divisions are still very prominent in Nuba and bring about conflict over land and resources. Another recurring conflict is between the farmers and nomads that seems to occur all over Sudan. Water is probably the most significant problem for both people and livestock. Most people will use drilled boreholes or hand-dug wells to access drinking water that is not always clean. Many of our projects focus on improving sustainable water supplies and improving the cleanliness of the water people are using.

"Rainfall in Nuba, as in all of Sudan, is seasonal, usually falling between about May and August, and watching the first rains come is one of the most amazing miracles to be seen. Within a week of the first showers the grass will start to peek through the ground, and slowly the whole area transforms into a green paradise. The leaves return to the trees and flowers bloom. People begin to cultivate crops that they will harvest in October or November and which will have to last them for most of the year. Although the coming of the rain brings life and nourishment to the ground, it also brings with it new challenges. As there are no paved roads, the roads become extremely muddy and often impassable. Some villages are completely cut off during the months of heavy rain. Mosquitoes come out, and with them, malaria. Almost everyone will get malaria in the months following the rainy season.

"Houses in Nuba are made of mud bricks with a grass roof, or with rocks and a grass roof. The more well-off Nubans build their houses with fired red bricks and cement, with a zinc sheet roof. The area is in great danger of desertification as the desert spreads from the north and west. Many of our food security projects focus on environmental issues of not cutting down the trees for charcoal and construction and controlling erosion and surface water runoff.

"In the past couple of years, the end of the rains has more or less coincided with the Muslim holy month of Ramadan, a very interesting time of year in Sudan. As the majority of people are Muslim, almost everyone will be fasting for the whole day from sunrise to sunset. They will not eat any food or even drink water. I am amazed that they can make it through the whole day without a drop of water in such extreme heat. You will even see people doing heavy physical labour in the hot sun who still do not touch water until they break their fast in the evening. Breaking the fast is done very traditionally with eating dates, balila [small lentils], and special fruity, very sweet drinks. It is a very social time, as men will gather outside on mats to break the fast together. Any person passing by is welcomed to join in.

"The women eat separately in the houses. Once the breakfast is over, all men stand in one line and pray together. Women also do this inside. Later in the evening people will eat one or two meals to tide them over, and the next day it all starts again. It is always a strange time for people who are not Muslim because all the restaurants are closed during the day and the streets can be full of families until late at night. Work in most offices ends early at three and everyone goes home to sleep, as by this time they have no energy to do anything else! The end of Ramadan is the Eid ul-Fitr Celebration when people feast with their families for several days that are public holidays, like Christmas or Thanksgiving for us in Canada. Eid ul-Fitr is also known as Little Eid because about two months later at the end of the holy month of pilgrimage to Mecca there is another Eid, the Eid al-Adha, when sheep are sacrificed in commemoration of God's call to Abraham to sacrifice his son. The feasting can go on for almost a week.

"Family dynamics in Nuba are interesting, as one man will often take two or three or even more wives and sometimes have up to 15 children. The wives can be in different villages, with the man travelling back and forth, or in the same village living together. Women are at times only viewed as having the duty to bear children, cook the meals, look after the household, and look after the man of the household. Although not all relationships I have seen are like this, and the more modern educated people I have met no longer practise such a traditional lifestyle, it is definitely still the reality in the villages we work in. The issue of gender is a cross-cutting issue in all our programs, and one of our primary goals is to empower women and overcome some of these gender inequalities and stereotypes. Women in Sudan are perhaps not always respected as much as they should be, but they are definitely taken care of. I find being a single female aid worker that I am more 'looked after' by my local friends and colleagues than in danger. They take care of me and make sure I have what I need, and I rarely go anywhere alone because I will always have a driver or other Sudanese colleagues with me.

"My title is 'program support manager.' This means that I support and monitor the programs at the field level, helping to write new proposals and write reports and liaise with donors. Most of our donors require quarterly, mid-year, and annual reports, and because I speak good English and am used to writing papers and reports, I can support the team by formulating these. I also assist with writing new proposals for funding based on local need and FAR's strategy. Living in the field, though, I end up doing a whole variety of things, including technical support, finance, logistical support, visiting and monitoring projects, and general organization to ensure we stick to our work plan. I really love what I do because of the variety and because of the way I get to interact with the people we are actually helping at the field level.

"The best thing about my experience with FAR has been the grass-roots community development work I have been able to witness and be involved in. I have learned probably more about development in the past year than the whole of my undergrad degree! Although FAR originated in Canada, I see it as more of a local Sudanese NGO that has a few Canadian expats who support the work going on. In this I mean that, at least on the field level, most of the managers are Sudanese and all of the projects we do originate from our fieldworker Sudanese staff. They design the programs, and I just support them in helping them to write it up into a project proposal and helping to send in donor reports.

"As Canadians, the work we do for FAR is to provide support in linking with donors overseas — writing new proposals and good reports because our English and computer skills are better. We also provide technical support. For example, one Canadian now working for FAR has expertise in water projects, so that helps us a great deal with the technicalities of the water projects we do. We also provide general moral support and encouragement, showing that someone from far away does actually care about what is happening in the Nuba Mountains in Sudan. However, it is largely the Sudanese themselves who carry FAR forward, who create, implement, and run the programs. We are just the support team. I believe this contributes a great deal to our effectiveness and sustainability as an organization.

"The best thing about my experience with FAR has been the grassroots community development work I have been able to witness and be involved in. I have learned probably more about development in the last year than in the whole of my undergrad degree. Our areas of programming mostly focus on food security and livelihoods, but we also cover health, water/sanitation, capacity building, women's empowerment, and peace-building. Our main mandate is to meet the needs of the most vulnerable populations in a holistic manner through the provision of relief, rehabilitation, and community development. In the past few years this has meant assisting thousands of IDPs in Khartoum, Kosti, and Darfur. It has also meant assisting returnees who have returned to their homes and need support to begin rebuilding their lives, such as in Nuba.

"Expatriates also provide general moral support and encouragement, because they show that people from far away actually do care about what is happening in the Nuba Mountains in Sudan. I believe this strong Sudanese flavour contributes a great deal to our effectiveness and sustainability as an organization, and not all NGOs I have seen are like this. Other Canadian ideals we uphold in our work include gender equality, i.e., through women's empowerment programs, and environmental sustainability. We also have a strategic focus on peace-building and 'development for peace,' particularly leading to the upcoming elections and the referendum on Southern Sudanese independence. In Nuba we work across the line, both in the government-controlled side (Dilling Locality) and in an area that is still controlled by the SPLM/A (Dilling County). By implementing equally in both areas we hope to foster peace and bring both sides together, and by improving livelihoods and access to services and opportunities we contribute to stability.

"Although we maintain positive relationships with both the government and the SPLM/A and involve them as much as possible in our programming, we do still struggle, as all NGOs do, with getting visas and permits and so on. We have new staff that get denied visas and have to wait months before they enter the country, and we have cars and supplies that get stuck in customs for months before they are cleared. These things can often be quite frustrating but are the reality of living and working in Sudan."

After working in Sudan for FAR from 2001 to 2004, Emmanuel Isch joined World Vision Canada (WVC) as director for humanitarian and emergency affairs, based out of its main office in Mississauga, Ontario. "One of my first emergencies to deal with," Isch says, "was Darfur, as WVC was getting re-established in Northern Sudan after having been out of that part of the country for some years. Darfur made it to the international media and public arena, although the problem had been brewing for some time. While still in Sudan with FAR, we were beginning to hear about rising tensions in that region in early 2003 and alerted donor countries and the United Nations, but little attention was paid to the issue, as there was a focus on getting the North-South deal sealed.

"It took some weeks of negotiations for WVC to get an official agreement with the Government of Sudan, but it was finally obtained in June 2004. So although I had left Sudan, having to deal with the Darfur crisis was as if I had not actually left. WVC mounted a fairly large humanitarian operation by July 2004, including an initial airlift of emergency supplies, and sent in a number of its Global Rapid Response Team staff on the ground. These are specialized staff who are deployed in major humanitarian emergencies and can get a program going from scratch.

"Going into Darfur, we were asked to become partners with the United Nations' World Food Programme, and we had some initial funding available from a number of sources. So WVC started distributing food rations — at one point providing rations to up to 500,000 people — and providing health and medical care to tens of thousands in camp and non-camp settings [as well as] clean water and emergency education. We have also focused on income-generation activities for the displaced, taking into account that many have been in camp settings for several years now and remain idle much of the day, so focusing on teaching a small trade not only occupies them but also helps them engage in small business activities and gain a skill they can use in the future. These camps are so big that they have developed their own little marketplaces. By the end of 2004, I was back twice in North Sudan, including Darfur, and was able to see first-hand the work we were doing on the ground. By then WVC was operating a multimillion-dollar emergency response program, was partnered with the United Nations and other organizations, and was operating in a couple of the IDP camps around Nyala.

"On my first visit to South Darfur, I was struck by the size of the camps we were working in. One of them had up to 100,000 people [Kalma] — an endless view of makeshift shelters where families survived in very poor conditions and were dependent on the assistance they received from organizations like WVC and others. I was further struck by the stories people shared of how they fled their villages due to conflict and how they often walked, and at times used public transport, to make it to the relative safety of places likes Nyala to seek refuge and assistance. They had lost pretty much everything when their communities were attacked. The tragedy of conflicts — and we often forget this — is that it takes years following the return to a level of normalcy for people to regain their livelihood, and many never get back to that point. There were certainly a number of challenges to deal with by being operational in this region, but at the same time there were clear opportunities to have an impact on the humanitarian side as needs were great and tens of thousands of people needed life-saving and life-sustaining assistance. WVC was quick to respond to our efforts in South Darfur and appealed to the Canadian public, while also eventually receiving funding support from CIDA, as well. We also sent staff on the ground to help with the humanitarian effort. So we clearly had a Canadian connection to our humanitarian efforts in Darfur, but also ongoing in the South of Sudan.

"WVC has made it a strategic priority to have a 'whole country' approach to Sudan, that is, looking at areas of need that we could address in the North and in the South. We have programs in Darfur, but also in the Khartoum area, Blue Nile, Equatoria, and other regions. Much of our emphasis outside of Darfur is on working with communities to help establish health services, improve access to clean water, and even focus on customary law. Much of the focus is also on capacity-building at the community level and with local authorities. Much of the South remains limited in terms of capacity, and if there is any hope of sustaining progress in our work, we have to ensure we help develop local capacities.

"One particular story I remember is of a young mother who had fled her community just a couple of weeks before I met her. She had woken up one morning as her village was being attacked, and men from the village were targets of the attacks, some shot and killed. She had just enough time to gather a couple of her young children — she didn't know where her husband was — and flee on foot as far as she could. She left a village that had just been burned down, ransacked, and devastated, with men killed and others fleeing. 'Who did this?' I asked her. 'Those men on horses,' she replied. She had managed to get on a transport truck, and several days later, following a challenging ride, she made it to Nyala and to the camp where she was now receiving assistance. I asked her if her hope was to one day go back to her community and find her husband, but she wasn't hopeful that this would happen anytime soon. This is one of countless stories one heard in those camps.

"Over time the number of those displaced by the conflict continued to grow, and so did the challenges for humanitarian agencies in providing continued assistance while also seeking opportunities to spread support to communities less affected by the conflict but nonetheless very needy. This is partly why the conflict started in the region — people and communities that had very limited or no resources and services. Community after community with limited access to clean water, education, and health care and wanting some attention and support. As an organization, we're conscious of the fact that we have to provide assistance to those displaced by the conflict but also to those still in communities who had little. It is important that we focus on basic activities that would improve the lives of people in those settings. So we received further funding support to begin digging wells, provide agricultural training, seeds, and tools, and improve health services in communities north and south of

Nyala in addition to continuing to care for thousands of displaced in camp settings. We believe these are activities with significant importance and impact. They also help ease some of the rising tensions we were seeing in various communities and among the displaced — humanitarian assistance can be tricky as far as who we assist and who we don't.

"On my most recent trip, in March 2008, I was able to visit some of the communities where we have such activities, in fact, funded specifically by CIDA. These are communities that had no direct access to clean water, and we saw that now several thousand people have access to water. We have also established a small health centre and provide basic health care to these people. We have worked with communities to improve their agricultural practices so they can grow crops more effectively, taking into account the challenges of doing so in a very arid environment. This area is relatively calm, so we're able to do this work, but it isn't far from areas with ongoing tensions and conflict. We in WVC believe it is important to focus on those displaced by the conflict and those who have remained in their communities."

Peter MacKay, who was Canada's foreign affairs minister in 2006, recounted Canadian aid to up to that year: "We are working on many different fronts to try to improve the situation throughout Sudan. We have contributed $238 million since 2004 in support of the African Union's Mission in Darfur. We have pledged $110 million through bilateral and multilateral channels to humanitarian assistance and reconstruction. We have earmarked a specific investment of $3.6 million in land-mine clearance to make Sudan's roads passable, including for the transport of humanitarian assistance. In concert with other donors, we have helped to deliver school supplies to over 20,000 students, teachers, and headmasters. We have repaired hospitals, delivered medical kits to health centres, and provided 18 months of pharmaceuticals. We will be providing $23 million to support peace-building activities for Darfur and Southern Sudan, including efforts to strengthen the capacity of the Southern Sudan government to provide for the needs of its citizens. In all we are funding 18 projects throughout Sudan in support of peace and reconciliation efforts."

To Emmanuel Isch, the imperative to focus on the larger population is key, "also taking into account that we have to establish seeds of rehabilitation and recovery for those people and communities. And the larger questions that loom — what do we do with the two to three million people who have been displaced by the conflict? If and when peace returns — where do they go, where do they resettle, taking into account that in most cases their villages were burned down to the ground and in some cases their land was taken over? And how are they supported to get their lives and livelihoods back to a minimum so they don't need assistance for the long term? We need to keep asking these questions so that we are in a position to eventually transition from humanitarian assistance to recovery and rehabilitation assistance. Lots of issues and variables to take into account.

"The significance of what has been happening in Sudan, not only in Darfur but also other parts of the country, has prompted agencies like WVC to have a significant involvement both in terms of humanitarian and rehabilitation assistance but also in engaging with our own government — through a consortium of Canadian organizations that focus on Sudan and through face-to-face meetings with Sudanese officials — and the United Nations to encourage a relevant diplomatic engagement and put further pressure on all parties involved in the Darfur conflict.

"The planned elections and referendum on secession to take place in the South are crucial milestones and ones that could either solidify politically in Sudan or lead to renewed conflict. The issue of oil has certainly become a major factor in the politics and economics of Sudan and is one that continues to be more of a divisive factor than a uniting factor and will likely continue to be a major point of contention between the North and the South and also other regions. Darfur also contains natural resources, including oil and precious metals and stones, and the conflict there needs to be also seen as one over access to land and resources. In fact, this is a primary issue related to the conflict there. The same continues to apply to South Sudan where access and control over natural resources remain a major political and economic issue, one that continues to bog down a process of true and effective reconciliation."

Peter MacKay concludes: "In most countries of the world, Canada and Canadians are welcome. In much of the developing world, our political, commercial, and development officers are viewed favourably, and are able to work effectively at the grassroots level with local groups and individuals. And yet, even here [Sudan], there are limits to what a foreign government can do. It is an enormous challenge, made even more difficult by the often-unhelpful — if not hostile — positions of the Sudanese government in Khartoum toward the international community, including the United Nations."

For humanitarian aid veterans like Emmanuel Isch, Sudan remains an enigma — a country with hospitable people, a country with a great history and culture, a country with much potential, but a country that continues to be subject to conflicts at various levels and that seems not to be able to deal with them. "The tragedy," Isch says, "is that millions of people continue to suffer as a result whereas we as an international community continue to wrestle with ways to better engage with the various entities who govern the country. We need to remain committed to help this country move forward."

8

POLICEWOMAN AND PRIME MINISTER

It was Sudan's erstwhile guest Osama bin Laden and the terrorist attacks of September 11, 2001, that set in motion events that would dramatically impact the relationship between Khartoum and the remainder of the world. By mid-2001, prospects for peace in Sudan appeared somewhat remote, and a week before the September 11 attacks in New York and Washington, the Bush Administration named former Senator John Danforth as its presidential envoy for peace in the Sudan. He was to explore the prospect that the United States could play a useful role in the search for an end to Africa's longest civil war, and stimulate the delivery of humanitarian aid.

The United States abandoned its veto in the Security Council against lifting sanctions against Khartoum on September 27, 2001. (But under the eye of religious groups and human-rights activists, Washington kept up its bilateral sanctions.) With Washington's clout, and under the auspices of IGAD, in 2002, the Sudan peace process made significant progress. On July 20 the Machakos Protocol was signed between the GOS and the SPLM/A, which set forth the principles of governance, the transitional process, and the structures of government, as well as the right to self-determination for the people of South Sudan concerning state and religion. Both parties agreed to continue talks on the outstanding issues of power-sharing, wealth-sharing, human rights, and a ceasefire. A major breakthrough occurred at Naivasha, Kenya, with the signing of the IGAD-sponsored Agreement on Wealth-Sharing on January 7, 2004, by the GOS and John Garang, followed by the Protocol on Power-Sharing on May 26. Both sides agreed on the division of oil revenues during a six-year transition period, separate banking laws (Islamic in the North and Western in the South), and reconstruction of the South.

Darfuri refugees who made it across the border to Chad in June 2003 brought with them horrifying accounts of "devils on horseback" destroying hundreds of villages and granaries and raping and gunning down whole families as they tried to flee. The word *Janjaweed* had entered the English vocabulary. The war in Darfur began on February 26, 2003, when the unknown Sudan Liberation Movement/Army (SLM/A) attacked a GOS garrison town in Northern Darfur. Encouraged by the easy victory, it and the Justice and Equality Movement (JEM) then attacked the GOS facilities in the western region of Darfur. The two rebel groups — soon to splinter into a dozen more with a confusing number of acronyms — had watched as Khartoum and the SPLM/A culminated the torturous process of negotiation leading to the signing of the Comprehensive Peace Agreement, which allowed for power- and resource-sharing between Khartoum and the hinterland regions. For the Darfuris this was the incentive to start their own rebellion. With few regular troops in Darfur, the GOS resorted to aerial bombardment by its Antonovs in support of ground attacks by the Janjaweed.

"I was born and raised on a farm near a small Southwestern Ontario village," recalls Debbie Bodkin, a sergeant with the Waterloo Regional Police Service for 20 years. She has worked on sex assaults, drugs, homicide, and intelligence, and in 2000, volunteered with five officers from the Royal Canadian Mounted Police to be part of a forensic team in Kosovo investigating war crimes and genocide for the International Criminal Tribunal for the Former Yugoslavia (ICTY) under the United Nations and the North Atlantic Treaty Organization (NATO).

"When I returned home from Kosovo," she says, "I learned about CANADEM, a Canadian organization that assists international organizations by identifying skilled Canadians who are interested in positions working overseas. I posted my résumé with them, and in early 2004 I got a call from the coordinator of the Coalition of International Justice [CIJ], a non-profit agency in Washington, D.C. The coordinator, Stefanie Frease, explained that the U.S. State Department had contacted CIJ to have it undertake an investigation to determine what types of war crimes were occurring in Darfur. Stefanie required female investigators to travel as part of a team to Chad for two weeks to conduct interviews with the refugees who had fled from Sudan. I accepted the position without hesitation and used my annual holidays to leave for Chad in July 2004. CIJ had hired four teams of four people and each team would spend two weeks conducting interviews. The goal was to compile at least 12,000 interviews that would be examined by the U.S. State Department statisticians. My interpreter, Mustapha, was a bright, ambitious, 24-year-old Sudanese who had been living in Chad so he could study English. He hoped that someday he would come to North America, go to university, then return to his country, become president, and make things better.

"I will never forget our first interview. The temperature was scorching, somewhere around 40 degrees Celsius, even though the sun had gone down. Mustapha and I sat together on the steps of the old schoolhouse, sweating, working by candlelight and flashlight, and swatting the bugs around us as I tried to fill in the questionnaire. Our minor discomfort was nothing compared to the pain that the man we interviewed had suffered and would forever suffer. He was 30 years old and had fled Sudan hours before. He wept as he told us about watching as his parents, wife, and young son were brutally killed in front of him when their village was attacked by Janjaweed. He escaped physically unharmed, but the pain in his voice and tears was tremendous. He didn't want to go on living and yet the inherent desire to survive pushed him to come to Chad. His last words were: 'Life is nothing anymore when you have no one.'

"Our wake-up time in the morning was based on the sounds of donkeys baying and roosters crowing at the break of dawn, which was around 4:00 a.m. We made it a habit to start our interviews early so we could get out of the almost unbearable heat in the late afternoon and head back to our camp and a little shade. We would take down our tents, pack our belongings in the back of the trucks, and then the 10 of us would climb into the trucks, drive into the village to find some bread and tea for breakfast, and then head for the refugee camps.

"Bahai refugee camp, like most others, sprawled across the desert and contained upward of 10,000 to 20,000 people living in a sea of U.N. tents. Upon arrival we parked the trucks and teamed up with our interpreters, then each pair headed in a different direction in the camp armed with a backpack of water bottles, pens, and questionnaire sheets. We would walk past a few tents and then randomly stop at one, explain who we were working for, and ask the occupants if one of them would allow us to interview him or her. We never had anyone turn down the opportunity to speak to us. They were all hopeful that if they told us their story of what horrible things they had endured we would then go back to North America and tell the people with power about it and the atrocities would be stopped. We shared the same hope.

"We conducted the majority of the interviews inside the sweltering hot tents in order to give the person answering our questions some privacy. The tents were full of flies, sick children, and nothing more than a mat on the dirt. Due to the number of refugees, there was a shortage of food and water for everyone, but almost every person we spoke to would offer us food or drink, even though it may have been their last ration for a while. I was amazed at the generosity and personal strength of each person we spoke to. They had been witness to or victims of horrible atrocities, and yet they would smile at me, offer me whatever they had to sit on, and thank me over and over for coming to their country to help them. I soon realized that the majority of people didn't know their own birth date or even how old they were. There were no calendars, and almost every day in their lives consisted of the same routine of tending crops and fetching water. Each interview took about an hour, and we tried to conduct an average of seven interviews a day. We worked every day we were there to ensure we were able to get the number of interviews required completed.

"I remember interviewing one very determined woman who had been gang-raped by 12 men. She invited me into her tent, which had nothing in it but a piece of straw mat and one tiny stool that she gave to me to sit on. She offered me some of her tiny ration of rice and some water. Understandably, most of the women who talked to me about being raped had great difficulty because they were so ashamed and embarrassed. This woman, however, sat rigidly and spoke so forcefully and with such determination that she amazed me. She wasn't married and had been a virgin. She had a great deal of anger in her voice as she talked about the men who raped her over and over, yet she was so strong-willed and full of determination that I couldn't help but admire her courage and composure. She wasn't going to be silent about what they had done to her, and she hoped by sharing it with me they would someday be punished.

"The majority of the stories followed the same sequence. The villages were first attacked by GOS planes dropping bombs, shortly after soldiers in cars with guns drove through shooting, and then Janjaweed on horses would continue the assaults on the people and burn down the village. Men and children were whipped, beaten, shot, and thrown into burning huts, while women and young girls were often held hostage for days and raped over and over by numerous men. In their culture, when a women was raped, she was 'spoiled.' This not only meant that no man would want to marry her, but often even her husband, family, and friends would disown her due to the shame. Also if the woman was impregnated by the rape, the baby would be deemed to be an Arab child, not African. The attacks were often accompanied by racial epithets such as 'From now and for 20 years we will kill all the blacks,' 'You are black people's wives and bear black children, but now you will have to bear a white people's child,' or 'Slaves run. You don't belong here.'

"Bahai was the first camp we went to, but the other two, Cariari and Tine, looked exactly the same. What we saw were miles and miles of tents in the middle of the desert. After being at each camp for a day or two, everyone knew the investigators were there, and people started following us, wanting to tell their stories.

"After two weeks, we returned to our homes and awaited the results of the CIJ investigation. U.S. Secretary of State Colin Powell released the Documenting Atrocities in Darfur Report on September 9, 2004, which affirmed that 'genocide has been committed in Darfur and the Government of Sudan and the Janjaweed bear responsibility.' We were all thrilled with the findings, as it was what we had all believed, and now we felt that the people of Sudan would be saved and the governmental killing machine would be stopped. Unfortunately, we were wrong."

On April 8, 2004, months before Colin Powell's condemnation, and faced with international criticism on the use of the Janjaweed, the GOS signed the Humanitarian Ceasefire Agreement in N'Djamena, Chad, with the rebels. Both sides broke it almost immediately. During the following month, the United States, the European Union, and a number of African states settled on a solution for stabilizing Darfur: send in the African Union.

The post-colonial-era Organization of African Unity (OAU), once called the best Third World dictators' club in existence, had morphed into the African Union (AU) on May 25, 2001. Sudan was to have an African solution for an African problem. Thabo Mbeki, the president of South Africa at the time, told the West: "Darfur is an African responsibility and we can do it." As with all easy solutions, it was acceptable to everyone. The Darfur conflict was threatening to spill over into neighbouring Chad and the Central African Republic, as the former accused Khartoum of supporting the Union of Forces for Democracy and Development and the latter charged that the Sudanese government encouraged the Democratic Forces for Unity, both rebel groups in each country. The SLM/A and the JEM were then meeting with the GOS in Abuja and demanded that the AU convene separately with both to draft an agenda. Unless the Janjaweed were disarmed, they said, they refused to sign any humanitarian accord giving aid organizations greater access to the IDP camps. Influenced by U.N. Secretary General Kofi Annan's visit to Darfur from June 29 to July 3, 2004, and the signing of the Joint Implementation Mechanism to resolve what Annan called the world's worst humanitarian crisis, the GOS figured that if it was forced to accept peacekeepers, the more pliant AU troops were preferable to those of the United Nations.

For the Western powers that saw their military being increasingly sucked into Iraq and Afghanistan, here was a situation where they could write cheques and field a few military observers who wouldn't take casualties. Given the right spin, "green hatting" (AU soldiers wore green berets in contrast with the blue of U.N. forces) Darfur with Nigerian, Senegalese, and Rwandan soldiers would also appease their vociferous film star, church, humanitarian, and student activists. The United Nations, then juggling 16 peacekeeping missions around the world, was relieved that another international organization would take the flak

Top: These Grizzly and Husky AVGPs were shipped from Canada to Africa in the summer of 2005 on the *Marinus Green*, a Dutch commercial ship. (Photo by Combat Camera) **Bottom:** A Grizzly, part of the shipment of 105 AVGPs for African Union forces in Sudan, is hoisted ashore at Dakar, Senegal. (Photo by Combat Camera)

Top: Canadian Forces' oldest C-130, No. 315, was used in Sudan. Captain Tim Hatheway, a Hercules pilot at CFB Trenton in Ontario, remembers fondly how the 40-year-old aircraft got him out of dangerous situations. No. 315 was finally retired in September 2005. (Photo courtesy Department of National Defence) **Bottom:** Canadian Forces Master Corporal Rock Bourdeau (with headphones and sunglasses) instructs an AU soldier driving a Grizzly AVGP in Thiès, Senegal. (Photo by Combat Camera)

Top: Chief Warrant Officer Grégoire Lacroix (left) and then Chief of Defence Staff General Rick Hillier (right) present Major Gregory Allan Penner (middle) with a Mentioned in Dispatches for his courageous actions in Sudan. (Photo by Corporal Marcie Lane, CFSU(O) Photo Services) **Bottom:** On August 19,

2006, National Redemption Front (NRF) "technicals" ambushed a convoy protected by AMIS. One Grizzly gunner rammed the nearest NRF vehicle in self-defence, igniting the extra fuel tanks and ammunition and engulfing the AVGP in flames. (Photo by Major George Boyuk, CEFCOM)

Major Sandi Banerjee of The Queen's Own Rifles replaces a sign next to what was an unmarked minefield in Malakal, Sudan, scene of heavy fighting in November and December 2006. (Photo by Major Jitin Kumar, Indian Army)

Rocket-propelled grenade warheads and anti-personnel mines have been dumped into a shallow pit in Sudan. Very unstable due to severe heat and years of erosion, the ordnance is extremely dangerous. (Photo by Major Sandi Banerjee)

Miriam Booy (centre) grew up in Tanzania where her father worked for World Vision Canada. After graduating from university in British Columbia in May 2006, she came to the Nuba Mountains in Sudan to intern with Fellowship for African Relief. (Photo courtesy Miriam Booy)

A Russian Ilyushin Il-76, with a United Nations helicopter behind it, stands on the tarmac in Sudan. (Photo by Major Sandi Banerjee)

Darfur in the late rainy season when briefly the arid land sprouts green. (Photo by Lieutenant-Commander Nicholas Smith)

Children in a makeshift school in an internally displaced person (IDP) camp in South Darfur. The Canadian Contingent, Operation Safari, raised funds to renovate the classrooms and supply books for the children. (Photo courtesy Major Sandi Banerjee)

Petty Officer Second Class Heidi Sorrell hands out treats from Canada to kids at an IDP camp in South Darfur. For these children it is their first exposure to foreigners, especially female role models in the military. (Photo by Major Sandi Banerjee)

Top: A curious child in Nyala, South Darfur, peeks out as a United Nations patrol drives by. (Photo by Major Sandi Banerjee). **Bottom**: Debbie Bodkin, a sergeant with the Waterloo Regional Police Service for more than 20 years, sits with little Mohammad in front of a refugee tent in Darfur. (Photo courtesy Debbie Bodkin)

A girl at an IDP camp in South Darfur fetches water with the help of a donkey. (Photo by Major Sandi Banerjee)

Nyala in South Darfur. Over the hills are the IDP camps that the local authorities tried to prevent the United Nations from reaching. (Photo by Major Sandi Banerjee) **Inset:** In 2007, when the World Health Organization estimated the number of people who have perished in Sudan from hunger, disease, and violence at about 200,000, Sudan's ambassador to the United Nations disputed the claim, saying the number didn't exceed 10,000. (Photo by Debbie Bodkin)

A local vendor sells camel milk and potatoes at a well-established IDP camp inhabited by refugees from Darfur. (Photo by Major Sandi Banerjee)

Top: At the U.N. General Assembly in 2004 Prime Minister Paul Martin said, "Well, you go into that camp in Darfur and you tell that mother who lost her family that it's going to take the Security Council six months to determine when they can go in." (Photo by Debbie Bodkin) **Bottom**: The U.N. Commission of Inquiry for Darfur concluded in January 2005 that while there was no evidence that genocide had been pursued by the Sudanese government, its forces and the Janjaweed militias had killed and tortured Darfurians and had destroyed villages and displaced thousands of people. (Photo by Debbie Bodkin)

Although the Nuba Mountains in Southern Kordofan are pretty as a picture postcard, much of the civil war in Sudan has taken place here. (Photo by Miriam Booy)

when this one encountered turbulence. Still smarting from the condemnation for not intervening in the genocide of Rwanda in 1994 and about to be heavily embroiled in Iraq, the United States mustered its considerable clout — political and financial — behind the AU solution.

The U.N. Security Council also got behind the AU plan, passing Resolution 1547 on June 11, 2004, to establish a special political mission — the United Nations Advance Mission in the Sudan (UNAMIS). Cheered on all sides, in July the AU entered into negotiations at Abuja, Nigeria, with Khartoum even as the first 60 military observers and 310 soldiers for their protection were deployed to Darfur to monitor the compliance of all parties to the N'Djamena Humanitarian Ceasefire Agreement. Keeping up the momentum, on July 30, in response to the escalation of atrocities in Darfur, the Security Council also adopted Resolution 1556, which imposed an arms embargo on all militias, and more important, endorsed the African Union's deployment of monitors and troops. That Darfur was the size of France, without its transport or communications infrastructure, and that the AU troops had neither capacity nor intent to patrol it, never seemed to occur to anyone.

By the time Paul Martin became prime minister in December 2003, Canada's role in peacemaking had shrunk a great deal from its glory days when Lester Pearson talked the United Nations into sending a force to the Suez Canal in 1956. Part of the blame could be attached to Prime Minister Jean Chrétien and Paul Martin, his finance minister, who slashed funding to the military, developmental aid, and Foreign Affairs to reduce the federal deficit. While campaigning to lead the Liberal Party in 2003, Martin attacked the United Nations for its "old thinking" and "out-of-date decision-making mechanisms." At the World Economic Forum in Davos, Switzerland, in late January 2004, barely a month into the job of prime minster, Martin evoked the vision of Canada playing "a very ambitious role in the world," its military once more in the forefront of the international stage both in peacekeeping and in an offensive role.

With these developments, Canadians were soon speculating whether their military would be in Sudan as part of the Hovelte, Denmark–based Standby High Readiness Brigade (SHIRBRIG.)[1] SHIRBRIG Headquarters had been planning an actual deployment of a follow-on mission to Sudan, and in 2003 Canada assumed the presidency of the brigade, with Canadian Brigadier-General Greg Mitchell as its commander. As assistance to SHIRBRIG, whose planning element staff formed the core of an advanced military component within the initial UNAMIS, the Canadian Forces provided, on short notice, two non-permanent personnel, Major James Simiana, a public-affairs officer, and Warrant Officer Robert Moug, an intelligence officer. Operation Safari (Task Force Sudan or TFS) was made public in a media release on July 23, 2004. Following pre-deployment preparations and training in Canada and further mission familiarization training in Denmark, both Operation Safari members were "on the ground" in Khartoum by August 2004.

In September, Defence Minister Bill Graham announced that Darfur would get about CDN$250,000 in military equipment from Canada, "but there are no plans to send our troops there." The equipment included vests, helmets, and other gear for AU troops patrolling Darfur. "There is no immediate plan to deploy troops there," Graham told reporters. "The international community has generally considered that it is important that this matter be managed by the African Union forces that are there." In any case, Canadian troops were stretched too thin with commitments in Afghanistan and the Balkans, Graham said. There were currently 650 Canadian peacekeepers still in Bosnia, with most scheduled to leave that December.

"When we reviewed the evidence compiled by our team, and then put it beside other information available to the State Department and widely known throughout the international community, widely reported upon by the media and by others, we concluded, I concluded, that genocide has been committed in Darfur and that the government of Sudan and the Janjaweed bear responsibility," U.S. Secretary of State Colin Powell said before the U.S. Senate Foreign Relations Committee on September 9, 2004. He further declared that the United States had pledged US$1.7 billion to spend on food, camps, and air transport for AU troops. Illinois Senator (now President) Barack Obama said that the issue wasn't sending U.S. troops to Darfur but U.S. leadership, "but in the interim, having NATO forces there [that] could be supplied by some of the middle powers, Canada, Australia, others that have experience in peacekeeping, would be absolutely crucial." The U.N. Security Council stopped short of using the word *genocide* at the General Assembly but resolved unanimously on September 18 that Sudan could face sanctions unless the GOS stopped the violence in Darfur. It also supported an expanded role for the too few AU troops then in the country. "We are afraid of neither the U.N. nor its resolution," al-Bashir, Sudan's president, replied the next day.

Like his father, Paul Martin is a confirmed multilateralist. Paul Martin, Sr., had been present with Prime Minister William Lyon Mackenzie King at the birth of the United Nations in San Francisco in 1945. Yet in his inaugural speech before the General Assembly on September 22, Paul Junior attacked that August body in blunt language, reprimanding it for delays in Sudan by quibbling over the legal definition of the word *genocide*. "I found it bordering on the immoral," he said, "whether it was genocide or not, that we could only go in if it was. Clearly, the rapes and killings were going on. Damn it, stop arguing and go in. While the international community struggles with definitions, the people of Darfur struggle with disaster," Martin lashed out at the Assembly. "They are hungry, they are homeless, they are sick, and many have been driven out of their own country. Tens of thousands have been murdered, raped, and assaulted." He shamed the U.N. leaders for dragging their feet, he later said. "My reaction was, 'Well, you go into that camp in Darfur and you tell that mother who lost her family that it's going to take the Security Council six months to determine when they can go in.' We are not going to stand by and watch those massacres take place any longer."

Along with other countries the Canadian government had applied the terms of Security Council Resolution 1054 in 1996 to reduce the size of the Sudanese embassy in Ottawa, trimming the number of diplomats and ordering Sudanese representation be lowered to the level of chargé d'affaires. There hadn't been a Sudanese ambassador to Canada since 1991 for "economic reasons," said the embassy's deputy ambassador Adil Bannanga. In October 2004 he announced that Dr. Faiza Hassan Taha was being sent by Khartoum to assume his country's top diplomatic post in Ottawa. Educated at the University of Khartoum and a senior researcher with the Center for Strategic Studies, Dr. Taha had been previously posted with her husband to Abidjan, Rome, and Washington, D.C. Stockwell Day, the Conservative Party foreign affairs critic, said the Sudanese government "should be made aware that we are not going to treat this as an automatic acceptance of credentials." The new ambassador should be compelled to appear as a witness before the House of Commons Foreign Affairs Committee, he said, "to take questions from MPs because we are flooded with questions from Canadians about the disaster in Sudan." He was too late. Foreign Affairs spokeswoman Kimberly Phillips said, "It is important that we are able to engage in dialogue with Sudanese authorities in Canada at the highest level. The nomination is accepted."

With more than 1.5 million people having fled their homes in Darfur since the raids began in 2003, and an estimated 70,000 dead through hunger and disease (there were no reliable figures on those killed by violence), the World Food Programme had been struggling to deliver aid, especially to North Darfur. Although a ceasefire was brokered on November 9 between the SLM/A and the government, and UNAMIS had increased its numbers the previous month to 2,341 military personnel and 815 civilian police, fighting broke out around the town of Tawilla, west of El Fasher. When the GOS Antonovs bombed rebel positions in the east and south — the towns of Allaiat and Tadit — the rebels retaliated by attacking WFP truck convoys going out of El Fasher and refugee camps. "All we are doing is protecting ourselves and the civilians," SLM/A spokesman Mahgoub Hussain told Al-Jazeera TV. "We have to retaliate." Although some 300,000 IDPs would be cut off from food aid, the WFP and all NGOs halted operations and moved their staff out of North Darfur on November 22.

The first Canadian prime minister to visit Sudan had just arrived in the country. U.N. Secretary General Kofi Annan had personally asked Paul Martin to go to Khartoum, hoping he might make a breakthrough in negotiations with the Sudanese government. British Prime Minister Tony Blair had been there the week before, and the GOS hadn't listened. Martin was determined. "Essentially," he told the accompanying media,

"Bashir was not letting our vehicles in, trying to stop everything we were doing. So I went to Khartoum to see him and said, 'Cut it out.' He said he wasn't stopping us, and I said, 'Of course you are. Cut it out.' Whether or not it had any effect, I suppose history will judge. Listen, war is not normal. Peace is. And we're going to pressure the government to sign a peace agreement. President Bashir indicated to us that he was not able to control the Janjaweed, that, in fact, they were acting on their own. The point I made to him is we expected that the Janjaweed would be controlled. Period. I just simply said that it is a responsibility of government to essentially control those kinds of extraneous militia forces."

Martin met with a number of the refugees at an IDP camp and even joined in an impromptu dance with the children. They applauded when he said his office had brought "a planeload" of schoolbooks, crayons, and supplies. Earlier Martin's team had a scare when a Sudanese Army truck in his convoy grazed a young girl in the street. She was taken to hospital because, it was thought, of the media attention. Martin later visited her, bearing candy and two teddy bears. "I feel very, very badly," the prime minister said after the visit, "as I know we all do, about what happened. She had stitches on her tongue, but she's going to be fine."

After Debbie Bodkin returned home in August 2004, she had mixed emotions. "Naturally, I was happy to see my family and friends, but my heart and mind were still filled with the thoughts of the fleeing victims of Darfur." In October 2004, at the request of the Security Council, the U.N. secretary general established a commission of inquiry to investigate reports from Darfur of violations of international humanitarian law and to determine whether or not acts of genocide had occurred.

"When I received a phone call from the lead investigator for the U.N. Commission of Inquiry for Darfur asking if I could return to Africa and this time go directly into Darfur to continue the investigation," Bodkin says, "I accepted immediately. On November 22 I arrived at the United Nations Headquarters in Geneva. After going through the mounds of U.N. procedural paperwork and physical examinations, I met the team members from various parts of the world: four police officers, three forensic experts, two of whom I had met in Kosovo, four analysts, and a lawyer. While we waited for our Sudanese visas, which were inexplicably slow in arriving, the inquiry's commissioners laid out the goals and categories of crimes to be examined: decide whether or not genocide was occurring, identify the perpetrators, and propose possible solutions. The categories of crimes to be examined were: indiscriminate acts on villages, execution and extermination, rape, forced expulsion, looting, and torture.

"Other than these goals and categories, details about how we were to get the job done or in what format the report was to be compiled weren't touched on at all. I was rather shocked when one of the commissioners stated that based on his brief visit he didn't believe that two of the required elements of genocide, specifically a target group of victims and *mens rea* [Latin for "guilty mind," a common legal test of criminal liability] were present, so he felt we wouldn't likely be deeming what was happening as genocide.

"In Khartoum we met the lead U.N. investigator John Ralston, an experienced Australian police officer. He had set up an operational headquarters in the basement of the Khartoum Hilton. Here we learned about security and emergency procedures for ourselves and some background about the Sudanese government. We then split into three teams and headed to the Darfurian villages of El Fasher, El Geneina, and Nyala where we would live and work for the next couple of months. Our U.N. equipment consisted of Land Rover vehicles, blue flak jackets, helmets, and portable radios. As we flew over the country, we saw vast areas of nothing but desert, the remnants of burned-out villages, and huge, sprawling IDP camps set up on the very edges of villages, which hadn't been attacked.

"My partner, Muhammad Lejme, a forensic analyst from Tunisia, and I got off the plane at the El Geneina airport, which consisted of a dirt runway with a small building alongside it. We were picked up by fellow investigators Sylvan Roy, a lawyer from Canada, and Peter Stewart, a police officer from New Zealand. We drove through the small village, found our accommodations, unloaded our equipment, and then set to work right away. We began our search for people to interview by making contact with various humanitarian agencies that had been in Darfur for some time. We asked them questions such as which villages had been attacked and in which IDP camps the victims from those villages would be found. We were fortunate that many non-governmental agencies were very helpful in directing us. They were far more helpful than the other U.N. organizations that had been working in the area for a long time. The U.N. personnel had been told by their supervisors that they weren't to assist those of us from the inquiry as then they wouldn't appear impartial to the people of the town. Our interpreters, Racha and Abdul, were hired a few days later and turned out to be wonderful. However, they were both from Arab tribes, which caused difficulty with the victims' comfort level talking through them.

"Muhammad and I were extremely lucky with accommodations as we had rooms in the best U.N. guest house in town. This house wasn't fancy, just a very large clay two-storey building with multiple rooms. However, it was the only house in town with two real toilets and real showers. Although the water was usually cold, showers were a great luxury. Approximately 13 people lived in the guest house at a time, with the numbers fluctuating. I shared a room with another Canadian girl, and we each had a single metal-framed bed, with very little support left in the springs and a thin mattress on top. My bed had been used the previous week by Angelina Jolie, the U.N. ambassador for refugees, so I knew these accommodations were luxurious for this town.

"We had two local women who came to the house daily and cooked the meals, swept the dirt off the straw mats, hand-washed all our clothes, and folded them neatly when they dried. The all-inclusive rent cost $14 a day. The ladies usually created our meals around goat meat with a few vegetables and some bread. They enjoyed doing their cooking on an open fire. A small stove was in the kitchen, but they didn't like it. And because of the wind, we became accustomed to all meals including some gritty sand. We also had a little store directly across the street that supplied us with a few treats from home, including Coke, Laughing Cow brand processed cheese spread, and low-grade cans of tuna. These, along with some of the leftover morning bread, were the usual lunch for Muhammad and me as we were often outside of town for the entire day.

"We worked a full, long day because we wanted to complete as many interviews as possible in hopes of determining names of perpetrators and portraying a clear picture of what was happening. Muhammad and

I were picked up each morning at the gate of our house by our driver and knowledgeable assistant Mahamoud. He drove us to our makeshift office, which was a small outside courtyard behind a U.N. office. The U.N. compound had a check-in desk run by a hired local, and he would bring people to our interviewing area. We started out having to search out victims and witnesses, but within a few days everyone in the village and nearby knew that the investigators from the United Nations were in town and where we were working from, so people began showing up at the office entrance in large numbers.

"Everyone seemed to have a strong desire to tell us what horrible things they had survived or witnessed with the hope that we would make it stop. We also had some informants who hadn't been personally victimized but who knew about the government people involved and were able to supply documented proof. Within the town there were government spies and also the rogue Janjaweed, who drove through in army vehicles with mounted machine guns just to remind the villagers of their presence. As a result, the people wanting to talk to us would often leave their name with the guard at the office and then stay out of sight until they felt it safe to return and come in to see us. Our driver, Mahamoud, had always lived in El Geneina, so he was able to tell us who to trust and who were the Janjaweed, since to us they looked the same as any other villagers. Mahamoud would quickly point out the army-issue boots or hat that they were wearing and the fact that they weren't originally from this town.

"The victims' stories were much the same as what I had heard from the refugees in Chad. The government planes bombed, government vehicles with mounted machine guns drove through shooting, Janjaweed on horses with whips and guns rode through torturing, raping, and killing, and finally the entire village was burned to the ground. A few days later those who had survived and fled returned to bury the remains of their family members, friends, and neighbours.

"One young girl I interviewed will always stand out in my mind. Marion was 17 years old, tall and slim, and had the most beautiful bright smile. When she came to us to be interviewed, I noticed that she walked slowly with a very pronounced limp, yet she seemed to be continuously smiling. Marion told me about how her village had been attacked and she and her surviving family had moved to the closest IDP camp. A few days later she and two friends left the camp to get firewood to cook the evening meal. Because the camp was filled with thousands of people, the supply of firewood close by became scarce, and this meant walking for hours before finding a few twigs. As the girls walked, two Janjaweed men riding on horses started to chase them and attack them. The men were yelling at them to stop and lie down.

"Marion's two friends managed to run away, leaving the two men chasing Marion. The Janjaweed caught up to her and pushed her to the ground. They told her to lie still and take her clothes off. Marion refused, continued fighting, and attempted to run. The men became angry, and one of them pulled out his gun, shot her twice, and left her to die. Marion then showed me the scars on her leg from the bullets. She then smiled brightly and stated, 'They didn't spoil me. I didn't let them spoil me.' She had a permanently injured leg and would never run again or even walk properly. Of utmost importance to her and her culture, she hadn't been raped, which would have spoiled her chance of ever having a husband, along with losing the respect of her family and friends.

"After we interviewed a large number of people from in and around El Geneina, we began to travel to other villages and IDP camps. If we were informed of a large massacre, mass graves, and bomb evidence at a certain village, we would make our way to it. This sometimes occurred by driving through the desert for hours to reach the village, conducting as many interviews as possible, and then travelling back as quickly as possible to be back in El Geneina before the nine o'clock curfew, imposed because of lootings and killings of people driving after dark. If the village we needed to get to was too far to drive, we would book a plane to take us and on a few occasions would stay overnight in that village. We would often stay within the compound of another humanitarian organization or in the army camp of the African Union.

"We encountered problems instigated by the Sudanese government whenever we travelled away from El Geneina. They had hired humanitarian aid coordinators [HACs], who had the job of 'assisting,' or spying on, agencies, and they would accompany the workers when they travelled to other villages. Although we, as the investigators for the Darfur Inquiry, were to be exempt from that, we spent countless hours arguing with the HAC when he tried to board our plane or follow our trucks. The HAC we continuously locked horns with also always managed to make himself present when we went to interview the El Geneina police chief and some of the tribal leaders.

"While we were at the IDP camp outside the village of Masteri, I conducted the most difficult and emotional interview of all the hundreds I had done while investigating Darfur and, in fact, the most emotional in my 20 years of policing. We had been told that there had been multiple rapes committed in this area during the attacks. The IDP camp was filled with some 20,000 people, so getting privacy for interviews was very difficult. We settled on working inside an unused school compound in a couple of little rooms. As word got out that we were there, the victims started arriving, wanting to tell their stories.

"One woman, Miriam, about 30 years old, walked in by herself and sat on the ground among all the male tribal leaders and waited. I went out and told her it was going to be a long wait as we had people waiting inside, as well. She sat up very stoically with no emotion on her determined-looking face and said she would wait. She sat for four hours in the hot sun. She never moved, never went to the washroom, never asked for a drink of water. Nothing. When my interpreter and I brought her inside, she immediately started to tell her story, and for an hour and a half she talked and cried and I cried along with her.

"It was nearing the end of the day, and we had to rush to get back to El Geneina before curfew, but I wasn't leaving until she had a chance to tell us everything she needed to. She said, 'I know 18 of the women who were raped, but there were many more. I think about 50 in total. First, they raped the young girls and then us. I was raped by nine men. Every woman was raped by many men. All of us women were kept for six days from Saturday until Thursday at the wadi [river]. Five of the young girls who were raped went to the hospital for six months and then they died. I went to the hospital in Mornei and was there for 28 days. A female doctor from MSF [Médecins sans Frontières] France did surgery on me and removed things.' We believe she had a hysterectomy.

"This woman was so strong. Throughout her horrific story she called me sister and kept saying, 'Sister, thank you for coming. Thank you for saving us.' When she was done, she held on to me and we both cried, and I didn't want to let her go. I felt if I hugged her enough I could take away some of her pain. At the end I asked her, 'Are you concerned about your safety after talking to us and everyone seeing you come here and wait?' She looked me straight in the eye and said, 'No, it really doesn't matter. I want to die, anyway, but save the rest of us.' That's all she wanted from me, and I still haven't been able to make that happen.

"We also made a point of attempting to interview as many government officials and known Janjaweed members as we could. Even though I always used an interpreter for the interviews, I could tell from my experience as an investigator and trained interviewer when the story I was being told was lies. The big difference between hearing the true victims' stories and those perpetrators who were trying to portray themselves as victims was the report being about family members killed versus livestock being stolen.

"One morning a father and his two young daughters showed up at the house. They were from a village that was a three-hour walk away, and they had made that trip without food or water, the father carrying one daughter on his back. He had done this because he wanted us to hear what had happened to both his daughters by the Janjaweed and the police. The daughters were 10 and seven years old. Both had been gang-raped by Janjaweed while they were out gathering firewood. The 10-year-old was permanently injured from it and couldn't walk properly. Both girls had glazed-over, vacant stares from being severely traumatized, and they looked as if there was nothing left inside them. The girls told me about having their clothes ripped off and 'being spoiled.' Then their father talked of finding them both bleeding and bringing them to the police to make the mandatory report before they could go to a hospital. A female police officer took the girls into a locked room and told them to stop their lying and making trouble and go home. The police refused to make a report. The father travelled until he found a Médecins sans Frontières doctor who tended to them. I knew those young girls would never receive any kind of counselling and would likely never be happy children again. I was so impressed with the father who refused to shun them or treat them with shame as many others would have.

"In mid-January 2005 we had completed our field interviews and flew back to Geneva, so each team could piece their portion of the report together. Muhammad and I had completed over 100 interviews and had named 48 GOS members and Janjaweed whom witnesses had seen committing crimes or had documented information proving they had ordered the attacks and killings. Each team put their portion of the report together in a different style, as there had been no laid-out guidelines. We stayed in Geneva for another week to be available for questions from the commissioners about our findings, but they asked very little."

The commission of inquiry submitted a full report on its findings in January 2005 to the U.N. secretary general and found that while the Sudanese government hadn't pursued a policy of genocide, both its forces and allied Janjaweed militias had carried out "indiscriminate attacks, including the killing of civilians, torture, enforced disappearances, destruction of villages, rape and other forms of sexual violence, pillaging, and forced displacement." It concluded that although there was no evidence that a genocidal policy has been pursued in Darfur by government authorities directly or through the militias under their control, "it should not be taken in any way as detracting from the gravity of the crimes perpetrated in that region." The panel also noted that the rebel forces in Darfur were responsible for possible war crimes, including the murder of civilians and pillage, and recommended that the Security Council refer its dossier on the situation in Darfur to the International Criminal Court.

While one war was ongoing, another concluded. On January 9, 2005, the decades-long civil war ended, and in an event that marked a turning point in the history of Sudan, the GOS, represented by Vice-President Ali Osman Taha, and the SPLM/A, represented by Chairman Dr. John Garang, signed the Comprehensive Peace Agreement in Nairobi. The old fox Garang had survived coups and assassination attempts and was sworn in as vice-president of Sudan. Aware that he had been carrying the hopes and aspirations of most Southern Sudanese, the once-aloof guerrilla leader had transformed himself from guerrilla fighter to elder statesman of a new Sudan. "There is a new sense of dignity and open-ness about him," noted Peter Verney, veteran editor of *Sudan Update and Independent Information Services,* "or perhaps it is just PR. With Garang, one never knew."

The CPA included agreements on outstanding issues remaining from the Machakos Protocol and had provisions on security arrangements, power-sharing in Khartoum, some autonomy for the South, and more equitable distribution of economic resources, including oil. Sudan would now be ruled by the Government of National Unity (GONU), made up of the former ruling party, the National Congress, the SPLM/A, and others, with a semi-autonomous Government of Southern Sudan. In the CPA's four protocols, two framework agreements, and two annexes, the parties acknowledged that, taken together, the documents were a model for solving the wider problem of conflict and that, if successfully implemented, the CPA would help create a solid basis for unity. A six-and-a-half-year interim period was agreed to (until July 2011), during which interim institutions would govern the country and international monitoring mechanisms would be established. At the end of the period the people of Southern Sudan would vote in an internationally moni-tored referendum to confirm the unity of Sudan or to vote for secession.

With Resolution 1590 the Security Council established the United Nations Mission in Sudan on March 24, 2005. It was to be tasked with supporting the implementation of the CPA, facilitating the voluntary return of IDPs and, without infringing on the responsibilities of the Sudanese government, to "coordinate international efforts toward the protection of civilians, with particular attention to vulnerable groups, including internally displaced persons, returning refugees, and women and children."

The interim National Constitution had been signed, and the Ceasefire Political Commission was about to be established in August to oversee the implementation of the CPA when, on July 30, 2005, returning from meeting with the Ugandan president, John Garang was killed in a mysterious helicopter crash. His death was seen as a major setback to the peace efforts and caused IDPs around Khartoum and other cities to riot.

* * *

"My program with Sudan was twofold," says former Prime Minister Paul Martin. "I wanted the AU to use its troops. I knew there would be fewer problems with al-Bashir if the AU was in the lead. Second, Africa has a lot of fragile states. But it has the capability to provide manpower — peacekeepers — if we embarked on a training program for them and provided the logistics."

In March 2005, Martin met with President Bush at his ranch at Waco, Texas. "I said to Bush, 'Look, we're going to go into Kandahar, but our priority is Darfur. We will step up to the mark and put a lot more troops and equipment in, but you have to come in behind us over Sudan. You are 10 times bigger.' He was very reluctant to do that, but I said, 'We'll take the lead.' I've got to say that George Bush kept his word. I wanted Canada to get credit for this."

The news that Martin had pledged an "aid package" for Darfur on May 14, 2005, was greeted with surprise and suspicion. Along with CDN$170 million in aid, Canada was to provide airlift capabilities, some old military equipment for the African Union observers in Darfur, and also up to 150 Canadian Forces personnel. The shock came from military analysts, since Canada had always deployed overseas under a multilateral banner — the United Nations, NATO, or ISAF. This would be the first time it was acting without coalition partners. As Prime Minister John A. Macdonald had pointed out in another century, sending Canadian troops to Sudan wasn't in the national interest, and the Opposition suspected a political motive.

The Liberal minority government was then facing imminent defeat in Parliament and to survive needed the votes of three independent MPs: Carolyn Parrish, Chuck Cadman, and David Kilgour. The last had just returned from Darfur and told reporters that Canada's response to the Sudan issue would determine his decision to support the government in any non-confidence vote. When he met with the prime minister earlier that week, the Edmonton West MP told the media he had come with a shopping list for Darfur: medicine, food, helicopters, and "boots on the ground," at least 500 Canadian troops. Parliament Hill buzzed with rumours that Martin was brokering a deal with Kilgour for his support in the upcoming confidence vote. The minority government was fighting for its life, and like it or not, Sudan had become part of Canada's domestic politics.

"Kilgour had been in the Chrétien Cabinet and supported me for the party leadership," recalls Martin. "I had read some of his stuff and was very impressed. However, he was opposed to the issue of same-sex marriage, and I made the government's position very clear to him and said that if he wanted to be in my Cabinet, he would have to support us. He refused, so I didn't put him in. That created a problem between us, and it was only a matter of time before he left the Liberal Party. As you know, he had already left the Conservatives. Well, he was very upset and chose the day that I made the announcement of the contribution to come and see me and Senator Dallaire. He said, 'You've got to send 500 Canadian troops to Darfur.' I said no, that I wanted the AU to take the lead and that I would rather pay for 5,000 African troops than send 500 Canadians to Sudan. 'If you don't do that,' Kilgour said, 'I'm not going to vote for you.' I replied, 'Fine.' It was clear that there was tension between us, so later I asked Dallaire to go and speak to him. He tried, came back, and said he couldn't deal with him. Kilgour then went public and said Martin wants to buy my vote. He was just looking for some personal publicity."

While her country welcomed the $170 million, Sudanese Ambassador Taha said, her government firmly objected to non-African soldiers in Darfur. When Foreign Affairs had called her three days before to tell her about Martin's announcement, she asked him to call Sudanese President al-Bashir first. The GOS had been fully advised, the Prime Minister's Office said, and not only had Martin spoken to President al-Bashir 24 hours before but Canada's chargé d'affaires in Khartoum had briefed Sudan's minister of state for foreign affairs, as well.

The Sudanese ambassador wasn't buying any of it. "This will not be decided by Mr. Kilgour or the Canadian government," Ms. Taha fumed. "It will be decided by all parties that are involved in Sudan." When asked if the Canadian troops would be armed, Canada's Department of National Defence would neither confirm nor deny it, and Foreign Affairs acknowledged there was no Memorandum of Understanding between Canada and Sudan that allowed Canadian Forces to carry weapons there. The deployment would be covered under "status of mission" agreements between Sudan and the African Union and the United Nations.

On May 19, Paul Martin's minority government survived two confidence votes in the House with a razor-thin margin. Kilgour didn't vote for the Liberals, but since Belinda Stronach "crossed the floor," his voted was cancelled out. After a couple of more near-death experiences, Martin's government was brought down by the issues of same-sex marriage and the report released by Justice John Gomery in November 2005. "We should have/could have done more for Sudan," says the former prime minister. "There is a massive Chinese presence there now. They're everywhere — building roads, employing the locals, for example. The Sudanese will tell you, 'You guys talk, but the Chinese do.' We are just turning our backs on Africa. It's a tragedy."

9

MAPLE LEAF MILITARY

"**M**any of the roads we travelled on were not confirmed clear of mines," Lieutenant Dave Coulter, UNMIS, recalls. "The main concern in this case was that the seasonal rains and floods would bring mines out of the hills and onto the roads. This doesn't sound possible until you see the floods during the rainy season starting in May. Some areas were cleared of mines on the road only. These were commonly marked by lines of stones on either side of the road. These stones were painted white and/or heaped on top of each other. Once, we stopped between two such lines of white stones to wait for the back of our convoy to catch up. A civilian convoy driver jumped out of his car to take a leak in the mined area. I pointed out the stones and gently suggested he get back in his car. He complied without complaint."

The United Nations Mine Action Office (UNMAO) estimated in 2007 that less than 9 percent of the mines sown in 21 of 26 states in Sudan had been surveyed and cleared. This was especially so in the conflict areas of the Nuba Mountains, Abyei, and the Blue Nile. De-mining and road rehabilitation in Sudan were being implemented through contributions from 15 countries that in 2006 totalled CDN$46,914,250, with Canada contributing $2,192,035. The CPA required both sides to turn in maps indicating where mines had been laid, and the Sudanese Army provided UNMAO with some, but the SPLM/A never systematically recorded where their minefields were, relying on collective memory instead. Then, in the course of the war, areas were repeatedly mined, cleared, and later re-mined. If there was a discernible pattern, it was that the SPLM/A had put anti-vehicle mines on the roads to restrict the movement of government convoys, while the GOS used antipersonnel mines defensively to protect its garrison towns.

Mines apart, large quantities of unexploded ordnance (UXO) and abandoned explosive ordnance (AXO) also littered the countryside — both UXO and AXO not only around abandoned military compounds, separation/disengagement lines, and battlefields, but also close to wells and bridges and near villages and schools, severely restricting aid from reaching needy communities and the return of the thousands of postwar IDPs. Now sensitive to age and weather, the ammunition requires little interference to explode. Since 2002, more than 1,800 mine and ordnance casualties have been reported, most in vehicles or as a result of children handling them. The country's borders with Chad, the Democratic Republic of Congo, Eritrea, Ethiopia, Libya, and Uganda are also heavily mined, and the new Government of Southern Sudan (GOSS) is reluctant to co-operate in de-mining the Ugandan border for good reason. In September 2005, units of the Lord's Resistance Army moved across the Nile, targeting communities in Southern Sudan, armed and encouraged, it was said, by Khartoum.[1]

Major George Boyuk was commissioned in 1995 with the Princess Patricia's Canadian Light Infantry (PPCLI) in Calgary. When interviewed, he was J3 Regional Operations 1 Desk Officer (Africa) for Canadian Expeditionary Force Command (CEFCOM) in Ottawa where he had been posted in the summer of 2007. Almost a monthly commuter between Canada and Sudan, Boyuk was responsible for the coordination and oversight of Operation Augural, the Canadian Forces (CF) mission in Darfur in support of the African Mission in Sudan (AMIS). When AMIS became the African Mission in Darfur (AMID), the major oversaw Operation Saturn, the CF mission in Sudan. Prior to CEFCOM, with the Third Battalion, Princess Patricia's Canadian Light Infantry Battle Group, he studied the situation in Sudan in detail as a potential area of operations.

"Regarding the background of Operation Augural, it is difficult to encapsulate seven rotations," Boyuk says, "but here goes. On June 4, 2004, a Status of Mission Agreement [SOMA] on the establishment and management of the Ceasefire Commission [CFC] in the Darfur area of Sudan was signed between the AU and the GOS, allowing for the initial deployment of AU troops into Sudan. In a letter dated December 31, 2004, the AU expressed its appreciation to the AU partners, including Canada, and formally requested that Canada and other partners in the Darfur peace process provide expert planners with specialist skills for deployment in Khartoum and El Fasher as well as with the Darfur Integrated Task Force [DITF] in Addis Ababa. On January 24, 2005, the office of the Canadian embassy in Khartoum sent a diplomatic note to the AU asking that the privileges and immunities of SOMA be extended to Canadian officials who might enter Sudan and who might be attached to AMIS. In a response dated February 8, 2005, the African Union confirmed that Canadian officials would be afforded the same terms and conditions as other participants as outlined in SOMA between the AU and the GOS. The CF support to AMIS was allocated the name Operation Augural.

"Operation Augural/Task Force Addis Ababa [TFAA] 'Roto 0' commenced on November 15, 2004, with a mission to support AU planning activities with regard to force generation and force employment of AMIS in the Darfur region. Initially, CF support to AMIS consisted of two staff officers to provide strategic planning assistance at the DITF HQ and air operations planning assistance to the AU HQ, both in Addis Ababa. Subsequent rotations would see the provision of experts to provide security planning advice to the AU HQ and air operations planning to Mission HQ in Khartoum. Much-needed contracting specialists for DITF and AMIS MHQ followed suit in addition to establishing a liaison officer to the Canadian embassy in Addis Ababa.

"Operation Augural staff also assisted Foreign Affairs and DND reps in the development of CF assistance packages to the AU. CF personnel also played significant roles in the establishment of the Joint Logistics Operations Centre [JLOC] downrange in El Fasher, Darfur, with the deployment of two logistics specialists and the Information Analysis Centre [IAC] in Addis Ababa through the deployment of key military and civilian personnel for a short time." The initial equipment provided to the IAC was donated by Canada upon transition of TFAA to TF

Darfur/Operation Saturn CANCON UNAMID in January 2008.

Initially referred to as "some old military equipment," 100 Grizzly and five Husky AVGPs were loaned to AMIS for a year to assist the AU in moving its troops quickly and safely. Working out of Zam Zam (just outside El Fasher), CF NCOs became a staple of the mission to train Troop Contributing Countries (TCC) gunners and drivers for the AVGPs. "They also had a maintenance schedule," says Lieutenant-Colonel Pickell. "They went out with the AU drivers and kept the Grizzlies up to speed, doing inspections on the vehicles just to see that the patrols would continue."

With the signing of the Darfur Peace Agreement, and later the adoption of United Nations Security Resolution 1769, Canada continued its support to AMIS vis-à-vis invaluable mentoring and advising at the strategic, operational, and tactical levels, the last with respect to the proper employment of the Canadian AVGPs.

* * *

There are no in-flight movies, complimentary champagne, or attractive, smartly dressed cabin crew at SkyLink Aviation. The company's aircraft have been riddled with bullets from Kosovo to Cambodia — one was even shot down by a missile in Angola. It is hardly surprising that SkyLink's motto is "Doing difficult jobs in difficult places."

The Canadian Forces and SkyLink are old friends. The company has provided the Department of National Defence with heavy-lift capability for years, most recently to meet its commitments in Afghanistan. Sturdy Russian- and Ukrainian-leased Ilyushin 76s transported CF equipment to Kandahar directly from Edmonton, and before Ottawa bought C-17s from Boeing, SkyLink proposed an economical strategic airlift interim solution to the Department of National Defence, even basing its aircraft at CFB Trenton to ensure availability on short notice. Flying disaster-relief supplies into Kosovo in 1999, evacuating 12,000 Lebanese Canadians out of Cyprus, and operating a Mi-26 (the world's largest helicopter) to get drilling equipment into the Mackenzie River Valley, SkyLink might as well have a motto that says: "We fly anything, anywhere, anytime." Run by Walter Arbib and Surjit Babra from an office on Yonge Street in Toronto, SkyLink Aviation essentially finds aircraft and crews quickly and efficiently. Sadly, when business is good for the company, there is a disaster, natural or man-made, somewhere in the world.

SkyLink's aircraft specialize in payload that is outsize (a 90-foot-tall ancient obelisk returned to Ethiopia from Italy), precious (sensitive sniffer dogs to assist at an earthquake in Turkey), and historic (potato seeds to North Korea, the first Western plane to land in that starving nation). Described as having a head for business and a heart for philanthropy, the Libya-born Arbib professes that he is in the charter and logistical trade to make money. "But what the news says is happening [in Darfur] is exactly what's happening," Arbib says. "People are using different terms [to describe it], but what I have to say is there's a need to give help." In 2006, using his own funds, with assistance from friends in Jewish groups and humanitarian agencies, Arbib shipped more than US$400,000 worth of antibiotics, de-worming medicine, and penicillin to the camps in Sudan.[2]

SkyLink arrived in Darfur in October 2004 and grew rapidly from five to 25 Mi-8 helicopters (19 T model and six MTVs) and two Antonov An-74 fixed-wing freighters, the former based in El Fasher, Nyala, and Geneina, the latter shuttling between Khartoum and those bases with millions of gallons of jet and diesel fuel. The CF people who fly SkyLink aircraft remember fondly that the crews are mostly Russian and Ukrainian, but they also have some Moldovans and a few others from the far reaches of the former Soviet Union.

Bob Waring, a retired CF transportation officer commissioned from the ranks, did U.N. tours in Cyprus, the former Yugoslavia, Haiti, and the First Gulf War. After years of service in Angola, Darfur, and Egypt, he knows Africa well. Bestowing on himself the title "Chief of the Darfur Air Force," the SkyLink general manager achieved almost legendary status during the company's four-year contract in Sudan, leaving on April 1, 2008, to take over the aviation firm's operation in Kandahar. Every member of the Canadian Forces who served in Sudan is unanimous in their admiration and gratitude to Waring and his colleague, Tracey Munday.

The SkyLink team, says a CF soldier, surmounted significant operational and political obstacles, local complacency and micro management at the mission level, dangerous rebel and GOS interference, attempted hijackings of aircraft, and pilots held up at gunpoint to ensure that equipment and supplies got to where they had to get.

"Bottom line is that they performed way beyond the call of duty," says CF Major George Boyuk, "bending over backward to support AMIS troops and affording the Canadians in Darfur an extra layer of security. We knew that if anything ever happened, be it a serious casualty downrange or, in one instance, facilitating the precautionary withdrawal of an unarmed CF back to Khartoum in October 2007 when the rebel forces had massed in El Fasher and were threatening to attack headquarters, SkyLink would be there for us."

When asked about his exploits in Sudan, Bob Waring eloquently says, "God knows it sure as hell wasn't the Hospital Administration SOI Air Ops who ran things!"

By mid-2005 it was clear that AU troops sent to Darfur were being overwhelmed. Expecting that the Ceasefire Agreement would be observed by all parties and that its mission was temporary, the African Union was suffering from "mission creep." Far from being stabilized by the AU troops, Darfur was descending into another Somalia situation as rebels and warlords recruited private armies to extort vehicles, fuel, and radios from aid agencies and terrorized the local population. The influx of thousands of refugees from Chad hadn't helped, either. Although the AU force had been increased to 7,000 soldiers (Senator Roméo Dallaire thought that a multinational force of up to 44,000 troops was more realistic to patrol Darfur), it lacked mobility, communications, and peace-keeping training.

However, the AU force's weaknesses didn't just entail a lack of secure communications (AMIS Internet connections were on Yahoo), an over-reliance on contracted logistics, and an insufficient degree of peacekeeping inexperience. "The biggest problem with the AU is that it didn't have the money to look after its forces," says Lieutenant-Colonel Paul Pickell, commander of Operation Augural from December 2006 to June 2007. "Money was always a big issue. There were a lot of delays in paying the soldiers and police to the point where operations weren't taking place because soldiers weren't willing to risk their lives, not knowing if they would ever be paid for what they were doing. They were also lightly armed. The African Union basically deployed foot soldiers, no tanks, no armour, so that was why Canada's contribution — the AVGPs — was so essential. As lightly armed infantry, they couldn't protect the unarmed observers who were there to monitor the ceasefire, let alone the thousands of refugees that its 'safe havens' attracted, and for which they had no mandate to protect at all. The AU civilian police actually operated in the IDP camps. They were there to restore local order and assist the civilians, but again they weren't as heavily armed as the rebels. There is a lot of criminal activity in Darfur, and the AU was reluctant to get involved. Not just the rebels, but drugs, aid convoys hijacked, and the AU troops didn't have the mandate or the will to put their own lives at risk."

So hamstrung were the AU troops that when they encountered rebels and bandits, they were under orders to inform AMIS headquarters in Addis Ababa and wait for a decision before taking action. Lightly armed, demoralized, unpaid, and isolated, the green-bereted soldiers were a joke to the prowling Janjaweed with their RPGs and brand-new SUVs, both supplied by the Sudanese government in Khartoum. The AU soldiers needed helicopters for mobility, and Rwanda's government warned that it would withdraw its forces if better logistical support wasn't forthcoming. The CDN$1.4 million in very basic military equipment, including helmets and protective vests, that Canada had provided was welcome, but by now Western "donor fatigue," the silver bullet that kills all international good intentions, had set in.

The United States had promised US$50 million to support AMIS at the donor conference in May 2005, but by November 2006, the U.S. Congress had removed the money from the Foreign Operations Appropriations Bill. Responsible for the salaries of AU troops, the European Union had suspended payments for months because the correct paperwork showing accountability hadn't been done. There wasn't money for interpreters or fuel, aviation or vehicle (essential for the observers to monitor the ceasefire), and the African countries were unwilling to send any more of their soldiers into such an untenable situation. It was expected that when Sudan took over the rotating presidency of the African Union in January 2006, it would do its best to stall any progress.

"The average African soldier was a good soldier," says Lieutenant-Colonel Pickell, "who just wanted to do his job. I believe there was a leadership issue, a real reluctance to come out of their comfort zone to enforce a mandate to protect the IDPs. 'We're under-equipped, we're out of fuel' — they had many different excuses as to why that wasn't happening. We [the Canadians] were often pushing them — you need to establish a presence patrol outside the camp to show the people of Darfur that you're there to help them. I can't say that always happened. They didn't want to take casualties, which is clearly understandable. No country wants to take casualties. But the reality is if you're in there to do a job, then there's a job to be done."

The AMIS troops had become targets themselves in the conflict. Fourteen AMIS soldiers had been killed, and entire patrols were kidnapped by the SLM/A and the JEM. Humanitarian agencies also complained that children as young as 11 years old and women at IDP camps were being approached by AU soldiers who demanded sex. In September 2005, when two AU troops died of AIDS-related illnesses, widespread fear was provoked in the region.

After the Canadian Forces issued a requirement for an armoured vehicle general purpose (AVGP) in 1974 to equip both regular and militia units, the Swiss MOWAG Piranha 6 x 6 won the evaluation. Licence-built by General Motors Canada Diesel Division in three versions (Grizzly, Husky, and Cougar), the last MOWAG AVGP rolled off the line in 1982. Each version has in common a maximum speed of 60 miles per hour on roads and six miles per hour in water and is armoured up to 10 millimetres maximum for protection from shell splinters. (Although not useful in Darfur, each AVGP was fully amphibious and could be propelled by two propellers mounted in the rear of the vehicles behind the third road wheel on each side.) The Grizzly version has a manually traversed Cadillac Gage turret armed with .50 calibre and 7.62 mm machine guns mounted coaxially.[3] It has a crew of three, can carry an additional seven troops, and allows for entry and exit for the infantry by two doors in the hull rear. The maintenance-and-recovery version, the Husky, has a roof-mounted hydraulic crane and is crewed by three. Both vehicles were put through the Wheeled LAV Life Extension Program in 1999 but were to be kept for reserve units only.

"We were getting rid of the Grizzly and the Cougar fleet," says Lieutenant-Colonel Pickell, "so this was an extra asset that the government of Canada had to loan. They can be used to defend camps or convoy escorts or for patrolling. It was to give the AU a capability with the rebel forces. Unfortunately, many times the rebels were better armed than the AU. Some of their heavy weapons were taken directly from the Sudanese Army. The vehicle of choice for the rebels in Darfur is the Toyota Land Cruiser with a heavy machine gun mounted on the back. Since they're 'soft-skinned,' taking one out with a Grizzly's .50 calibre machine gun shouldn't be an issue. But a lot of it was a 'willingness to use' by the African Union. I think that they were uncomfortable using the Grizzly. They were afraid it would break down, and it was very odd to see their unwillingness to patrol for long distance. There seems to be the African mentality to want to ride in the open air in the back of a truck that offered no protection whatsoever. So it was a bit difficult to understand."

Referred to "as some old military equipment," the 100 Grizzly and five Husky AVGPs were loaned to AMIS for a year initially to assist the African Union in moving its troops quickly and safely. The vehicles were shipped by sea to Dakar, Senegal, where an Intermediate Staging Base and Training Centre (ISBTC) was established by the Canadian Forces. Here, at Stage One, the vehicles were prepared for the final leg of their journey to Sudan by air. Stage Two consisted of setting up a training centre in Thiès (70 miles outside Dakar) where in a train-the-trainer program the Canadian Forces taught AU soldiers to operate the AVGPs.

The biggest thing Sergeant Chad McNamara, the "course warrant" for the driver operator course, learned was how to be very patient. "Things in Africa don't happen as quickly as in Canada," he says. Captain Geoff Hampton adds: "It was a very challenging mission. We were teaching to a wide range of students, including Muslims and Christians who spoke different languages, such as Swahili, but we were able to accommodate everyone's unique status." In late September 2005, with more than 150

AU troops from Senegal, Nigeria, and Rwanda trained on operating the AVGPs, Stage Two was completed.

The Department of National Defence issued an invitation to tender on August 15, 2005, for air freight services to carry the AVGPs, stores, and ammunition from Senegal to Sudan in support of Operation Augural. The CDN$15.5 million contract was awarded to SkyLink Aviation on September 27, and it was expected that it would take about a month to move all vehicles, spare parts, and ammunition to El Fasher.[4] Once there, the AVGPs would be maintained by an arrangement with the U.S. State Department and a contract with Lockheed Martin–owned Pacific Architects and Engineers.

The Sudanese government said that it feared rebels would get their hands on the AVGPs, so the GOS stonewalled the arrival of the vehicles as long as it could — "It was death by a thousand cuts," commented one CF officer — and it would be November 17 before the first shipment was on its way. Watching the two SkyLink Il-76 transports carrying a half-dozen armoured vehicles lift off for Sudan, Major Mark Nicholls, who handled the move, said, "As of today, everything went swimmingly. We've had no real problems to speak of. But we're always prepared for the worst." The aircraft refuelled in Libya before proceeding to El Fasher. There they were unloaded, then turned around and flew back to Senegal to start the process all over. Nicholls worried that the GOS would still slow everything down. "There was hope that we were going to start an air bridge about two months ago," he said at the time. "That didn't happen. So, yes, everyone's anxious to see when that first vehicle rolls off in El Fasher that everything goes well."

Intensive diplomatic lobbying brought about the Darfur Peace Agreement (DPA) on May 5, 2006, signed in Abuja by the GOS and the SLM/A, encompassing economic, structural, and security arrangements for Darfur. But since three of the rebel groups — the JEM, a hold-out faction of the SLM/A, and the Sudan Federal Democratic Alliance (SFDA) — remained out of the accord to form their own organization, the National Redemption Front (NRF), and "reject the faulty process" of the DPA, the ceasefire had little effect on curbing violence. On the contrary, the level of hostility rose and the number of violent situations in Northern Darfur multiplied, causing the non-signatories to view their "expulsion" from the DPA as linked to an expected GOS/SLM/A offensive. Aid workers reported that tensions in the IDP camps escalated significantly and that Arab militias were increasingly active throughout all of Darfur. On August 15, 2006, for example, 300 Janjaweed wearing GOS military uniforms attacked villages at Shakrin. The next day GOS vehicles and 500 Janjaweed (again in GOS army uniforms) on horseback moved near Kulus to ambush vehicles. On August 18 they raided an IDP camp close to El Danein, killing 10 and wounding seven inhabitants.

General Erwin Rommel would have understood the situation well. In the Second World War his armoured columns, defeated by a lack of fuel, had ground to a halt in their push to take Egypt. After that the Desert Fox relied on captured British fuel supplies, which sustained him throughout the North African campaign. While the signing of the DPA allowed the GOS and the SLM/A to consolidate their own fuel resources, both AMIS and the NRF were critically short of fuel. There had been a recent large-scale battle between the GOS and the rebels in nearby Sayid, which had left the already resource-poor NRF even more depleted of combat supplies. The pressure on the non-signatories to amass fuel intensified with each day their enemies rearmed. First the NRF banned U.N. flights from "their" areas, citing the "expulsion" reason and the belief that AMIS was "biased" in favour of the GOS and the SLM/A. The NRF knew this measure would hinder air mobility and reconnaissance of potential ambush areas.

Since AMIS had no stockpiles in El Fasher, fuel and air mobility were vital, especially in the August rainy season. If its fuel convoys from Khartoum were attacked, a critical link would be broken, which would hamper future patrols. On August 19, a convoy of 27 fuel tankers was on the main highway from Khartoum, via Kordofan, to El Fasher. It was protected by four Buffalo soft-skinned vehicles, each with 22 Rwandan Protection Force (PF) soldiers sitting in the back bed on bench seats facing outward. At 7:30 a.m. the convoy was ambushed by 15 "technicals" (soft-skinned Land Cruiser–type 4 x 4s) equipped with mounted heavy machine guns (HMGs). With NRF painted on the sides of their vehicles, the ambushers made no attempt to hide their identity. They were also armed with anti-aircraft guns, mortars, and lethal 106 mm recoilless anti-tank guns. The escort patrol initially thought the National Redemption Front vehicles were GOS until one of them drove to the front of the convoy to cut off escape. All doubt was dispelled when the NRF opened fire on the PF vehicles, taking care not to hit the tankers but easily recognizing the positions of the Buffaloes in the convoy. The PF soldiers dismounted and returned fire on the NRF, which made the rebels advance. In a prolonged firefight, the convoy PF fought the ambushers off, though a few were wounded.

During the battle, the NRF was reinforced by more technicals until it easily outnumbered and outgunned the PF. Meanwhile the airmobile Quick Relief Force (QRF) was having difficulty deploying because the GOS wouldn't let armed PF on the tarmac. The problem took an hour to resolve. Then, when the QRF was in the helicopter at last, the pilot wouldn't fly due to the explosive ammunition onboard. The QRF finally took off at 8:30 a.m. but was stood down when the locations of friendly and enemy forces couldn't be determined and the presence of enemy HMGs was confirmed. The land QRF from Zam Zam included Canadian AVGPs, some of which got stuck during the ground movement. They arrived at the scene at 9:20 and immediately engaged the NRF. However, thanks to weapon malfunctions, the QRF AVGPs became vulnerable to the NRF's 106s. After being temporarily immobilized due to tire damage from a 106, one AVGP rammed an NRF vehicle in self-defence and was destroyed by the resulting conflagration.

The land QRF secured the ambush site, and after reinforcement by the air QRF, pursued the rebels in the general direction of Sayid. The QRF exchanged fire with the NRF and is believed to have inflicted a number of casualties. Medevac arrived at approximately 1:30 p.m. and took away the injured. The aircraft shut down for about 20 minutes to load and get the wounded stable. The second damaged AVGP had to be abandoned at a GOS checkpoint near Kouma.

In a scene out of one of Mel Gibson's Mad Max movies, the 27 tankers escaped as best they could. Three made it to El Fasher, seven others eluded capture eventually, but the remaining 17 were seized by the NRF. Later, 10 of the tankers, drained of fuel, were recovered by AMIS. Some of the released and/or escaped tanker drivers noted that their captors spoke French and had an accent associated with Chad (during the initial ambush, the PF had also heard French spoken by the attackers), indicating that the NRF was linked to Chad.

There had been several previous attacks on AMIS fuel convoys, specifically the capture of one in Sector VI (next to Sector I) in which a South African patrol was outnumbered, surrounded, and subsequently surrendered without inflicting casualties on its foes. Previous convoys had been seized by armed parties by a show of force or by firing over the heads of PF soldiers. As one CF officer says, "I don't think the raiders wanted to kill anybody from AMIS, but I don't think they were bothered by it, either."

The shooting wasn't confined just to Darfur; the signing of the CPA didn't usher in an era of peace and security in the South, either. "Fog of war," says Major Greg Penner, CEFCOM. "No one really knew anything. No one really knew what to do. At first it was simply a matter of ensuring we weren't targets. Over time we moved from confusion to action." Malakal had been a Southern garrison town for the Sudanese Army during the civil war, but by 2006, as part of the autonomous Southern region, it now held SPLM/A soldiers, who mostly weren't local but from Bahr El Ghazal. On November 26, 2006, when a firefight erupted with a Northern militia group, the Northern combatants took shelter in the former Sudanese Army garrison and were surrounded by the SPLM/A troops, who began a siege. The next day the Sudanese Army arrived with tanks and shelled Malakal, inflicting heavy civilian casualties. As fighting escalated into full warfare between the Northern Sudanese militia and the SPLM/A, delegations from Khartoum, Juba, and the United Nations arrived to help defuse the situation. Eventually, a ceasefire was arranged, with all forces returning to their original positions. By then U.N. officials had estimated that 150 people had been killed, with about 400 to 500 wounded. There were also concerns about corpses contaminating the Nile, a major water source for the population.

The sole Canadian U.N. military observer in Malakal at the time was Major Penner, who found himself "in places and times where quick decisions and small patrol teams were needed. At first it was to locate and evacuate a wounded U.N. civilian from his home after the clashes began. I did first aid and drove the ambulance through the battle lines between the Sudanese Army and the SPLM/A troops. While en route back to the U.N. hospital, we were persuaded by some of the local fighters to aid a badly injured soldier from the South. The doctor at the hospital assured me that had we not evacuated this soldier he would have died soon after. As it became apparent that we were in the middle of a deepening crisis, we adapted to the situation. Our teams collected U.N. civilians from their homes and prepared them for relocation, and we moved into the Protection Force camps away from the direct lines of fire. Over time, and as we gained more situational awareness, it was possible to start addressing the causes of the fighting, engage the Joint Military Co-operation Committee, and sit down with the local military commanders. Eventually, the U.N. force commander came down to conduct the negotiations personally.

"As the days passed, the fighting ebbed and flowed but eventually stopped and the cleanup began. The United Nations assisted with the disposal of human remains that were found throughout the town. We started to assert ourselves with 'presence patrols' into areas where the fighting continued to calm things down. Our presence was visibly and warmly received by the local community. I dismounted on one patrol into the centre of town to meet people and pinpoint areas of continued fighting. Everyone seemed happy to see us and eager to point out where the unexploded ordnance was lying around in the roads or yards. In one case we found an unexploded RPG stuck in the mud wall of a home with about 11 children. There were many others.

"It was a strange and surreal time. Eventually, we returned to our houses in the community to assure ourselves we weren't scared to live in the town after the fighting. I was apprehensive during the first few days back in our brick house. We returned to find it riddled with bullets — our front door was ventilated. A hut not far away was still burning, and ammunition was 'cooking off' inside. Several bodies were still lying in the road not far from our home. We were happy to find that our pet cat, Lissie, and our dog, Sam, managed to survive the crisis. They were cowering behind our generator when my German housemates and

I returned. Eventually, they both stopped shaking. I came home intact. For that I'm very grateful."

For his actions in the battle, Major Penner received a Mentioned in Dispatches in October 2007.

On December 3, 2006, U.N. Secretary General Kofi Annan blamed the GOS for Darfur's slow spiral into chaos. "They are refusing to let the international community come in and assist," he maintained. "They will be held responsible for what is happening and what happens." Some progress was made by Governor Bill Richardson of New Mexico who, acting for the Save Darfur Coalition in January 2007, negotiated a 60-day ceasefire. Richardson even got President al-Bashir to consider allowing U.N. peacekeepers into the region. The New Mexico governor was supported by President George W. Bush, who announced further sanctions against Sudan, listing 31 companies doing business with the country and making it illegal for any U.S. citizen or firm to do business with it.

Mohammed Hamdan, one of the leaders of the estimated 20,000 Janjaweed who controlled most of Southern Darfur, confirmed what had always been suspected: that his men received direct orders and heavy weaponry from Khartoum. Hamdan had met al-Bashir twice, once at the Sudanese president's home to obtain his orders to carry out ethnic-cleansing campaigns in Um Sidr and Kiryari in Northern Darfur after they were taken by Darfur rebels. On March 14, 2007, in front of a British television crew, his men showed off their Sudanese Army identity cards, rocket launchers, Chinese-made heavy artillery, and a fleet of 126 brand-new Toyota Land Cruisers. "The hardware that we have?" Hamdan said to the crew. "Where did we get it from? Do you think we just 'magicked' it out of the air? It belongs to the government. Even the weapons, the cars, all that you see, we got it from the government."

Naturally, Hamdan refuted all accusations that his men were involved in atrocities in Darfur, including mass rape and murder. In fact, he insisted, he had refused to carry out government orders to attack civilian areas, arguing that the Sudanese government, having used him and his men to fight its battles, were now making them scapegoats for atrocities committed by others and excluding them from the political process.

Resentful, the Janjaweed militia men were said to want proportional representation at peace talks.

Officials from the U.N. Security Council visited Khartoum in June 2007 to get acceptance for a hybrid U.N.-AU peacekeeping force. When the Security Council achieved its aim, it unanimously adopted Resolution 1769, which led to the authorization of the United Nations–African Union Mission in Darfur (UNAMID). To augment the embattled AU soldiers in Darfur, 20,000 international troops commanded by General Luther Agwai of Nigeria were to be deployed by January 1, 2008. While France and Britain were to take the lead, the secretary general stressed that the joint mission would have to have as large a contingent of AU troops as possible. No mention was made of essential helicopters (the SkyLink fixed-wing and helicopter contract wasn't renewed).

The hybrid force would be much needed, especially since Oxfam had announced on June 17, 2007, that it would withdraw its staff from the refugee camp at Gereida in Darfur because it could no longer protect them. Four years after the conflict in Darfur had begun, the situation had deteriorated alarmingly, with ever more mass killings, rapes, and car-jackings, not to mention the splintering of rebel groups into even more warring factions, all ignoring any kind of peace negotiations. To make matters worse, President al-Bashir then suffered a change of heart concerning UNAMID and refused to allow the deployment of essential Nordic, Thai, and Nepalese units, blaming a Danish newspaper for publishing cartoons satirizing the Prophet Mohammed.

The Canadian Forces' Captain Douglas Oggelsby was posted to Julud in the Nuba Mountains in Kordofan and to regions in Darfur. "Julud," he says, "was a village, probably around 500 people, but the outlying areas had many more. The village consisted of about eight little stores, and when I say stores, I mean little sheds selling minimal supplies. It was amazing that I could buy a Coke but couldn't find bottled water in that village. That was the first thing I remembered when I arrived — my Canadian counterpart saying to me, 'Have a good tour and I'll buy you a Coke.' I said, 'Water?' He said, 'No, no water.' I had to drive three and a half hours to get my supply of water. I did that a couple of times a week. 'Bird baths' were common. The village had one little school where all the children would walk to from the country. The teachers were from Kenya. The kids really enjoyed school. You could see them walking to school happy that they had a chance to learn. It was an amazing thing to see. I walked to the school and donated some pencils and pens and the children were very content.

"I used to go out on patrols daily to see many of the small villages near Julud, working with the local population, meeting with the Sudanese rebels and the Sudanese Army. It was very interesting when I went to the different camps. The way we were treated was different in each location. The rebels in many cases were glad to see us, whereas the army soldiers were very suspicious and were always watching where we went and what we did."

In the Canadian Navy since 1983, Lieutenant Dave Coulter served as the marine systems engineering officer on HMCS *Terra Nova* during the First Gulf War in 1991. "All Canadian UNMOs [United Nations Military Observers] posted to Sudan receive a month-long course in Kingston, Ontario, to prepare them for their duties," he says. "On arrival in Khartoum we were introduced to the U.N. bureaucracy at UNMIS headquarters, which included completing a similar course crammed into one week followed by a further week of tedious indoctrination training intended for U.N. civilians, military, or police. This was punctuated by long waits outside, and then inside, various U.N. buildings or the bank as we cleared in. Canadian UNMOs in Khartoum stayed in a rented house just down the street from the expansive Chinese embassy in East Khartoum. Once finished our UNMIS in-routine and training in Khartoum, we were sent in pairs to one of the six UNMIS sectors in Southern Sudan. I was sent with another Canadian, Major Matt Joost, to Southern Kordofan [Sector IV]. We were to be the UNMOs at Kadugli in the Nuba Mountains. Kadugli was a garrison town of the Sudanese Armed Forces [SAF] during the last war in Southern Sudan and is located in the centre of the mountains in the state of Southern Kordofan.

"Our job as UNMOs in UNMIS was to monitor the military and security elements of the Comprehensive Peace Agreement. Southern Kordofan is one of three disputed areas just north of the 1–1–56 line [named after the date of Sudan's independence from Britain on

January 1, 1956] that demarcate North, or Arab-dominated, Sudan from South, largely black, Sudan. The other three UNMIS sectors are south of the 1–1–56 line. While flying into 'Kadugli International' Airport from Khartoum in January, large patches of blackened earth and fallen trees could be seen. It was the height of the dry season, and the land had been burned by the Arab nomads as they headed south in search of water for their cattle. The plains were punctuated by massive black rock outcroppings 300 to 500 metres high — the Nuba Mountains. Our residence was high-rent for Kadugli and most of the South. It was surrounded by a two-and-a-half-metre wall. Frequently, I had to jump this wall as there weren't enough keys to go around. The wall surrounded an external propane burner kitchen, external shower and toilet, and the main house of two separate sections. All the buildings were made of cinder blocks with tin roofs and concrete floors. There was no air conditioning, but we had ceiling fans and reasonably reliable electricity. There were about eight of us renting the house at any one time. All the doors were metal, and the windows were without glass, just bug mesh and grilles.

"At the other end of the spectrum, our housekeeper, her three kids, and her extended family lived in a few simple, separated, single-room huts made of local brick with tin roofs in an area defined by cut thorn bushes laid down to discourage snakes. During the war, her husband had heard shots outside, and on getting up to see what was the matter, was shot dead outside their home. Typically, we would drive to her home on the outskirts of Kadugli. Once, I dropped her off to find her teenage boy and his friend taking apart a bullet so they could fire off the gunpowder for fun. Nobody at her home thought this was unusual.

"Most affluent households in Kadugli like ours had their water delivered by donkey cart by a boy every second day or so. Even the water boys without donkeys had cell phones. Given our cistern was just six metres from our septic tank, we only used this for cleaning and showers — cold in the morning, hot in the evening, after the sun warmed the tank on its tower. Water for cooking was hand-pumped by us through camping micro filters. This water came from the local well about 15 metres from our cistern just outside our wall. For drinking water we always used commercial bottled water. Though we lived far better than most of the locals, 50-degree-plus Celsius heat at the height of the dry season is still 50 degrees plus. During the last part of the dry season, I would take two 1.5-litre bottles of water and freeze them. That night I would sleep with my two 'girlfriends.' At first they were always cold to me ... but they always warmed up. It was necessary to drink at least three 1.5-litre bottles of water a day during the dry season.

"Since there was no garbage collection, we burned the garbage outside our walls as everyone else did. I found that if I left the garbage outside to get some more before lighting it, the local kids would dive in and scatter it everywhere, looking for something to play with or use. The taking part was fine. It was the scattering part I disliked, since I was left alone to clean it up. Stale bread and biodegradable garbage were generally just thrown over the way ... and gone the next day either as food for animals or people.

"Street boys would also come by to make some money cleaning our cars inside and out. Though we could get this done for free at HQ, we paid for them to do it, anyway. One morning we found one of our cassette/tape radio sets removed and a window smashed. The thief was evidently intimately familiar with the alarm system hidden in the car so as to turn it off in time to avoid the alarm going off. To get the police to investigate we had to purchase a 'permit' from the government. The thief was taking a great chance, since amputation is the formal penalty for theft in that area of Sudan.

"Sector IV is divided into five areas of responsibility [AORs], with one 'Team Site' of UNMOs per AOR. My duty station was to be the Kadugli Team Site. Major Joost was to work in the sector HQ. Kadugli Team Site had 16 majors and captains from various countries such as Egypt, Uganda, Mali, Zimbabwe, Ghana, India, Pakistan, Bangladesh, Germany, and Fiji. One of our Team Site UNMOs was a prince of Guinea. Those from India and Pakistan had fought against one another in Kashmir. More than a few had serious political troubles, i.e., coups, attempted coups, insurgencies, et cetera, back home.

"The Team Site AOR was the southwestern portion of Southern Kordofan that bordered the east of the Abyei Region [Sector VI] and the northwest of Unity Province [Sector III]. All these regions, including the south of our AOR, are rich in oil. Sudan's main pipeline taking this oil to Port Sudan on the Red Sea passed directly through our AOR. The only significant road in the Kadugli AOR was the one built by oil companies to service the oil regions south of Kadugli — the 'pipeline road,' so called because it ran parallel to the pipeline for much of its length. It was unpaved and largely unmaintained. The nearest paved road outside of Kadugli was the one between Dilling and Khartoum. That road had been financed by Osama bin Laden during his days in Sudan.

"UNMIS has about 700 UNMOs, and there were less than 30 that were Canadian, yet we seemed to have a fairly high profile despite our small numbers. This became apparent to me during UNMO training in Khartoum in the way the instructors and staff referred to us. Part of our advantage was that we were fluent in English, the working language of UNMIS. Sector HQ staff from the Troop Contributing Countries [TCCs — troops for protection of UNMOs and other UNMIS personnel], in particular, didn't always have this advantage, making reading and writing reports for the U.N. difficult. Another reason is that Canadian service personnel come from a society that is already fairly multicultural. Perhaps yet another reason maybe hinted at by a SAF lieutenant-colonel I worked and ate with on many occasions. He said, 'Canada has done no evil in the world.' Then he paused and added, 'Or not much.'

"The main job of the Team Site was to conduct patrols to monitor the location and movement of troops and weapons [military unit visits], monitor the security situation of civilians [village visits], and investigate allegations of violations of the CPA. A Joint Military Team [JMT] patrol from a Team Site was generally comprised of two Nissan Patrol vehicles equipped with HF and VHF radios. On long-range patrols we would always take the one car with the satellite phone, since VHF communications wasn't reliable in the south of our AOR and working with HF can be difficult. The satellite phone also provided slightly more discreet communications, at least locally.

"There were normally two UNMOs per vehicle. The passenger UNMO of the first vehicle was the patrol leader, and the passenger of the second was the navigator. The language assistant, a local Sudanese, would be in the first vehicle to actually guide the patrol to its location.

Regardless of what position I filled, I always carried my own GPS — just in case the language assistant's wife's directions weren't well understood before he left home. National monitors from the SAF and the Sudan People's Liberation Movement/Army would normally ride together in the second vehicle. Occasionally, we would bring a truck or two of Egyptian TCC troops for force protection if travelling on long-range patrols — anything longer than a day.

"On one patrol I led a convoy of seven vehicles with over 25 people of nine nationalities. The only serious difficulty I encountered was the tendency of a few Sudanese on our team to wander away in search of the hospitality of the local ladies and so delay our departures. Along the same lines, one of our Arab UNMOs had a fondness for camel's milk such that anytime time he saw a nomad riding a camel he'd leave the convoy in hope of buying some. There wasn't much one could do about this except to ask that he announce 'Charlie Mike,' for camel's milk, on VHF so at least we knew he'd dropped out.

"Once, I and other UNMOs from our Team Site had a chance to star in an Egyptian promotional video featuring the TCC truck leading the patrol with canvas cover off the truck, weapons ready, and a manned light machine gun resting on the roof of the cab facing forward. On any real patrol the TCC followed the lead UNMO vehicle, the canvas was on, and the weapons were safely stowed away. In our AOR no one except SAF or SPLM/A soldiers in uniform generally openly displayed their weapons. Indeed, it was very common to find soldiers in the markets with their AK-47s slung over their shoulders. For the U.N. to arrive in a village, or worse, a military unit, with weapons showing, would have been both very insulting and very foolish.

"On my second day at the Kadugli Team Site we learned of an unannounced SAF convoy of several tanks on flatbeds coming south from Khartoum. Most of the rest of the Team Site was on a long-range patrol, so Matt and I had a chance to go on patrol immediately, but unfortunately without a language assistant or national monitors. The two Egyptian officers who led the patrol spoke Arabic, however. We went north to where the pipeline road joins the road to the main road from Kadugli to Dilling and then Khartoum. Here we waited until the convoy arrived promptly as night fell. Generally, the U.N. in Sudan doesn't travel at night, and so, after an unsuccessful attempt to convince the convoy commander to stop travelling, we slept outside on the steps of the SAF barracks near a converted school. That night we ate under a clear sky with the Egyptian soldiers there as our force protection. Live local singing and music played all night as there was a wedding celebration in the village.

"We caught up with the convoy easily the next day, since the pipeline road didn't allow it to go more than 20 kilometres per hour. We spent the rest of the next day leap-frogging parts of the convoy. On one occasion we gave a lift to a driver of one of the flatbed trucks that had a flat tire so he could tell his commander to wait. We spent much of the afternoon trying to arrange a turnover of the convoy with Sector VI UNMOs. We didn't know it at the time, but they weren't permitted to travel outside their Team Site, so no turnover was possible, in any case.

"On most patrols south we stopped at a truck stop at Keliak to eat and fix flat tires. This patrol was no exception. It had a dozen restaurants selling fresh fish, goat, or sheep cooked on the premises. Generally, these restaurants consisted of a 20-by-40-metre post-and-beam room furnished with plastic chairs and tables. The walls and ceiling were made of straw mats. The open kitchen — wok and charcoal fire — would be at the front. The main meal was hung up at the entrance. Water was sprinkled on the ground out front to keep the dust down. A jug of water was out front to clean your hands before and after meals. The toilet was the large expanse behind the restaurants.

"The maps Matt and I had unsuccessfully tried to order when in Khartoum would have come in handy later in the day, since by that time we were well off our one portable map that the Team Site had. UNMIS is an integrated mission of civilian and military personnel. In practice this meant the civilians controlled the assets that the military used like helicopters, cars, and maps — and they tended to be jealous of these. At times there was a clash of cultures. I can remember being about to board a helicopter for an air recce patrol and being told by the UNMIS air movement staff 'checking' our 'tickets' before boarding that he was going to decide who was going on my patrol and who wasn't — he lost. Were we boarding an airline or going on a military patrol? On another occasion the air movement staff decided where we would go on patrol — he won that time. Allocation of cars and office space followed a similar pattern.

"When night fell again, we had to say goodbye to the convoy at a SAF checkpoint as it headed into Sector VI. The commander of the SAF troops in Heglig was kind enough to offer us his officers' mess for accommodation that night. The Heglig oil facility was so large that we had no problem getting separated and just slightly lost before finally arriving at the SAF officers' mess. Our accommodations were rudimentary — made of two tractor trailer cargo containers set in an *L* and screened in — but we did have a shower. The SAF colonel, an aide, and a Government of Northern Sudan intelligence officer shared our late supper. As far as I know, we were the first and only UNMOs to visit Heglig. Heglig, located in Sector III, is a major oil production centre for Sudan. As we drove in at night, we could see the plumes of gas being burned off wellheads all around us.

"The next morning, after knocking the red sand out of the air filters of our cars, we set off back to Keliak for the night and then back to Kadugli the following day. On the way north from Heglig I took the GPS grids to two red roads I noticed leading east. On later air patrols we used the grids I obtained to discover the oil production facility there — and its troops. Had the Internet link at the U.N. camp been faster, Google Earth would have shown these.

"My second patrol was more typically a village visit. Such visits consist of meeting with the village leader and some of his supporters, generally under the largest tree in the village on some homemade chairs made out of rebar and nylon string, or sitting on the ubiquitous plastic lawn chairs. We would be kindly offered some water and maybe some nuts to eat. The patrol leader would ask the village leader some standard questions about the status of the village — how many wells, clinics, schools, et cetera. These questions were for the benefit of the civilian side of UNMIS.

"The real point of these visits, from the point of view of UNMOs, was to determine the security status of the village. Was anyone threatening it? Generally, the answer was no, though in some cases there was some violence between nomads and the villagers, i.e., 150 stolen goats the year before leading to the arrest and ad hoc village 'trial' of five nomads harvesting wood for charcoal. Or it could be armed threats from a neighbouring village, i.e., a truck full of men carrying AK-47s and RPGs to boost a claim to more territory. In the case of the stolen goats, the assembly of village elders denied any arrests until the village leader strolled into the meeting and set the record straight, or at least a version closer to the truth. In one case the villagers had burned down a SAF barracks located where they wanted their market. The SAF commander stated frankly that had the U.N. not been present he would have burned down the village in retribution. He was very angry that the U.N. was involved. Such incidents weren't uncommon and in some ways not central to the UNMO mandate. Nonetheless, the U.N. presence did tend to defuse these situations.

"In this village visit the 'newbie keeners' — two Canadians and an Indian major — wanted to see the village clinic and school, both built by Norwegians decades ago. The other members of the JMT reluctantly agreed. The clinic was filled with boxes of unrefrigerated antibiotics in 30 Celsius heat and malaria drugs past their expiry date. There was no nurse in the area to dispense these drugs. I asked a German UNMO if the aid agency that left the medicines didn't feel some responsibility for them. He replied, 'You must be delusional. The donor agency had their photo op and left.' The nearby school was long deserted. Though the village leader wisely declared his village neutral — a SAF national monitor was present — he told us that the SAF had imprisoned the teacher in Khartoum during the war and that the teacher hadn't been seen since. In discussing the needs of his village, he stated, 'We don't need infrastructure. We need teachers.'

"We visited Miseriya nomad camps, as well. They echoed the same sentiment — they wanted their children to be educated but were having difficulty getting them taught. We once met the emir of the Miseriya in Kadugli while we drank tea in the market in the evening. Apparently, he has a master's degree from Harvard in economics.

"Many of the patrols I led or participated in involved a town on the pipeline road called Kharasana ['gravel' in Arabic]. It was the source of much of the distinctive red gravel that the pipeline road had been built from. Kharasana was described by one local as 'Sudan in miniature.' People from all over Sudan lived there. Miseriya Arabs, mostly nomads, occupied the north part of the town. Black Sudanese — Nuer and Dinka — occupied the south. There were no less than five other armed groups [OAGs] in the small town — former SSDF, former PDF, elements of the Debab Force [Arab-dominated, aligned but not integrated into the SPLM/A], a SAF unit, and the Miseriya nomads themselves. The political wing of the SPLA, the SPLM, was also present.

"On my first visit to the town our language assistant pointed out the town's chief plainclothes GOS security/intelligence man. How did he know him? So we had a meeting with the GOS man during which he berated the U.N. for not entering the former SSDF's armed camp. 'Real men go to the real place,' he said. Real men or not, we hadn't been invited into the camp, and the former SSDF commander had made it very clear we wouldn't be. Nonetheless, it was true that we had a responsibility to determine as much as we could about the OAG, particularly given its claims.

"Although we never did get into the camp, months later I arranged for flights over it to determine the size of the force, weapons, et cetera. On the same visit there was some unrest in the town. The leader of the Arabs in the north of the town threatened war in 24 hours during a meeting with UNMIS personnel, including myself, unless the town's plans to install firebreaks were halted. The U.N. was helpful in stopping the plans from being implemented in the north end of the town, and those who lived there later expressed their gratitude. That meeting continued for some time after we left. It was dispersed by the local former SSDF commander's arrival with his armed escort in a Toyota pickup. He then followed us directly into the SAF compound without so much as a nod to its armed sentry.

"Given the importance of the area, Keliak, Kharasana, and other towns on the pipeline also had more than their fair share of GOS security/intelligence men in civilian dress. These generally sat next to wherever UNMOs stopped to eat or drink. They were easy to spot, since they generally had upscale footwear, meaning they wore socks and shoes.

And they spoke excellent English. My job as the G2 [military information officer] for the Team Site was to figure out who was who of the military groups in our AOR — their strength and what their command structure was. This was no small task even for the participants themselves. For instance, the Debab Force claimed to be part of the SPLM/A. Apparently, this was news to the SPLM/A in the Nuba Mountains/ Southern Kordofan, since it arrested several Debab Force recruiters for operating in SPLM/A-dominated areas in the Nuba Mountains. Their arrest by the SPLM/A surprised the recruiters, since they really thought they were part of the SPLM/A. They carried ID cards to prove it. The SAF also arrested several former PDF who jointed the Debab Force who also thought they were legally joining the SPLM/A. Such recruiting was contrary to the CPA, so it was illegal.

"On one patrol I once took a SAF colonel and an SPLM/A colonel to meet the former SSDF commander in Kharasana. They asked, 'When did you defect to the SPLM/A' and 'Who do you report to?' respectively. The colonels knew the answers more or less. The questions were loaded. Had the SSDF commander answered these questions, which he didn't, claiming they were too insulting, he would have admitted his organization, its presence in Kharasana, and its activities — taxing all oil industry vehicle traffic south and charcoal ones going north on the pipeline road — were illegal.

"The real issue was the commander's claim that Kharasana was part of Unity Province. If valid, this would have put the as yet unsurveyed 1–1–56 line north of the nearby oil facility and the Heglig facility and associated oil fields farther south, and these would all belong to the SPLM/A. Most maps of Sudan show the border between North and South well south of Heglig. It was an extreme and dangerous claim. The commander wanted the U.N. to have a permanent presence in Kharasana. I believe he wished this because such a presence would have diminished the potential for him to be forcibly removed by the SAF, which maintained pickets and barracks all along the pipeline and associated oil production fields.

"In Kharasana the local people made a distinction between the 'old' SPLM/A, the former SSDF, and the 'new' SPLM/A, the former PDF. They generally thought of the new SPLM/A as little more than common criminals, since several of them had put two of the town's policemen in hospital by beating them with swords, a dispute that started with a local baker not acquiescing to the wage demands of his 'new' SPLM/A employee. However, neither group, old or new, was integrated into the SPLM/A. All this was to say that the military/political/social situation in our AOR was complicated.

"Much of the work I did involved investigating incidents such as the police beating, sometimes with UNPOL [United Nations Police]. We also often worked with the human-rights officers of UNMIS, since arrests by Sudanese military or police often involved beatings and some-times torture. One arrest was for jaywalking in front of a SAF junior officer's car. Another arrest was for being part of a church established by a defrocked Anglican priest accused of child molestation. Frequently, such investigations were initiated by allegations of infractions of the CPA by either the SPLM/A or the SAF. Typically, we would start with the military intelligence officer who wrote the complaint and then visit the village where the infraction occurred. There was a creative element to many such reports and complaints.

"At other times our work involved monitoring troop movements. I was personally involved in intercepting two unannounced tank con-voys moving south and one unannounced convoy of over 20 trucks with ammunition, heavy weapons, and 100 troops moving north. Sometimes we were unable to respond quickly to reports or obvious signs of troop movements simply because of the paperwork required to get security clearances for our language assistants.

"Other duties involved monitoring the strength of military units, including the Joint Integrated Units [JIUs] composed of mixed former SPLM/A and SAF soldiers operating under one command structure per unit. The JIUs were to form the interim armed forces for the Government of National Unity of Sudan, composed of both SPLM/A and the GOS. At the time I was there the JIUs in our AOR were neither joint — SAF and SPLM/A soldiers were at different locations — nor integrated. They had two command structures save for a unit commander nominally commanding both elements, so they weren't really a 'unit.' Nonetheless, shortly before I left, real progress was being made in at least 'verifying' these units. Verification meant that both the SAF and the SPLM/A JIUs paraded their troops with their weapons for us to count.

"While coming back at night from a long-range patrol we heard on the radio of SPLM/A JIU troops moving to protect the SPLM/A governor's residence in Kadugli from protests connected with a teachers' strike for non-payment of wages. For months they couldn't move to join the SAF JIU, but now they could move on short notice and in the dark.

"Several times I met with GOS and SPLM/A politicians at the state level. They proved as capable of saying everything and nothing at the same time as any politician. In terms of actions during my tour, three shot dead in the streets and 20 wounded by gunfire from the authorities say plenty. The wounded and dead were mostly students who had protested with their teachers. They died or were wounded protesting a situation that prevented them from completing their education. Though one UNMO in our sector was arrested and beaten during my tour, generally the danger to UNMOs in our AOR were relatively low.

"The greatest danger was rolling a patrol car on the poor roads. This was real enough as I witnessed such an accident and took the injured to the hospital at the UNMIS Sector HQ Camp where our Team Site was co-located. When travelling on the pipeline road, at least one flat tire per day was common. For large stretches on the pipeline road, it was easier for transport trucks, and our Nissan patrols, to drive beside the road rather than on it. Sustained speeds above 60 kilometres on this road, or 40 kilometres on any other road outside the town of Kadugli, resulted in our vehicles rolling over. Behind the Sector HQ mechanics shop was the UNMO and UNPOL 'walk of shame' — a score of vehicles the observers or police had destroyed in accidents involving nothing more than one vehicle and the road — and excessive speed."

For his service in Sudan, Lieutenant Dave Coulter was awarded the United Nations Mission in Sudan (UNMIS) Task Force Commander's Commendation, and he returned to that country in 2008 for a second tour.

Understanding that CF deployments in support of UNMIS are six months long, the environmental and operating conditions faced by the UNMOs are particularly harsh and demanding, requiring ingenuity, tolerance, and an ability to work well with others in order to

accomplish difficult tasks. As of the summer of 2008, Canada's contribution to UNMIS stood at 35 personnel, including eight staff officers, 24
UNMOs, and three National Support Element personnel.

"The general consensus from my numerous visits and countless
discussions with TFCs and redeployed members," says Major George
Boyuk, "is that the CF contribution to UNMIS is greatly appreciated
and meaningful, once again demonstrating that our soldiers are great
ambassadors of Canada and held in high regard by other contributing
countries. Many have enjoyed their deployment and feel grateful for the
opportunity to have served in Sudan with the U.N., referring to it as the
experience of a lifetime both personally and professionally."

"It might seem odd for a naval reservist to spend his first deployment
3,000 metres above sea level and 800 kilometres inland," says Lieutenant-
Commander Nicholas Smith, "but from a selfish point of view I'm glad
that the opportunity came along and I was able to take a sabbatical from
my civilian job once selected." Smith joined the Canadian Naval Reserve
in 1989, following his emigration from the United Kingdom where
he had been an officer in the Royal Naval Reserve. Most of his career
had been spent on "Class A" (part-time) service at HMCS *Donnacona*
in Montreal. Operation Augural was his first operational deployment
where he served as operations officer, Task Force Addis Ababa (TFAA).

"I worked with what became a close-knit group of people both in
TFAA and the wider community supporting AMIS and was able to
observe the evolving situation in one of the world's hot spots from close
hand. On the negative side, although I've seen enough of the world to
know that it was unlikely that the situation would be transformed during
my six-month deployment, it is still a disappointment that, despite all
the hard work of TFAA, other partners, and AMIS itself, the situation
facing the people of Darfur continues to be a bleak one.

"My experience of Sudan and Darfur was a second-hand one
based on my observations of events from Ethiopia where I served from
August 2007 to January 2008 as the operations officer for Task Force
Addis Ababa. During my time in theatre [Roto 6], there were 11 of
us in TFAA — five in Addis, four in El Fasher/Zam Zam, and two
in Khartoum. Most of the positions were directly in support of AMIS

either as advisers to its planning and logistics staffs in the DITF, AMIS HQ, and Forward HQ or as trainers for the AVGPs that Canada had lent to the mission.

"As the operations officer, I also served as military liaison officer to the Canadian embassy in Addis, and I worked mainly out of the Chancery building in the south of Addis near the Adams Pavilion where DITF was located. Set in a secure compound with 24/7 guards and its own generators, this was a convenient location and allowed me access to Foreign Affairs communications, including secure voice and email, our only such facilities.

"The typical daily routine involved leaving Canada House around 0730 with the CO and contracts officer who both worked at DITF, getting to the embassy about 10 minutes later, and invariably opening the Chancery since I was the first member of Canada-based staff to arrive. We were driven to our locations, since standing orders didn't permit us to drive ourselves in Addis for security reasons.

"My main task every day was to perform a situational and threat analysis, looking at a number of sources, invariably unclassified because of the absence of secure communications in AMIS, and speaking to several contacts to compile a summary of what was going on in Darfur and the evolution of the threat to TFAA members working there. This was circulated each day to TFAA and a number of other parties such as CEFCOM, our EU and NATO colleagues supporting AMIS. This was an ongoing process. Events didn't arrange themselves to fit into my schedule, so the sources had to be monitored throughout the day to ensure we were on top of them. There was also work to do on checking sources when I was back at Canada House, providing that the Internet wasn't down or we weren't sitting in darkness, since we didn't have a generator. My other duties included preparing and maintaining a background analysis of the situation in Darfur and drafting the weekly SITREP and monthly War Diary.

"At the embassy I worked closely with the first secretary, political, who was the contact point for Foreign Affairs' support to AMIS, which included the supply of the SkyLink helicopters, vital to the sustainment of the force in the field, the provision of fuel, and financial support for the building and maintenance of civilian police stations. For a large part of my deployment there were discussions and negotiations about how these were to be transitioned into UNAMID, which involved Foreign Affairs colleagues in Ottawa and the Canadian mission to the U.N. and meant a sharp learning curve for all of us in Addis with U.N. procedures, particularly financial and contracting. These discussions also embraced the question of how the 105 Canadian AVGPs deployed with AMIS could be transferred to UNAMID. A large part of the embassy side of my work included liaison with the 'partner' nations through the weekly Partners' Technical Support Group meetings hosted initially at the EU Delegation and then at the U.S. embassy and the weekly Partners/DITF Liaison Group meetings.

"El Fasher, Darfur, was a contrast — a more noticeable security presence and one or two multi-storey buildings going up, I was told, to accommodate the expanded AMIS/UNAMID force, but otherwise rather sleepy and traditional. My recollections are of streets of low mud-brick houses, all behind walls; large numbers of children walking to and from school in colourful uniforms; women off to the fields on donkeys or on foot; and sand, sand, and more sand.

"I spent a day flying to several of the AMIS camps by helicopter, so I saw quite a large part of Northern Darfur. Amid yet more sand there was sparse vegetation — this was the rainy season — and small settlements — it wouldn't be appropriate to call them villages — consisting of a number of houses fashioned from branches inside compounds made of the same, set against a background of rocky hills springing sporadically from the desert. I recall coming in to land at one of the camps — Shangil Tobaya, I think — and wondering why there were mounds of plastic sheeting scattered nearby, before realizing that this was an IDP camp. There were no neat rows of tents on concrete bases behind perimeter fences like the AMIS camps, but a mass of primitive shelters made from whatever was to hand or supplied by aid agencies."

The Oxfam coordinator would have agreed with Lieutenant-Commander Smith. Most of the refugees arrived in the camps with virtually nothing. Some were able to bring animals (if they hadn't been killed or stolen in attacks) and a few pots or blankets, but many came with just the clothes they were wearing. Even for those lucky enough to bring animals such as donkeys and cows it was difficult to find food with which to feed them, and taking them out to graze put the owners at serious risk of attack. In many camps the makeshift huts in which the families sheltered were made of little more than sticks and plastic sheeting. By the fifth year of war, some camps, such as Abu Shouk on the outskirts of El Fasher, were taking on an air of permanence, with stone buildings replacing the tents. With the conflict showing no sign of ending, Oxfam concluded that many people expected to be stuck in the camps for a long time to come.

"There were very few men to be found in the IDP camps," Captain Doug Oggelsby recalls. "Most of them were out fighting. It was very sad to walk into one of those camps and see how these people had to live. Plastic sheets over sticks. I opened several sheets and saw sick women and children. It was terrible. The countryside was beautiful, but the war was taking its toll on the land."

Indeed, despite the billions of dollars in aid, the situation was as desperate as ever. The humanitarian groups said that the sheer scale of suffering remained incredible, and the numbers of people affected were higher than ever before: Over 4.5 million people in Darfur and eastern Chad now relied on humanitarian aid, and 2.5 million people, more than one in three Darfurians, had been forced from their homes by the violence. More than two million of them sheltered in camps inside Darfur. A further quarter of a million refugees from Darfur were in camps over the border in neighbouring Chad. In 2007 alone a further 300,000 people fled their homes across Darfur. Another 185,000 Chadians fled their homes as the conflict increasingly spilled over into Chad. A World Health Organization estimate places the number of people who have perished in the Sudanese region from the combined effects of the conflict, including hunger, disease, and violence, at around 200,000.

But Abdalmahmoud Abdalhaleem, Sudan's ambassador to the United Nations, disputed the estimate. He said that his government placed the death toll at only 10,000 people killed. "In our own calculations the number does not exceed 10,000," the ambassador said. "Of course, here we are not including those who died because of malnutrition and starvation, because in Darfur there are no epidemics, no starvations, no violence, so that is why any additional number would be just very minimal."

There are Canadians who disagree with the ambassador. Although U.N. resolutions ban all GOS military flights over Darfur, Antonov bombers, MiG fighters, and attack helicopters have been used with impunity to indiscriminately eviscerate villages suspected of sheltering JEM rebels. Once a member of the Harker team, now Africa director at Human Rights Watch, Georgette Gagnon doesn't mince her words. "The attacks were carried out by Janjaweed militia and Sudanese ground troops supported by attack helicopters and aerial bombardments. This return to large-scale attacks on villages will be catastrophic for Darfur's civilians because they are completely unprotected."

An excerpt from Captain Doug Oggelsby's journal confirms Gagnon's assertions: "A disturbing day in Darfur. We were in a village about one hour outside of Nyala. The SLM/A were to meet us. There had been a battle the day before, and the AU, accompanied by myself and a major from Belgium, were to go over and do an investigation. When we arrived, the SLM/A didn't show us any of the graves of their people, but only from the Arab Militia that had attacked the day before. The village was still burning, and there had to have been 20 to 25 graves that they wanted to show us. They wanted to show us that they could hold off attacks from the Arab Militia. They did not show us any of their graves, but my senses made me aware that there had been a lot of killing the day before. It was not a good scene. The village was still burning and the children seemed to be very stressed out. The little town was not functioning like it should have been. I could not imagine what was taking place a day before I got there."

Until the last hours of AMIS, CF personnel remained committed to assisting the AU with its significant challenges in Darfur. Their tireless efforts and dedication as staff officers and trainers had earned them kudos from the AU military and diplomatic stakeholders, coupled with a solid reputation as serious "horsepower." In the end, Operation Augural had seven personnel deployed to Addis Ababa, two to Khartoum, and four to El Fasher, Darfur. Five of them transitioned to commensurate positions within CANCON UNAMID. The Canadian government announced the creation of Operation Saturn on January 28, 2008, to support the new hybrid U.N.-AU Mission in Darfur (UNAMID), which had taken over from AMIS on January 1, 2008. With the stand-up of Operation Saturn, the CF began phasing out its participation in AMIS, conducted under Operation Augural.

"The significant and tangible contributions Canadian Forces personnel have already made in Darfur will continue in the new mission," said Lieutenant-General Michel Gauthier, commander of Canadian Expeditionary Force Command. "The co-operative approach taken to mount the U.N.–African Union mission in Darfur is an important development in efforts to bring peace to Sudan, and we are proud to be part of it."

The Canadian contingent in UNAMID, called Task Force Darfur, was to be based in El Fasher and would be commanded by Lieutenant-Colonel Ken Moore. Its members included three staff officers who worked at UNAMID's Joint Logistics Operations Centre and Combined Integrated Support Services. Additionally, four non-commissioned soldiers would teach soldiers from Nigeria, Rwanda, and Senegal to operate the Canadian AVGPs under loan since 2005 under Operation Augural, and which would continue with UNAMID under Saturn.

The task force consisted of five positions divided between staff officers (SO) and AVGP specialists, later raised to seven. Three SOs worked in the Integrated Support Services (ISS) Section of Mission Support Division, two with the Joint Logistics Operations Centre (JLOC), and the other in Air Operations. There were three combat arms AVGP operations and training NCOs who organized AVGP driver, gunner, and TCC instructor training, and conducted camp visits to reinforce the training with the soldiers and inspect the vehicles and the weapons. These three specialists normally did the weapons and driving training, and a fourth specialist, a vehicle technician, concentrated on the vehicle portion. He also trained the drivers on driver maintenance, how to do self-recovery, and conducted the Husky courses. The vehicle technician also worked closely with the maintenance contractor that was responsible for the repair of AVGPs throughout the theatre. Referred to as MCAV

(Maintenance of Canadian Armoured Vehicles), the repair organization was at that time funded by the Canadian government.

As of the summer of 2008, a single CF officer was deployed to Addis Ababa, Ethiopia, as a U.N. liaison officer to the AU HQ to work within its Joint Support Coordination Mechanism (JSCM) in support of UNAMID. Canada also committed to another four positions within the UNAMID Sector South HQ of Nyala, Darfur, which brought the total of CF personnel as part of Task Force Darfur to 12.

Not including the few formed units from outside Africa (i.e., Chinese engineers, Bangladesh Formed Police Unit) that many other non-African countries involved with AMIS continue to provide to fill key staff positions, Canada, in 2008, remained one of the largest non-African contributors to the mission in Darfur. Canadian positions have been earmarked for the significant mission effects they have achieved in their respective specialties. The increased training of AVGP drivers, gunners, Husky operators, and instructors directly contributed to intensified patrolling by Rwandan, Senegalese, and Nigerian soldiers, assisting the force commander to create a more secure environment within the Darfur region.

Through their unwavering determination, Canadian staff officers achieved enormous mission effects by being in a position to influence the stand-up and subsequent performance of their respective logistic sections. From influencing how support processes were developed and how support was provided to the force, to the coordination of the movement of Troop Contributing Countries into the theatre, to the revitalization of cells staffed by inexperienced and/or unqualified personnel, Canadian staff officers mentored and brought along those on the ground to develop strong teams. As with the previous operation, Operation Saturn continues to make an indelible impression on the Africans they support and train.

With the transition from AMIS to UNAMID, SkyLink was slated to be replaced by aircraft contracted and managed directly by the United Nations. As it prepared to leave, the Canadian company was commended by Ambassador Hassan A. Gibril, deputy head of AMIS. "I feel that it is appropriate that the exceptional professionalism, dedication, and effectiveness of SkyLink and its management team here in Darfur be acknowledged. In reviewing SkyLink's performance, I note from records that between October 2004 and the present date, the company has safely flown without accident more than 45,470 block hours, transporting in excess of 161,963 passengers and 12,410,318 kilograms of cargo to destinations throughout the AMIS area of responsibility.

"Even though the working environment has been austere and extremely difficult, SkyLink has nevertheless been more than a match for the tasks at hand, thus performing in addition, in excess of 300 Medevac flights. The project management team led by Bob Waring has consistently provided exceptional service, advice, and support well above the call. Tireless and highly dedicated, they have worked exhausting hours without complaint to meet the endless, normally short to no notice demands of the mission."

"As for our Canadian soldiers serving and who have served with AMIS and, more recently, UNAMID," Major Boyuk concludes, "they have personified selflessness by giving everything they can of themselves to assist in a noble cause — the development and mentoring of African soldiers and officers, many of whom are proud to serve and play their respective roles in solving their own issues as fellow Africans. Granted the CF did not deploy to Darfur or Khartoum or Addis in large numbers relatively speaking, our personnel have traditionally been selectively placed to achieve significant mission effects, be it through mentoring, training, and/or the provision of unproportional horsepower. Notwithstanding the obvious challenges and frustrations, those CF members I have spoken with have felt that they made a difference in some way and that their experience was truly unique and one to be remembered. I have never been prouder to be a Canadian than in my five visits to Sudan and Darfur since coming to CEFCOM in the summer of 2007.

"Wherever I travelled I heard two things. One was how hard Canadians had worked in the HQ and that they wished they could have more Canadian horsepower and original thinking on staff to deal with the complexity and seemingly never-ending challenges of the mission. The other is usually when speaking to the African soldiers in the camps that had the AVGPs. They would point out how much they enjoyed being trained by our Canadian NCOs and how proud they were to be drivers and gunners. Our soldiers have made an indelible mark on the Africans they have supported, and Canadians should be proud."

On May 1, 2008, the U.N. Security Council voted to extend the mandate of UNMIS until April 30, 2009. In a resolution passed unanimously, the Security Council emphasized the importance of "full and speedy" implementation of the Comprehensive Peace Agreement monitored by UNMIS. Whether as humanitarian workers, diplomats, or U.N. observers, Canadians were going to be in Sudan for the foreseeable future.

* * *

Ultimately, the tragedy of Sudan is the tragedy of most of Africa: war, famine, corruption, overpopulation, and tribal disputes that straddle colonial borders. Along with Angola, Somalia, Congo, and Chad, Sudan has become a focus for U.N. peacekeepers and Western humanitarian aid, both attempting to stop the country from disintegrating while an inept and corrupt government enriches itself extracting the nation's oil. Instead of Band-Aiding the devastation of Darfur, the world, both Western and Chinese, should concentrate on distant but more critical issues such as water conservation and climate change, which by 2020 will devastate all of sub-Saharan Africa. The tragedy is that for want of a better alternative, Canada, like other world powers, is forced to appease an authoritarian regime, since the opposition is non-existent and those who want political change are equally murderous. Until the Sudanese of all regions, religions, and ethnicities attempt to cohabit in the interest of their own peoples, the future of this sad country will be gloomy.

AFTERWORD

Harry Feversham was standing under the trees, guarded by four of the Ansar soldiery. His clothes had been stripped from him; he wore only a torn and ragged jibbeh upon his body and a twist of cotton on his head to shield him from the sun. His bare shoulders and arms were scorched and blistered. His ankles were fettered, his wrists were bound with a rope of palm fibre, an iron collar was locked about his neck, to which a chain was attached, and this chain one of the soldiers held. He stood and smiled at the mocking crowd about him and seemed well pleased, like a lunatic.

— A.E.W. Mason, *The Four Feathers*

*T*he Four Feathers is considered A.E.W. Mason's masterpiece because he successfully blended impersonation with high adventure (Anthony Hope, one of his friends, did the same with *The Prisoner of Zenda*). Mason so loved disguises and subterfuge that in the 1920s he set up espionage networks for British Naval Intelligence in Spain and South America while turning out novels, rather like Ian Fleming, another Naval Intelligence officer. There were occasions on my bus ride from Addis Ababa to the Sudanese border that Harry Feversham came to mind. Mason has his hero disguise himself as a local to get into Omdurman to rescue friends being tortured in the Mahdi's House of Stone. Visiting Sudan in 1901, the author used it as a backdrop for an adventure that combined cowardice, heroism, and redemption, making it his most successful work ever. I wondered at my own fate. Was the House of Stone still taking in guests?

The idea for a book on Canadians in Sudan began a year before my African bus trip in far-off, safe Ottawa. I Googled the Sudanese embassy to be greeted with a reassuring message: "The aim of the website, as well the Embassy [*sic*], is to enhance the relationship between the Sudanese and the Canadian government and the people of the two countries. Please don't hesitate to contact the Embassy through our different emails. We are here to serve you." I could only hope that the website of the Canadian embassy in Khartoum was as welcoming. Aiming for the top, I sent off an introductory email to the ambassador, giving as my credentials a list of books I had written and explaining my ambition to research Sudanese-Canadian relations.

Weeks passed, and when there was no acknowledgement, emails followed one another in rapid succession. I then started calling the embassy, leaving messages since the phone was never answered. Months went by, and I forsook the diplomatic route and began contacting Sudanese travel agencies instead. When they replied, I gushed that as an author there was much I wanted to see in their country: the old British residence's steps in Khartoum where General Gordon had been speared, the gunboat *Melik* from Kitchener's campaign, Al-Mogran where the Blue and White Niles merge. The agencies ignored all of that and replied, when they did, with the standard itinerary of a bus tour to the ancient city of Meroe, with its pyramids and accommodation in four-star hotels.

When I wrote back that I would also like to travel to Gedaref where the Canadian government had spent millions of dollars on an agricultural project, there was confusion. No one knew where it was, and the email replies soon dried up. Then, out of the blue, I heard from a gentleman who worked for one of the Khartoum travel agencies. He told me he understood exactly what I was about. I wanted to see the "real Sudan," not what *khawaja* ("foreigners") were shown, and he could arrange it all.

I was overjoyed. This man was a "fixer" who was well connected locally and obviously fluent in English — the dream of every journalist in the Third World! With the Sudanese embassy in Ottawa still ignoring my emails and phone calls, teaming up with a local guide who could open all doors was ideal. So I appealed to him. Could he get me an entry visa? He told me there would be no problem. All I had to do was send him the details and a visa would be waiting for me at Khartoum's airport. What about the travel permit necessary for overland trips? I knew that Sudan's Ministry of Humanitarian Affairs was responsible for them and often worked with the country's intelligence people. How would the latter take to a Canadian journalist? My fixer said he had contacts in the government that could arrange all the permits I needed.

It was also my intention to book a first-class seat on the Khartoum-Atbara train. Built to keep General Kitchener well supplied with men and ammunition as he smashed the khalifa's armies, the railway was the brainchild of Canadian engineer Percy Girouard, a Montrealer. Again, my fixer said, this wouldn't be a challenge. What about trekking in the Jebel Marra? When did I want to fit that in? the man asked.

Suspicions were beginning to set in by now, but I agreed to send the travel agency a deposit for the three-week trip and started getting all the immunizations I needed. And then I got a cautionary email from my fixer. He would get into serious trouble if his bosses at the travel agency knew he was helping me. He could even be fired. Could the deposit be sent to his personal bank account rather than the agency's? This didn't seem too far-fetched. The guidebooks warned of problems with Sudanese banks. Would it be easier, I asked the agent, if I brought the money in travellers' cheques to the airport in Khartoum? Back came the immediate reply — the Sudanese banks weren't a problem, since he lived in Doha. His friends in Sudan "fixed" tours for *khawajas*, and they would arrange everything. But the money had to be sent to him.

By now I was desperate. Alan Moorehead's books on the two Niles, Christopher Ondaatje's *Journey to the Source of the Nile*, and Winston Churchill's *The River War* were informative, but there was only so much that I could learn from them. There was little on Sudan specifically, as for centuries historians had treated the land below Wadi Halfa as the outer part of Egypt, or worse encompassed it into the whole colonial fabric of Africa. Canadian author Peter Dalglish's *The Courage of Children* did centre on the country, but it was now more than 10 years old, and though Deborah Scroggins's *Emma's War* and Douglas Johnson's *The*

Root Causes of Sudan's Civil Wars were more contemporary, there was nothing Canadian in their context.

The success and authenticity of my previous work, *Canada in Afghanistan: The War So Far*, owed much to being embedded with the Canadian Forces in Kandahar. This new book was taking shape, and I still hadn't got anywhere near the Nuba Mountains or interviewed members of the National Democratic Alliance or even tucked into a bowl of *ful*, the national dish. I began haranguing the North American offices of the humanitarian agencies operating in Sudan and asked if they could help. A letter of invitation from one of their offices in Khartoum would facilitate getting a visa. Could they be my in-country guarantors? Hostages to the Sudanese bureaucracy for their own visas, they all sympathized but were understandably leery of helping.

Perhaps if I entered from a neighbouring country, advised a Canadian who had been there, say, through Egypt, Ethiopia, or Chad. The Sudanese embassies in those countries were known to be more co-operative. They didn't have to contact Khartoum for permission to issue a visa. The Chad border had been closed since 2003, and I had been to Egypt before, years ago to work at an archaeological dig. I had never considered seeing the ancient Kingdom of Ethiopia. I saw Emperor Haile Selassie when he came to Montreal for Expo 67, and many years after that had contributed to Bob Geldof's Band Aid, and I was forever grateful to the Ethiopians for discovering coffee beans.

"The Land of the Burnt Faces," as the ancient Greeks had named the country, was said to be majestic, mysterious, and awe-inspiring. Its religion, language, and culture were unique in Africa, and unlike Sudan, it was relaxed and welcomed visitors and any humanitarian aid. The Ethiopian embassy in Ottawa not only put a visa in my passport within a day but told me I needn't have bothered. I could have had a visa stamped in on landing at Addis Ababa's Bole Airport. How easy was that? I booked a flight on Ethiopian Airlines and soon arrived in that ancient land.

Kitchener had planned the city of Khartoum in the form of interlocking Union Jacks so that a battery of cannon at the centre of each flag would be able to command the streets in any direction. Addis Ababa, on the other hand, had been laid out, it was said, by the Italians in the form of an upturned spaghetti bowl. I called the Sudanese embassy and, clutching my passport, an extra passport photo, and the required amount of American dollar bills, set off in a wheezing Lada taxi.

The driver first drove the length of Sudan Street in the hope that it meant the embassy was there. Then, after an animated cell phone conversation, he found Ras Lulseged Street and deposited me in front of the embassy. I made for the embassy door and expected entry to Sudan. But although friendly and courteous, the clerk behind the counter was adamant: as of a certain date, all visa applications had to be sent to Khartoum for approval, even from Addis Ababa. How long would that take? I asked, thinking of the mounting hotel bills if I had to stay in Ethiopia for a week. Surely, they had Fedex? A month at the earliest was the reply. And, after all that, my application might still be rejected. Without a visa I couldn't catch the Ethiopian Airlines flight to Khartoum. As hope rapidly faded about ever entering Sudan, that evening I drowned my disappointment in *araki*, the local spirit.

My second day in Addis was spent at the Sheraton Hotel. Still recovering from the previous night's *araki*, I arrived to use (I had been told) the only functioning ATM in the country. At the hotel's swimming pool and the bar called Breezes beside it, I was taken in by sympathetic "expats," none of whom I later discovered were actual guests of the Sheraton. Escaping, as one said, "the beggars, smell of urine, and sound of Amharic" outside the Sheraton's walls, all were pleased to recount their persistence in attempting to get into Sudan.

Stories were flung at me, whether truth or fiction I had no way of knowing, and several rounds later I found myself trying to memorize only half-heard details about various locations along the Ethiopia-Sudan border. What I do remember is being told that it was better to chew *chat*, the narcotic leaf that really was Ethiopia's number one export than to drown one's sorrows in *araki*. No one had read Mason's *The Four Feathers*, but a few recommended Paul Theroux's *Dark Star Safari*.

Ethiopia is landlocked, and all bulk imports enter either via Port Sudan or the country's only railway line from Djibouti. Most of the pool loungers were media agents for aid organizations and were especially up-to-date on border crossings. When the success of one's project depended on the arrival of goods, it was wise to know in what month they might appear. There had never been any love lost between Sudan and Ethiopia. Mengistu Haile Mariam, Ethiopia's former dictator, had given the SPLM/A shelter, and John Garang had even written the SPLM/A's manifesto in Addis. It had once been possible to drive from the Ethiopian city of Gambela into Sudan with a minimum of formality, but no longer. The only border post now open was at Metemmeh in the country's northwest, and supposedly with the right amount of U.S. dollars spread about on both sides of the frontier, it was possible to get an entry visa there.

Two Canadian students told me how they had heard of the tragedy in Sudan when Waterloo police officer Debbie Bodkin had spoken at their university. Impressed by her heart-wrenching speech and humility, they were eager to help me. They worked for an NGO in Bahir Dar, not far from the tourist town of Gonder, and had heard of a bus that went from there to Metema. Whatever happened, they thought I had to see the Blue Nile Gorge, the castles at Gonder, and the monasteries at Lake Tana. And there was a Sudanese connection to the area, one added. In 1889 a great battle had taken place in the region between a Mahdist army of dervishes and the defending Ethiopians, with both sides inflicting such enormous losses on each other that they were unable to resist the European invasions soon after. In retrospect, it must have been the exuberance of the young Canadians combined with the *araki* hangover that made me even consider getting into Sudan without a visa from its embassy in Addis.

Since Ethiopia has barely entered the Railway Age, its citizens depend on an extensive national bus system and a very few paved roads to accommodate it. Avoid the state-run buses, I was warned. The privately owned minibuses were faster but more dangerous as their drivers tried to make Gonder within daylight hours. A sense of humour and lots of patience and understanding were essential for bus travel in Ethiopia, the guidebooks advised. (If I really wanted an adventure, I should get a lift in the back of a *bouksi*, a Toyota pickup truck favoured by the Janjaweed in Darfur.)

I arrived at the bus terminal early enough to attract the expected swarm of touts, and no amount of refusal and rudeness deterred them. My Isuzu minibus left only when crammed to the aisles, its schedule obviously customer-driven. The country was supposed to be in the midst of a $500 million road construction program, and the road to Gonder was surfaced in fits and starts. When there was no tarmac, the driver ignored the possibility of undiscovered land mines and made for the dirt track used by the camel and donkey caravans. Where the road was being levelled (curiously by Chinese engineers), he sought to make up time by speeding along at 50 miles per hour, whether it was a straight stretch or a hairpin bend.

I was told by a pair of Dutch midwives, the only other foreigners onboard, that we had to arrive at Bahir Dar before nightfall not only because of *shiftas* ("bandits") who set up roadblocks to demand valuables but because the dump trucks and earth-moving machinery were parked in the middle of the road, undetectable in the blackness until too late. As the day wore on, the countryside became almost ethereal, marked with caves that had apparently been mines. This was where author Henry Rider Haggard had gotten the idea that King Solomon had mined for gold, popularizing Africa for a generation of Europeans. As we wound through the Blue Nile Gorge and made for the river and bridge far below, I watched the vultures soaring above and prayed that we would make Bahir Dar before nightfall, as well. We did but only just.

The next day I took a bus to where Lake Tana gave birth to the Blue Nile, beginning its 4,000-mile-plus journey through Sudan and Egypt to the Mediterranean Sea. It was here in 1770 that the Scottish explorer James Bruce had come, thinking he had traced the only source of the Nile. The place was rather shabby and disappointing, though. Expecting to see the spray of Niagara Falls, I found that the Nile at this point in its journey was a sad trickle, spayed by hydroelectric turbines.

Gonder, on the other hand, wasn't a disappointment. Although ransacked by the Mahdists and bombed in 1941 by the British from Sudan, its castles still managed to give the impression of being "Africa's Camelot." Here I negotiated a seat on the only bus that went daily to Shihedi, 25 miles from the border. Because it catered to tourists, Gonder had Internet facilities that worked, and the night before my departure I emailed everyone I knew about my intentions of crossing into Sudan the next day. I had learned in other travels to put down an electronic "trail of bread crumbs" should I vanish into the House of Stone.

During the six bone-shaking hours it took to reach Shihedi, I reflected on what I should tell the Sudanese border authorities, i.e., that I was an author who wanted to enter their country to write a history of Canadians in Sudan. I realized that this would be a sure way to be refused, and must have been the reason why the Sudanese embassy in Ottawa had ignored my requests. With the adverse publicity from Darfur, granting media access would be comparable to inviting CNN to cover the Second World War Katyn massacre of Poles in Russia. That settled it. I would be a tourist who wanted to see the Temple of Amun and the pyramids of Nuri — and that, too, was the truth.

A border truck stop, the single street that made up Shihedi consisted of bars, brothels, and money changers, exactly what I imagined Dawson City must have looked like during the gold rush. I had been warned that because of the truck drivers the town had the highest rate of HIV/AIDS in Ethiopia. But in contrast with border towns in Afghanistan at least, there were no guns in evidence. I spent the day wandering around, talking to other foreigners and searching for anyone who had U.S. dollars. I had been advised that the border officials would only accept greenbacks.

The next morning I found a driver of a Toyota Hilux who took me "on contract" the last 25 miles. Once at the Ethiopian side, I walked to the Sudanese post at Gallabat, cursing at the skittishness of the driver who refused to go any farther and at the unsuitability of my wheeled airline suitcase. This was the most dangerous part of the journey, since it was known that *shiftas* taking advantage of the no man's land between the countries pounced on travellers to rob and hold them (the Westerners at least) for ransom. No help could be expected from either the Sudanese or Ethiopian authorities, I had been warned.

Fortunately that day I wasn't alone. A stream of men, women, and children, all seemingly dressed as "extras" for a Cecil B. DeMille biblical epic, the men fiercely armed with staffs and the women overburdened with boxes and blue plastic jugs, were making for the border post. The *shiftas* were nowhere in sight, though that didn't stop me from constantly glancing up at the ridges above the path.

Without a wall or fence the Sudanese border was hardly noticeable. On the other side, buses were being filled to take my biblically dressed companions to farms in Gedaref, the route well used by agricultural workers. There were armed men in camouflage uniform in abundance (whether Sudanese soldiers or Ethiopian police, it was impossible to tell), but the immigration office was firmly closed. While the locals (if they were that) went through easily, I knew I could not. To enter any country, let alone Sudan illegally, meant a prison sentence, and no research was worth that.

Conceding defeat and thinking of imbibing gallons of *araki* and chewing whole bushels of *chat*, I returned to Shihedi, becoming the source of amusement to the never-ending stream going in the opposite direction. On the journey I had ample time to reflect on my options: I could spend a month in Addis while the Sudanese embassy granted me a visa, or I could use my time in Ethiopia to do something else.

It was while changing buses at Bahir Dar that I ran into the two Canadian students again and had the uncanny sensation they were expecting me. They were completing an assignment with the Ethiopian National Association of Persons Affected by Leprosy. Did I know anything about leprosy? they asked. I thought that in 2008 leprosy no longer existed. The Bible mentioned lepers, and I vaguely recalled that some of the medieval churches I had visited had "leper holes" in the walls where those afflicted with the disease were hidden away during church services. The students were part of an NGO project called EVERY ONE, which worked to remove the social stigma that afflicted millions of Ethiopians by housing, educating, and employing them.

I now knew what I would do …

NOTES

Introduction

1. Wilfred Thesiger was already legendary in Darfur not as a travel writer but as a crack shot. In those days only British officers were permitted to own rifles with enough power and accuracy to bring down a lion.
2. *Janja* is Arabic for "crazy man" and *weed* for "horse." Thought to mean "a man with a gun on a horse" or "devil on horseback," *Janjaweed* has become a blanket term to describe gunmen in Darfur, usually from the nomadic Arab tribes of the Abbala (camel herders) and the Baggara (cattle herders).
3. Largely unknown to the public, Sudan is the most important producer in the world of gum arabic, a product essential to the fabrication of candies, Coca-Cola, and pharmaceuticals, all of which are indispensable in the West and consequently have powerful lobbies in Washington, D.C.
4. Nick Coghlan, *Far in the Waste Sudan: On Assignment in Africa* (Montreal and Kingston: McGill-Queen's University Press, 2005), 25.
5. Notes for an address by the Honourable Peter MacKay, minister for foreign affairs, to Canadian Economic Development Assistance for Southern Sudan (CEDASS), March 30, 2007, London. Ontario.
6. The Export and Import Permits Act allows the Canadian Cabinet to create an "Area Control List," which is a list of countries to which the Canadian government "deems it necessary to control the export of Canadian products." Talisman Energy would have navigated around it by substituting foreign for Canadian goods and continuing its operation.
7. Coghlan, 74.

Chapter 1: Land Below Egypt

1. The most common *tariqa* in Sudan is the Qadiriyah, which can trace their heritage to twelfth-century Baghdad. The famous whirling dervishes of Omdurman are part of the sect.
2. Douglas H. Johnson, *The Root Causes of Sudan's Civil War* (Oxford: The International African Institute, 2003).
3. Alan Moorehead, *The White Nile* (London: George Rainbird Ltd., 1960), 92–95.
4. Moorehead, 90.
5. Samuel Baker would gain royal favour by naming the two great lakes that the Nile originates in after Her Majesty Queen Victoria and her consort, Prince Albert.

Chapter 2: Gordon, Wolseley, and the Siege of Khartoum

1. Garnet Wolseley had been posted to the United States during its Civil War. He was deeply affected by the first modern war in history in which the use of railways and the telegraph counted on the battlefield far more than raw courage. An observer at battles, he saw what happened when Southern cavalry, however gallant, charged against Northern infantrymen, well dug in and protected behind barbed wire.
2. Years after, Garnet Wolseley was seen shooting the weirs on the Thames River in his birchbark canoe.

Chapter 3: Voyageurs on the Nile

1. Library and Archives Canada, Macdonald Papers, Volume 84.
2. The idea of a railway from Cairo to Khartoum had been envisaged by the Egyptian Khedivate, which poured millions of pounds into the scheme, only to see them vanish in graft. But tracks for one had been laid from Wadi Halfa as far as Akasheh when the Mahdi's war began. The lines were destroyed, and because wood was very precious in the desert, the sleepers were torn up and used for campfires.
3. As the train stopped in Hull directly across the bridge from Ottawa, the boatmen used the opportunity afforded them to stock up on alcohol. Then, as now, Hull had more lenient laws than Ottawa regarding the sale of liquor. The boatmen paid dearly for this with hangovers and seasickness later in the voyage.
4. Garnet Wolseley wouldn't forget Lord Melgund's help, and when Queen Victoria refused to allow her son, the Duke of Connaught, to accept the post of governor general of Canada in 1898, he recommended Melgund (later the Earl of Minto) to Her Majesty for the position.
5. The only casualty on the voyage across the Atlantic Ocean was a Manitoba First Nations boatman, Richard Henderson, who died from a malady that Dr. Neilson diagnosed also afflicted the other voyageurs: homesickness. He was buried at sea.

6. Roy MacLaren, *Canadians on the Nile, 1882–1898: Being the Adventures of the Voyageurs on the Khartoum Relief Expedition and Other Exploits* (Vancouver: University of British Columbia Press, 1978), 79–80.
7. MacLaren, 83.
8. Major-General Gordon professed to be indignant about the British Empire's effort to save him alone (which it undoubtedly was). "It has come to SAVE OUR NATIONAL HONOUR," he wrote, not himself.
9. Egmont Hake, ed., *The Journals of Major-General G.C. Gordon* (London: Kegan, Paul, Trench, 1885), 275.
10. MacLaren, 168.
11. MacLaren, 109.
12. Frederick Charles Denison, the Nile Expedition hero, is little known among Canadians. The Denison Armoury (Allen Road and Sheppard Avenue) commemorates his older brother. Lieutenant-Colonel George Taylor Denison. Perhaps this is because in his last years the younger Denison was the object of an unpleasant controversy. He claimed that James Gibson Slater, a British army veteran who had enlisted with the Body Guard for 1885–88, was a drunkard and ordered him to return his kit at the end of his term. He did not, and Denison had him brought before magistrate's court and fined. In turn Slater brought a civil suit against Denison, claiming $250 for drill instruction and caring for his troop's arms and accoutrements. This suit failing, Slater had his case printed as a pamphlet in 1891 and distributed to all Members of Parliament. He also charged that officers of the Body Guard had pocketed money that should have gone to the men. When the Liberal Opposition brought up these charges in the House of Commons, Denison was put to some pains to refute them. Unable to get satisfaction in Canada's Parliament, Slater threatened to shoot Denison and then took his case to the governor general, the Colonial Office, and the British Parliament. In 1893, William Mulock aired the whole question again in the house. Denison called him a "cowardly blackguard … for two pins I would break his head."
13. Prime Minister Gladstone had hoped the French would be drawn into the Egyptian situation and allow the British to leave. To the British public, the Grand Old Man, or GOM, was now the MOG, the Murderer of Gordon. General Wolseley was quick to shift the blame for Gordon's murder on him, writing: "If God punishes men in the world … he will send down this old hypocrite in shame to his grave … as he dies despised & hated by every good Englishman."
14. The Royal Engineers Headquarters, Gilligham, Kent, has much of Major-General Gordon's memorabilia, including the court dress given him by the Chinese emperor, his pasha jacket, and a Mahdist robe. A portrait of Gordon hangs in the Royal Engineers Officers' Mess.
15. Sir Joseph Pope, ed., *The Correspondence of Sir John A. Macdonald* (Toronto: Oxford University Press, 1921), 337.
16. MacLaren, 158.
17. When asked what medals the current Canadian Forces in Sudan were entitled to, in April, 2008, the Department of National Defence responded thus: "There are 3 groups currently in the Sudan: 1. Those under Op SAFARI (UNMIS) get the UNMIS Medal and the CPSM. 2. Those NATO personnel deployed from Europe to provide Log Sp to AMIS (as far as we know that is only a handful of people, 4 or 5) get the NATO Non-Art 5 Medal for AMIS and the CPSM. 3. Those who served under Op AUGURAL (those actually under the AU) until it was replaced by SATURN on 1 Jan 08 qualified only for the CPSM (CANFORGEN 169/06 refers). The African Union Medal awarded to some Canadian Forces members has not been approved for wear by the Government of Canada and is unlikely to be as another proposal is under consideration to recognise service with Operation AUGURAL. The Department of National Defence has conducted a major review of overseas service recognition which has resulted in a number of proposals submitted to the Chancellery of Honours at Rideau Hall for consideration by the Government. Although we are not at liberty to discuss the details of the proposals at this point as such proposals are always considered 'Honours in Confidence' until formal approval, one of the recommendations pertains to the provision of a Canadian form of recognition for those members of the Canadian Forces who served in the Sudan and have yet to receive a medal for their service (such as those who are not under UN or NATO command). Since 1 Jan 08, AUGURAL has been superseded by Op SATURN which is a joint UN/AU mission. The process has started to have this new mission approved for the CPSM and we are still awaiting news from the United Nations as to whether or not they will issue a UN medal (the UNMIS or a new one) for this joint mission. More patience will be required before a final decision is made by the Government for Op AUGURAL recognition but we are confident the outcome will be positive. When/if that occurs, official announcements will be made through the usual means (CANFORGEN, Web Site, Maple Leaf, etc.)."

Chapter 4: A Canadian Engineer in Sudan

1. There remain several versions of how the Mahdi died. Smallpox or typhoid fever (as both raged during the siege) are the most likely causes, but knowing of his harem, which increased in number after the fall of

Khartoum, Victorian readers were titillated by the sensational story that on June 14 he was poisoned by one of the women he had "debauched" and suffered a lingering death a week later.

2. If Garnet Wolseley and Charles George Gordon had typified the generation that had fought the Crimean War, Herbert Kitchener and his generation were a rehearsal for the world wars to come. With him were a number of young men soon to be famous — Winston Churchill, Reginald Wingate (the great-uncle of Major-General Orde Wingate of Burma), Douglas Haig, Major J.D.P. French, and David Beatty. The last three distinguished themselves in the First World War.

3. Major-General Gordon's nephew, Major Charles "Monkey" Gordon, R.M., commanded the gunboat HMS *Melik*, which still exists in Khartoum today as the clubhouse of the Blue Nile Sailing Club.

4. Winston Churchill, who had a special dislike for Kitchener, would write years later: "I had been scandalized by his desecration of the Mahdi's tomb and the barbarous manner in which he had carried the Mahdi's skull in a kerosene can as a trophy." There was also the story that the skull is not buried in Sudan at all but was taken to England by Sir Reginald Wingate (who succeeded Kitchener as governor general of Sudan) and who drank champagne out of it for the rest of his life on each anniversary of the Battle of Omdurman.

5. Winston Churchill, then Member of Parliament for Lancashire, was representing Manchester, the Lancashire textile industry, and the British Cotton Growing Association was seeking alternatives to Britain's reliance on raw cotton from the United States. Northern Nigeria was deemed to offer a rich and reliable production source.

6. As governor, Sir Percy Girouard recruited many Canadians to work in northern Nigeria. One was Dr. Andrew P. Stirrett, formerly of the Sudan Interior Mission (SIM). Considered by many as the Norman Bethune of Nigeria, Stirrett did missionary work in Nigeria until his death at the age of 83. Girouard also hired a fellow Canadian and Royal Military College graduate, Arthur Leith-Ross, as the protectorate's chief transport officer. In 1907 he appointed A.W. Robinson, another Canadian, to oversee the dredging operations on the Niger River. In addition, "lumber-men from Canada" were hired to build the Baro-Kano Railway. In 1962, when the first Canadian volunteers came to an independent Nigeria as part of CUSO, many Nigerians still recalled the work of their countrymen half a century before.

Chapter 5: Rebels, Oil, and Darfur

1. Philip Warner, *Kitchener: The Man Behind the Legend* (New York: Atheneum, 1986), 107.

2. Sudanese Christians who converted from Islam run the risk of being arrested and their Bibles and baptism certificates confiscated. They can also be convicted of apostasy, which under Sudanese law carries a sentence of 100 lashes and the death penalty.

3. Jaafar Nimeiri's regard for the Jews was singular in the Muslim world. Just before he was removed from power, he allowed the transfer of 7,000 starving Ethiopian Jews to transfer from that country to Israel via Khartoum's airport. El Al 747 aircraft were provided facilities at the airport to do so. Both Nimeiri and his vice-president, Omar el-Tayeb, paid for this action with their lives after the coup.

4. Robert D. Kaplan, *Surrender or Starve: Travels in Ethiopia, Sudan and Eritrea* (New York: Knopf, 2003), 142.

5. Peter Dalglish, *The Courage of Children: My Life with the World's Poorest Kids* (Toronto: HarperCollins Canada, 1998), 177.

6. Dalglish, 322.

7. The rebels also planted a bomb on one of the doctor's bodies so that the aircraft taking the bodies to Khartoum would explode in midair. But it malfunctioned and blew up while the corpses were being loaded onboard.

8. Like Hassan al-Turabi and Sadiq al-Mahdi, both John Garang and Reik Machar held doctorates from prestigious Western universities, and even the current Sudanese minister for defence, Abdel Rahim Mohammed Hussein, graduated from Cranfield University in the United Kingdom with a master in aeronautical engineering, leading a Sudanese to quip that "all the ones who are making the mistakes are the so-called Ph.Ds — poverty, hunger, and disease." See Deborah Scroggins, *Emma's War: A True Story* (New York: Vintage, 2004), 317.

9. Scroggins, 24.

10. Arakis claimed that it had secured financing from a Saudi prince, causing its price to jump and insiders to profit. When the British Columbia Securities Commission (BCSC) showed that neither the money nor the royal connection was there, Arakis was fined CDN$250,000, and several persons associated with the scheme were penalized. Former CEO James Terrence Alexander had to pay CDN$1.2 million in fines for his role in these securities law breaches.

11. According to the *Sudan Democratic Gazette*, the decree, which was made public in August 1993, "legalises all the crimes of genocide which have been committed against the Nuba people over the past two years."

12. Coghlan, 64.

13. In 2000 the Harker Assessment Team first alerted Canadians that GOS helicopter gunships and Antonov bombers were being armed and refuelled at the Talisman-operated Heglig airstrip and flew from there to attack civilians.
14. Coghlan, 84–85.
15. On October 16, 1994, Reuters reported that the GOS had released 332 female prisoners in Omdurman Prison. Most had been found guilty of brewing or selling alcohol.
16. Johnson, 116.
17. Coghlan, 112.
18. However, the Saudi terrorist's influence continued long after his departure, since in March 1999, the Ugandan government reported that in Nsitu (south of Juba) Osama bin Laden's men were buying the children kidnapped by the Lord's Resistance Army for one AK-47 per child. The children were then taken to work as slaves on bin Laden's sunflower and marijuana farms outside Khartoum.
19. When interviewed by the Arabic *Al-Awsat* newspaper in 2007, Hassan al-Turabi remained unrepentant, saying that the "military cliques in Khartoum have more to do with totalitarianism than Islam." The old mastermind was too dangerous to be allowed his freedom, since even under house arrest he continued to make contact with the SPLM/A, as well as the rebel groups in Darfur and the East. Mohamed Hamdi's *The Makings of an Islamic Political Leader: Conversations with Hassan al-Turabi* is recommended as a study of this controversial figure in Sudanese history.

Chapter 6: Enter Talisman
1. Bruce Gall, "The Resurrection of Buffalo CN 85." *Flightlines* (Port Hope, ON: Canadian Warplane Heritage Museum, May 2008).
2. On April 15, 1986, the United States bombed Tripoli and Benghazi, and as a reprisal Libyan security men in Khartoum shot and killed a U.S. embassy employee. The U.S. embassy organized an evacuation of all Americans to Nairobi, allowing Canadians to accompany them.
3. Coghlan, 280.
4. Dalglish, 283–84.
5. Coghlan, 33.
6. In 2003, Georgette Gagnon received the Walter S. Tarnopolsky Human Rights Award. She returned to Sudan in 2001 to lead a mission that investigated and reported on the human-rights violations in the oil region for Canadian and British NGOs. In 2002 she served as the legal adviser to an International Eminent Persons Group that investigated slavery, abduction, and forced servitude in Sudan and recommended practical measures to stop these abuses.
7. The Special Economic Measures Act was introduced in 1992 to allow the Canadian government to impose sanctions against a foreign state in the absence of a U.N. Security Council resolution in response to a request from an international body. The act had been used twice before 2000, once with regard to Haiti at the request of the Organization of American States, and the other in regard to Yugoslavia at the request of the G8. It was never designed to be used unilaterally.
8. All quotations are taken from the report "Human Security in Sudan: The Report of a Canadian Assessment Team," distributed by the Government of Canada Depository Services Program, LC Class, No. JZ5588 C3 A36.
9. Laird Hindle (desk officer for Sudan) in Foreign Affairs told the Subcommittee on Human Rights and International Development of the Standing Committee on Foreign Affairs and International Trade on June 3, 2003, that there were two main groups of arms suppliers into Sudan. "One would be the more illicit organizations. A lot of weapons have been left over from previous conflicts in Africa elsewhere and are quite easily transported from one conflict to another, one part of the continent to another, and quite a bit of that is in Sudan. On the SPLA side, quite a bit of it was captured from the government when they raided various depots or captured a town. Most of their sources are from the illicit or grey trade. As for the government, the majority of its arms have come from a much more legal arms trade, if you will, and the majority of their suppliers seem to be — at least those reported in such things as the U.N. Register of Conventional Arms — from Russia, from China, from North Korea. There are no real surprises here, and there is also a strong domestic arms production capacity within northern Sudan but more limited towards small arms. We are not talking tanks or missile capability but small arms rather than the larger conventional weapons."
10. The lawsuit was based on the Alien Tort Claims Act, which usually only applied to disputes affecting the rights of aliens within the United States for acts that take place in this country. The obscure 1789 law originally was enacted to prosecute pirates but was rediscovered in 1980 by Holocaust survivors and relatives of people killed or tortured under despotic foreign regimes. The Presbyterian Church was encouraged to

use it when it was invoked against multinational corporations, including Chevron, over alleged abuses in Nigeria.

11. Talisman Energy's later involvement in Peru would not "turn into another Sudan," company officials said in May 2008, following a protest by leaders of indigenous communities in the Peruvian Amazon. Talisman CEO John Manzoni, who took over from Jim Buckee on September 1, 2007, vowed that Talisman would not perform oil and gas exploration without the consent of the people living in the area. "I think the lessons [of Sudan] have been learned deeply inside the company, call it the school of hard knocks, but we've learned." On April 29, 2008, the anti-corruption international watchdog, Transparency International, recognized Talisman Energy and the Canadian government "as examples for the rest of the world to emulate." The first for its above-average transparency in its dealings with Algeria, Indonesia, and Malaysia, and the second for making disclosure of revenues by Canadian companies paid to host countries mandatory.

12. Alison Azer, "Talismanized: Talisman's Exit, Sudan's Legacy." *Corporate Knights: The Canadian Magazine for Responsible Business*, March 1, 2004.

13. Mike Blanchfield, "Tories Ignoring Darfur." *Ottawa Citizen*, December 10, 2007.

14. While there Nicholas Coghlan wrote *The Saddest Country: On Assignment in Colombia*.

15. Coghlan, 14.

16. Coghlan, 309.

17. Ali Ahmed Karti was one of 51 Sudanese referred by the United Nations to the International Criminal Court for war crimes prosecution.

18. Aileen Carroll, former federal minister for CIDA in the Liberal government (and in 2008 the culture minister for Ontario), revealed that she had been advised during a visit to Khartoum that the Sudanese government might ask her to take Abdelrazik home on her government Challenger executive jet.

Chapter 7: Missionaries, Aid Workers, and NGOs

1. In 2000, SIM adopted the name (or slogan) "Serving in Mission" for English-speaking countries.

Chapter 8: Policewoman and Prime Minister

1. SHIRBRIG was established in 1996 as a non-standing multinational high-readiness brigade based on the U.N. Standby Arrangement System. On a case-by-case basis, member countries decide whether to participate in specific missions. Current full participants in SHIRBRIG include Austria, Canada, Denmark, Finland, Italy, Ireland, the Netherlands, Norway, Poland, Portugal, Romania, Slovenia, Spain, and Sweden. Chile, the Czech Republic, Hungary, Jordan, and Senegal are observers.

Chapter 9: Maple Leaf Military

1. In his speech on the celebration of the signing of the Comprehensive Peace Agreement on January 9, 2007, Salva Kiir Mayadit, president of the Government of Southern Sudan, publicly accused Khartoum of continuing to support the Lord's Resistance Army with arms to destabilize the South.

2. SkyLink's first humanitarian initiative happened in 1994 when it shipped hundreds of plane loads of personnel and equipment for the Canadian Armed Forces from Trenton, Ontario, to the massacres in Rwanda. SkyLink's in-country project manager learned of two aid workers struggling to care for 900 abandoned children in a village. "We got a request from our guys to do something," recalls Jan Ottens, the company manager. In partnership with a group of Canadian soldiers' wives, SkyLink set up a temporary orphanage and airlifted food, clothing, and medical supplies free of charge, along with a water-purification truck. Months later, as the killing subsided, most of the absent parents returned and reclaimed their children.

3. When Defence Minister Bill Graham first announced the loan of the AVGPs for AMIS in June 2005, legal problems arose. The armament and drive train were from the United States and fell under Foreign Military Sales rules. Given the age of both, and that the AVGPs were on loan for a year only (since extended), the legalities vanished.

4. Another Canadian company, C2 Logistics Incorporated, filed a complaint on September 16, 2005, with the Canadian International Trade Tribunal concerning the Invitation to Tender–Operation Augural–Deployment by the Department of National Defence for the provision of air charter services. DND submitted that, for the purpose of securing air charter services in support of its operations, it maintained a permanent list of eight potential suppliers and that the list includes C2. The tribunal awarded C2 its reasonable costs incurred in preparing and proceeding with the complaint to the amount of $2,400.

BIBLIOGRAPHY

Clammer, Paul. *Sudan: The Bradt Travel Guide*. London: Bradt Travel Guides, 2005.

Coghlan, Nicholas. *Far in the Waste Sudan: On Assignment in Africa*. Montreal and Kingston: McGill-Queen's University Press, 2005.

Collins, Robert O. *The History of Modern Sudan*. Cambridge: Cambridge University Press, 2008.

Dalglish, Peter. *The Courage of Children: My Life with the World's Poorest Kids*. Toronto: HarperCollins, 1998.

Dau, John Bul, and Michael S. Sweeney. *God Grew Tired of Us: A Memoir*. New York: National Geographic Society, 2008.

Johnson, Douglas H. *The Root Causes of Sudan's Civil War*. Oxford: The International African Institute, 2003.

Kaplan, Robert D. *Surrender or Starve: Travels in Ethiopia, Sudan, and Eritrea*. New York: Knopf, 2003.

MacLaren, Roy. *Canadians on the Nile, 1882–1898: Being the Adventures of the Voyageurs on the Khartoum Relief Expedition and Other Exploits*. Vancouver: University of British Columbia Press, 1978.

Moorehead, Alan. *The White Nile*. London: George Rainbird Ltd. 1960.

Reeves, Eric. *A Long Day's Dying: Critical Moments in the Darfur Genocide*. Toronto: Key Publishing House, 2007.

Scroggins, Deborah. *Emma's War: A True Story*. New York: Vintage, 2004.

Warner, Philip. *Kitchener: The Man Behind the Legend*. New York: Atheneum, 1986.

GLOSSARY OF ACRONYMS

ACL	Area Control List	HAC	Humanitarian Aid Coordinator
AGI	Arab Group International for Investment and Acquisition	IAC	Information Analysis Centre
AMIS	African Union Mission to Sudan	ICTY	International Criminal Tribunal for the Former Yugoslavia
AOR	Area of Responsibility		
APSO	Agency for Personnel Services Overseas	IDP	Internally Displaced Person
AU	African Union	IGAD	Intergovernmental Authority on Development
AVGP	Armoured Vehicle General Purpose		
AXO	Abandoned Explosive Ordnance	IGADD	Intergovernmental Authority on Drought and Development
BBC	British Broadcasting Corporation	IMF	International Monetary Fund
		IRC	International Rescue Committee
CARE	Cooperative for American Relief Everywhere	ISAF	International Security Assistance Force
CBC	Canadian Broadcasting Corporation	JEM	Justice and Equality Movement
CEAWC	Committee to Eradicate the Abduction of Women and Children	JIU	Jointed Integrated Unit
		JLOC	Joint Logistics Operations Centre
CEDASS	Canadian Economic Development Assistance for Southern Sudan	JMC	Joint Military Commission
		JMCC	Joint Military Co-operation Committee
CEFCOM	Canadian Expeditionary Force Command	LRA	Lord's Resistance Army
CF	Canadian Forces		
CFB	Canadian Forces Base	MOU	Memorandum of Understanding
CFC	Ceasefire Commission	MSF	Médecins sans Frontières
CIA	Central Intelligence Agency		
CIDA	Canadian International Development Agency	NATO	North Atlantic Treaty Organization
		NCO	Non-Commissioned Officer
COPA	Crude Oil Pipeline Agreement	NCP	National Congress Party
CPA	Comprehensive Peace Agreement	NDA	National Democratic Alliance
CPR	Canadian Pacific Railway	NGO	Non-Governmental Organization
CSIS	Canadian Security Intelligence Service	NIF	National Islamic Front
CUSO	Canadian University Students Overseas	NMRD	National Movement for Reform and Development
DITF	Darfur Integrated Task Force	NRF	National Redemption Front
DLF	Darfur Liberation Front	NSRCC	National Salvation Revolutionary Command Council
DND	Department of National Defence		
DOP	Declaration of Principles	NUP	National Unionist Party
DPA	Darfur Peace Agreement		
DUP	Democratic Unionist Party	OAU	Organization of African Unity
		OLS	Operation Lifeline Sudan
EU	European Union	ONGC	Oil and Natural Gas Corporation
FAO	Food and Agricultural Organization	PDF	People's Defence Force
FAR	Fellowship for African Relief	PDP	People's Democratic Party
		PNCP	Popular National Congress Party
GNOPC	Greater Nile Operating Petroleum Company	P/O	Pilot Officer
		PPCLI	Princess Patricia's Canadian Light Infantry
GONU	Government of National Unity		
GOS	Government of Sudan		
GOSS	Government of Southern Sudan	QRF	Quick Relief Force

RCC	Revolutionary Command Council	WUSC	World University Services of Canada
RCL	Royal Canadian Legion	WVC	World Vision Canada
RMC	Royal Military College		
ROM	Royal Ontario Museum		
RPG	Rocket-Propelled Grenade		
SAF	Sudanese Air Force, Sudanese Armed Forces		
SANU	Sudan African Nationalist Union		
SEMA	Special Economic Measures Act		
SFDA	Sudan Federal Democratic Alliance		
SHIRBRIG	Standby High Readiness Brigade		
SIM	Soudan Interior Mission		
SIPRI	Stockholm International Peace Research Institute		
SKI	Street Kids International		
SLM/A	Sudan Liberation Movement/Army		
SNP	Sudanese National Party		
SOMA	Status of Mission Agreement		
SPDF	Sudan People's Democratic Front		
SPLM/A	Sudan People's Liberation Movement/Army		
SSCC	Southern States Coordinating Council		
SSDF	South Sudan Defence Force		
SSIM/A	South Sudan Independence Movement/Army		
SSLM	Southern Sudan Liberation Movement		
SSU	Sudan Socialist Union		
TCC	Troop Contributing Country		
TFAA	Task Force Addis Ababa		
TFC	Task Force Commander		
TFD	Task Force Darfur		
TMC	Transitional Military Council		
TNA	Transitional National Assembly		
TNC	Transitional National Council		
U.N.	United Nations		
UNAMID	United Nations–African Union Mission in Darfur		
UNDP	United Nations Development Programme		
UNICEF	United Nations Children's Fund		
UNMAO	United Nations Mine Action Office		
UNMIS	United Nations Mission in Sudan		
UNMO	United Nations Military Observer		
UNPOL	United Nations Police		
UNRA	United Nations Relief and Rehabilitation Administration		
U.S.	United States		
USAID	United States Agency for International Development		
UXO	Unexploded Ordnance		
VMT	Verification and Monitoring Team		
VSE	Vancouver Stock Exchange		
WFP	World Food Programme		

INDEX